55

 **Oracle Press**™

Oracle Database Administration for Microsoft® SQL Server® DBAs

Michelle Malcher

New York   Chicago   San Francisco
Lisbon   London   Madrid   Mexico City   Milan
New Delhi   San Juan   Seoul   Singapore   Sydney   Toronto

Library Resource Center
Renton Technical College
3000 N.E. 4th Street
Renton, WA 98056

The McGraw·Hill Companies

Cataloging-in-Publication Data is on file with the Library of Congress

005.758541 MELCHER 2011

Melcher, Michelle.

Oracle database
  administration for

McGraw-Hill books are available at special quantity discounts to use as premiums and sales promotions, or for use in corporate training programs. To contact a representative, please e-mail us at bulksales@ mcgraw-hill.com.

Oracle Database Administration for Microsoft® SQL Server® DBAs

Copyright © 2011 by The McGraw-Hill Companies, Inc. (Publisher). All rights reserved. Printed in the United States of America. Except as permitted under the Copyright Act of 1976, no part of this publication may be reproduced or distributed in any form or by any means, or stored in a database or retrieval system, without the prior written permission of Publisher, with the exception that the program listings may be entered, stored, and executed in a computer system, but they may not be reproduced for publication.

Oracle is a registered trademark of Oracle Corporation and/or its affiliates. All other trademarks are the property of their respective owners, and McGraw-Hill makes no claim of ownership by the mention of products that contain these marks.

Screen displays of copyrighted Oracle software programs have been reproduced herein with the permission of Oracle Corporation and/or its affiliates.

1 2 3 4 5 6 7 8 9 0   DOC DOC   1 0 9 8 7 6 5 4 3 2 1 0

ISBN   978-0-07-174431-7
MHID   0-07-174431-2

Sponsoring Editor Lisa McClain	**Copy Editor** Marilyn Smith	**Illustration** Glyph International
Associate Acquisitions Editor Meghan Riley	**Proofreader** Paul Tyler	**Art Director, Cover** Jeff Weeks
Editorial Supervisor Janet Walden	**Indexer** Jack Lewis	**Cover Designer** Pattie Lee
Project Editor Emilia Thiuri	**Production Supervisor** Jean Bodeaux	
Technical Editor Kimberly Floss	**Composition** Glyph International	

Information has been obtained by Publisher from sources believed to be reliable. However, because of the possibility of human or mechanical error by our sources, Publisher, or others, Publisher does not guarantee the accuracy, adequacy, or completeness of any information included in this Work and is not responsible for any errors or omissions or the results obtained from the use of such information.

Oracle Corporation does not make any representations or warranties as to the accuracy, adequacy, or completeness of any information contained in this Work, and is not responsible for any errors or omissions.

Renton Technical College
3000 N.E. 4th Street
Renton, WA 98056

This book is dedicated to all of the hard-working DBAs
who learn of ways to work smarter and then share
that information so that others can learn as well.

About the Author

Michelle Malcher is a Senior Database Administrator at DRW Holdings with more than 12 years of experience in database development, design, and administration. She has expertise in performance tuning, security, data modeling, and database architecture of very large database environments. She has administered environments supporting multiple database platforms, including Oracle, SQL Server, and Sybase. As a DBA, she has strived to design, implement, and maintain stable, reliable, and secure database environments in order to support the business and important business processes.

Michelle enjoys contributing to the database technology user community by speaking at conferences and being on the Independent Oracle User Group (IOUG) Board of Directors as the Director of Education. She feels that being able to learn from others and teach what you know are key ways to enjoy working with databases. There is always something to learn and challenge us to come up with better solutions.

About the Technical Editor

Kimberly Floss is a Manager of Database Services for a large Fortune 500 company. She has managed teams responsible for both database administration and database engineering for Oracle, DB2, Teradata, and SQL Server. She has been largely responsible for database/system administration, general architecture, system performance monitoring, tuning, backup and recovery, and capacity planning of hundreds of database environments.

Kimberly is a former President of the Independent Oracle User Group (IOUG) and has been a board member for six years. She currently serves as a member of the Conference Committee for IOUG. She also serves on the board for the North Central Teradata User Group and has served as a content reviewer for the Professional Association of SQL Server (PASS). She is a frequent speaker at conferences such as Oracle OpenWorld and Collaborate.

Kimberly has a BS in Computer Information Systems from Purdue and an MBA with emphasis in MIS from Loyola University. She teaches a Database Applications and SQL Programming class at a local community college.

Contents

ACKNOWLEDGMENTS xi
INTRODUCTION xiii

1 The Database Administrator **1**
General DBA Skills 2
Where Do DBAs Belong in an Organization? 4
Database Installation Planning 5
Leveraging Skills 5
Database Migrations 9
Summary 13

2 Oracle Internals **15**
Memory Structures 16
    Oracle Memory Parameters 17
    Sizing the SGA and PGA 20
Where Are the master, msdb, and tempdb Databases? 22
    System-level Information 23
    Data Dictionary Views 26
    Jobs and Schedules 28
    Templates and Temporary Tables 28
Services and Processes 29
sp_configure Options and Parameters 32
    Viewing and Setting Parameters 33
    Getting Started with Some Parameters 34
Undo, Redo, and Logs 38
    Transaction Logs Versus Redo Logs 38
    Undo and Beyond 39
Summary 42

3 Oracle Installation **43**
    Operating Systems   44
        Windows Setup   46
        Useful Linux/Unix Commands   48
        Linux Setup   50
    Storage Requirements   55
        Disk Storage   56
        Storage Management with ASM   57
        Oracle Files   61
        Oracle Database Components   63
    Oracle Software Installation   64
        Using a Response File   67
        Removing Software   68
        Upgrading the Database   68
        Applying Patches   70
    Summary   71

4 Database Definitions and Setup **73**
    Servers, Databases, Instances, and Schemas   74
    SQL Server Setup Versus Oracle Setup   77
    Creating Databases   79
        Using the DBCA   79
        Duplicating Databases with Templates and Scripts   83
        Creating the Listener   85
        Choosing a Character Set   89
    Security   94
        Permissions for the Server   95
        Permissions for Schemas   98
        DBA Roles and Responsibilities Revisited   101
    Summary   102

5 DBA Tools **103**
    Overview of Tools for Typical Database Tasks   104
    Oracle Enterprise Manager   105
        OEM Navigation   105
        Storage Management   107
        Database Configuration   108
        Oracle Scheduler   109
        Statistics and Resource Management   109

Security 109
Enterprise Manager Configuration 111
SQL*Plus 112
SQL Developer 117
Client Connections 119
Client Connection Configuration 120
JDBC Connections 123
Aliases 123
My Oracle Support 124
Summary 125

6 Database Backup, Restore, and Recovery **127**
Backing Up Databases 128
Backup Strategies 128
Backup and Restore Commands 129
RMAN Configuration for Backups 131
Backup Options 135
Backup Examples 137
OEM Backup Jobs 137
Restoring and Recovering Databases 141
What Can Go Wrong? 141
Restore and Recover Options 143
Data Recovery Advisor 147
Copying the Database 149
Managing Backups 152
Viewing Backups 152
Purging Obsolete Files 155
Backing Up and Restoring Objects 156
Copying Objects at the Table and Schema Level 156
Using Data Pump 157
Protecting Users from Users 161
Recycle Bin 161
Flashback 164
Summary 169

7 Database Maintenance **171**
Maintenance Tasks 172
Consistency Checks 173
Health Checks 174

Update Statistics 176
     System Statistics 177
     Object Statistics 178
Object Maintenance 181
     Index Rebuild 181
     Table Reorganization 184
     Invalid Objects 187
     Grants 189
     Synonyms 190
Job Scheduling 191
     Creating a Job in Oracle Scheduler 191
     Using DBMS_SCHEDULER 194
     Setting Up System and User Jobs 196
File Maintenance 197
     Shrinking and Resizing Files 197
     Tablespace Monitoring 200
     Error Logs, Alert Logs, and Trace Files 203
Summary 204

8 Performance and Tuning **207**
Better-Performing Systems 208
Indexes 209
     Index Monitoring 210
     Index Types 210
Locking 219
Current Activity Views 221
     Current Sessions 222
     Activity Monitors 223
     Waits 225
SQL Plans 226
     Viewing Explain Plans 226
     Tuning Using Explain Plans 228
Automatic Workload Repository 233
     AWR Reports 233
     Active Session History View 236
     Library Cache for SQL Statements 236
Summary 238

9 PL/SQL **239**
Database Coding Practices 240
Packages and Package Bodies 243

Triggers 246
Updates and Conditions 249
Transactions 250
    Beginning a Transaction 251
    Defining Commits 253
    Cursor Processing 254
    Processing with FORALL 257
Functions 258
Debugging Procedures and Unit Testing 262
Error Handling 264
    Error Handling Packages 266
    Standard Error Messages 268
Using DBMS Packages 270
Summary 271

10 High-Availability Architecture **273**
Options for High Availability 274
Clustering with RAC 276
    Configuring RAC 278
    Testing RAC 282
    Setting Up Client Failover 283
    Setting Up RAC Listeners 285
    Patching RAC 286
    Deploying RAC 286
    Configuring and Monitoring RAC Instances 287
Primary and Standby Databases 289
    Using Active Standby Databases 290
    Setting Up a Standby Database 292
ASM in an RAC Environment 297
    Managing ASM Disk Groups 297
    Viewing ASM Information 302
Streams and Advanced Replication 304
    Oracle Streams 304
    Advanced Replication 307
Summary 307

Appendix **309**

Index **315**

Acknowledgments

It is because I have been able to share this experience with my family, friends, and coworkers that I have felt such a sense of accomplishment in completing this book. I truly would like to thank all of them, and I am glad that they share in different aspects of my life.

Thanks to my junior DBAs, Emily and Mandy, who have also heard what an Oracle SGA is as I have read some pages to them for bedtime stories. Thanks for listening to me even without understanding, and now we can get back to other bedtime stories. Thanks to my husband, Bernd, for his understanding as I pursue new challenges.

Thanks to my technical editor, Kim Floss, for reviewing and making the book even better. Thanks to my sister, Carrie Steyer, for being available as a sounding board for some of my ideas.

Thanks to the awesome DBA team at DRW, which I am proud to be a part of—Laura Culley, Randy Swanson, and Henry Treftz—and for their help in testing some of the examples contained in this book.

Thanks to the IOUG Board of Directors, Ian Abramson, Judi Doolittle, Andy Flower, Kent Hinckley, Steve Lemme, John Matelski, Todd Sheetz, Jon Wolfe, and my mentors in the user group community, who have encouraged me to share my ideas and have provided me with opportunities to grow and develop in my career.

Introduction

Database environments are constantly growing. There is definitely not a shortage of data, and many companies need their systems to be constantly up and available. For various reasons, companies may have different database platforms that they use for storing the data. This means that DBAs need the skills to support mixed environments.

Oracle database solutions are a large part of a robust enterprise database environment. Oracle provides high-availability solutions, efficient ways to manage very large databases, and configurations for better performance. New features in Oracle Database 11g have simplified some of the configurations and maintenance for the database. However, even with some of the areas being automated and easier to manage, there is still much to learn about Oracle and the different options and components of Oracle databases.

Some database concepts, such as data modeling and database backup and recovery plans, carry across different platforms. Also, there are common tasks that DBAs perform to maintain any database environment.

This book covers tasks in Oracle as they relate to the SQL Server ways of doing things, providing translations between the two platforms. It compares some of the standard practices and looks at how the internals of the database require some different maintenance and health checks. The point is not to say that one platform's feature is better than the other's, but to help you learn how to use and implement both similar features and different features. Each chapter includes comparison tables listing the SQL Server and Oracle commands or components related to the topic. This makes it easy for those who are familiar with how to do something in SQL Server to find the information they need for working with Oracle.

The book covers a broad range of topics related to administering databases, including the following:

- The internals of Oracle and system information that is available to configure the database settings

- Installations, including some basic Linux commands and details that are needed for the installation on Linux

- Database creation and the different terminology and security associated with Oracle databases

- The tools available to perform administrative tasks, such as Oracle Enterprise Manager and SQL Developer

- Backup and restore planning and procedures

- Management of statistics and database objects, and performance tuning

- Use of PL/SQL, including how it varies from Transact-SQL

- High-availability solutions for the architecture and design of the database system

This book is designed to help DBAs leverage the skill set they've already developed on another database platform and advance that knowledge to the Oracle database systems. The goal is to ease your transition to Oracle and show you how to effectively administer the Oracle database system.

CHAPTER

1

The Database Administrator

atabase administrators (DBAs) have significant responsibilities. They must not only provide reliable access to company data, but also protect that data, monitor the database environment, troubleshoot problems, and more. If the lives of DBAs were simple, what fun would that be? That is probably why I enjoy the job so much—because of the different opportunities and challenges that I get to face day to day.

To provide a stable and highly available database environment, along with planning backups and performing recoveries and all the other maintenance tasks, DBAs are usually exploring how to use new features, and even learning multiple database platforms. Yes, I said it: as a DBA, you probably need to know more than one database platform. The days of being just an Oracle or SQL Server DBA are probably gone. Companies are adopting more than one database platform, and applications may import or export data from one database system to another. But why am I telling you this? You have already decided to add Oracle to your arsenal. The big question is, How hard will this be?

If you are a SQL Server DBA, you don't need to start back at square one to support Oracle databases. Certainly, there are differences between the platforms, but many of the DBA tasks are basically the same. You can apply the skills you already have to learning Oracle, using this book as your guide. This book will even translate terms from SQL Server to Oracle, because sometimes being able to speak the language is half of the battle.

Before we look into the specifics of Oracle, in this chapter, we will review the role of the DBA, so you can see how to leverage the skills you already have as you learn the new database platform. We will also look briefly at the migration process.

General DBA Skills

The role of the DBA is more than just backing up the database and making sure the database is available. There are several hats that are worn by a DBA—from tuning queries to server configuration, as well as making sure the database is secure.

Here are some of the tasks a DBA performs:

- Installing databases
- Backing up and restoring databases

- Troubleshooting problems and errors

- Coding and tuning SQL statements

- Monitoring space and growth

- Establishing best practices

- Configuring highly available environments

- Developing security strategies

- Performing maintenance tasks

On a given day, a DBA may need to validate backups, handle some support issues, add users, and possibly roll out some new code to the production database. Some days may be spent just troubleshooting performance, tuning code, or working on the database model. Even if the production database might not need to be restored on a regular basis (a very good thing!), a test environment may need to be refreshed frequently. Being able to resolve an issue as quickly as possible is important, which may require research and drilling through database logs and trace files.

Other general skills for a DBA might include managing projects and creating and following processes. DBAs are not working in an environment where only one person is accessing the database system. The database is normally supporting enterprise-level applications with many users and various workloads.

Software vendors have stated that installing databases and monitoring them are simple tasks, but somehow there seems to be more moving parts these days. Also, new areas, such as compliance and business intelligence, provide different challenges for DBAs.

The DBA may have the responsibility to back up databases and restore and copy them into another environment. The DBA may be required to design the database model and coding procedures. A DBA may even be more of an enterprise architect, who knows how to use data at an enterprise level to support the business and add value through business intelligence solutions. This type of role would also involve assessing if the right tool is being used, understanding the differences in platforms, and managing these to help make better design decisions.

Where Do DBAs Belong in an Organization?

Are DBAs in production support, the architecture team, the engineering team, or the development team? Actually, they could probably be a part of all these teams or in a separate group altogether. But in any case, they still need to work with all the teams.

DBAs work with system administrators for configuring operating systems and providing input to hardware decisions for the environment. DBAs work with developers to design systems and provide coding standards and best practices for developing applications that use databases. DBAs work with networking and interface teams for connections and hooks into the database. DBAs work with users, operations, and anyone else who needs access to the database. DBAs are considered to be experts in the area of databases, and they are expected to know enough information in other areas to be able to support and communicate needs for the database environment. Some DBAs may even be considered engineers instead of administrators, which implies more of a design and architecture type of role than production support.

Depending on the size of the company and number of databases, there might be one DBA who does it all, or separate DBAs, such as a system DBA, an application DBA, a development DBA, and an architecture DBA. In following compliance regulations, the separation of these roles for the DBAs is becoming more important.

Just as application developers shouldn't have access to the production system, the development DBA may just be working in the development space, and passing scripts to production support DBAs for execution. The development DBA could be working with the developers on the design of the database application, developing the data model and data flows. The role might involve looking at performance and coding SQL, as well as seeing how best to implement new features.

The system DBA will concentrate on backups, space monitoring, and maintenance jobs like reviewing statistics and rebuilding indexes. This DBA would probably be the one who provides production support and runs prepared scripts for changing objects or implementing upgrades.

The roles for DBAs also depend on whether applications are developed in-house or third-party applications are running in the environment.

Database Installation Planning

Several pieces need to be coordinated and communicated to install and upgrade databases. Basic installations wouldn't need much planning if we were just installing software on a desktop somewhere and the application was used by just one person. Also, an organization will probably need more than just one database, so a repeatable process would be useful.

DBAs need to manage installations to be able to communicate needs to other teams for hardware and operating system configurations. They must get details about the application to make sure that the database has the features needed. Properly managing database installations is important for planning upgrades and implementing enterprise monitoring systems. On a smaller scale, this planning is useful for patching, making changes to security configurations, and rolling out auditing tools. Developing standards and building a process will create a more consistent and stable database environment.

When installing SQL Server, you can choose where to put data files and log files, if the instance is the default unnamed or named instance, which patch set is to be applied, if Reporting Services and Analysis Services are to be installed, and so on. You probably have a checklist so that a standard installation can be repeated on multiple databases. Creating a checklist or standard installation document is just as important for Oracle databases. Instance names, parameters that should be set, components that should be installed, Oracle home directories, directories for data files and log files, as well as recovery areas, should all be included. Table 1-1 shows high-level checklists for preparing to install SQL Server and Oracle databases. Notice that many of the same tasks are listed for both platforms. (Chapter 3 covers Oracle installation in detail.)

Leveraging Skills

We've reviewed some general DBA skills and practices, which you are probably currently applying to support the SQL Server system you are managing. Now let's look at how these skills provide a starting point for learning Oracle.

SQL Server	Oracle
Obtain software and release notes	Obtain software and release notes
Configure Windows, memory, etc.	Validate operating system configuration
Set up domain account and privileges	Create user for installing Oracle and processes (other users might be needed for other components)
Allocate storage	Allocate storage
Configure network	Configure network
Install software	Install software
Validate install	Validate install
Back up system, excluding .mdf and .ldf files	Back up system, excluding data files

TABLE 1-1.   *SQL Server and Oracle Installation Checklists*

Table 1-2 compares the skills needed for managing SQL Server databases with those required for managing Oracle databases.

You probably expected that these tasks and skills are needed no matter which database platform is being supported and managed. The trick is discovering the differences, such as new best practices, variations in features, and differences in syntax for these tasks in Oracle. This way, you can distinguish what you already know from what you need to learn.

For example, whether the database is Oracle or SQL Server, part of the DBA's job is to make sure things are backed up properly, including having a strategy for the types of backups required. Recovery and restore procedures are also part of this strategy. You already understand general backup concepts. You know that you want transaction log backups and to be able to recover up to a point in time, as you've set up in SQL Server. Now you need to know the details of backup and restore options in Oracle. For example, to create a backup in SQL Server, you execute a backup database command; in Oracle, using the RMAN utility, you execute a backup database command—that's simple enough, right?

Task/Skill	SQL Server	Oracle
Backing up	X	X
Restoring	X	X
Disaster recovery planning	X	X
Monitoring	X	X
Performance tuning	X	X
Patching	X	X
Installing	X	X
Troubleshooting	X	X
Coding	X	X
Developing standards and best practices	X	X
Implementing security	X	X
Capacity planning	X	X
Managing projects	X	X

TABLE 1-2.   *SQL Server and Oracle Skill Sets*

System monitoring is another example. Understanding why certain areas need to be monitored for better-running databases is half of the battle. If you know the information you want to monitor, then you just need to find out how to do it in Oracle. Knowing which areas to check comes from the experience of dealing with databases and troubleshooting issues in the past. Performing health checks against the database and reviewing database logs are good first steps.

Health checks are not just looking into current issues, but also monitoring several areas and verifying that databases are running well. Health checks in SQL Server could be verifying if jobs are running properly, checking disk space, reviewing last-analyzed-for statistics, making sure old backups have been purged, and running other monitoring scripts. Oracle's high-level list of health checks include validating backups, checking available space in tablespaces and file systems, making sure statistics are up to date, and verifying that other scripts are running and completing as expected.

The home page of Oracle Enterprise Manager, shown in Figure 1-1, provides a quick look at the status of the database. It shows if the database is up or down, a list of errors in the alert log, and general server information about CPU and active sessions. Checking system-level resources, such as CPU and memory usage, in a Microsoft Windows system is probably already part of your SQL Server health check routine. Knowing that these details are available in Oracle Enterprise Manager gives you a good place to start. You'll learn more about Oracle Enterprise Manager in Chapter 5.

If you have scripts created in Perl or another programming language to monitor and manage SQL Server, these scripts can be leveraged to create similar scripts for Oracle. Having such scripts is a great start.

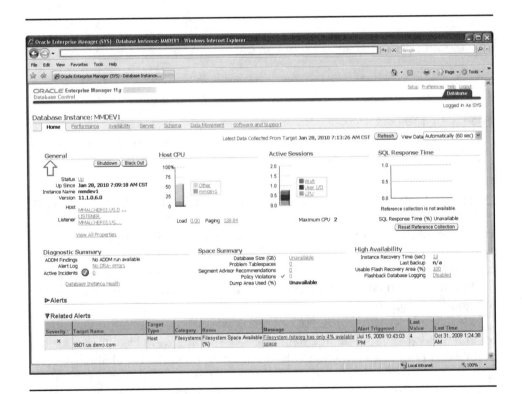

FIGURE 1-1. *Oracle Enterprise Manager home page*

DBA Monitoring Checklist
DBAs typically monitor the following:

- Backup jobs ran successfully (full and logs)
- Space on server and tablespaces/data files
- Errors in the alert log/server log
- Any new information in the alert log/server log
- Security auditing
- Scheduled jobs ran successfully
- Current statistics

Database Migrations

You might need to learn Oracle because your company's current database will be converted from SQL Server to Oracle. There are various ways to migrate, but all begin with a solid plan. The options available have varying inputs and outputs, as well as varying amounts of downtime and risk.

You will need an Oracle database, a way to convert the definitions of the tables from SQL Server datatypes to Oracle datatypes, a way to move the data over to the new system, and a way to convert the stored procedures and packages. Depending on how big and complex the database is, this could be a very simple or a very complicated move.

Not all of the datatypes can translate exactly from one platform to another. Table 1-3 shows just an example of some of the conversions.

Moving the data is probably the least of your concerns, unless you have several terabytes of data to transfer. Data can be moved out of SQL Server with the bcp utility, and then SQL*Loader can load it on the Oracle side. SQL Server Integration Services (SSIS) packages can be created to export from one database into the other.

SQL	Oracle
DATETIME	DATE, TIMESTAMP
FLOAT	NUMBER
VARCHAR	VARCHAR2
CHAR	CHAR
VARBINARY	BLOB
NUMERIC	NUMBER

TABLE 1-3. *Example Datatype Conversions*

The Oracle SQL Developer tool is available to assist with any of these types of migrations, as shown in Figure 1-2. The Migration Wizard sets up a repository for the work area of the conversion process. It pulls in the source information, translates the structures to Oracle structures, and then allows for movement of data online or offline, depending on how much data needs to be transferred. The constraints, primary keys, foreign keys, and check constraints are included in the migration process, and stored procedures are translated into Oracle structures. If there are issues in converting a datatype, you will get an error when attempting the migration process. (Oracle SQL Developer is discussed in more detail in Chapter 5.)

NOTE
Oracle SQL Developer can be used to manage SQL Server databases. Java Database Connectivity (JDBC) drivers will need to be configured with Oracle SQL Developer before the SQL Server tab is present to connect to the SQL Server database. Details on the procedure are available from the Oracle SQL Developer Help menu. Search for "database: third-party JDBC drivers."

Well, pulling the SQL Server database over into an Oracle database with the provided tools sounds simple enough. Then the fun begins. Just because

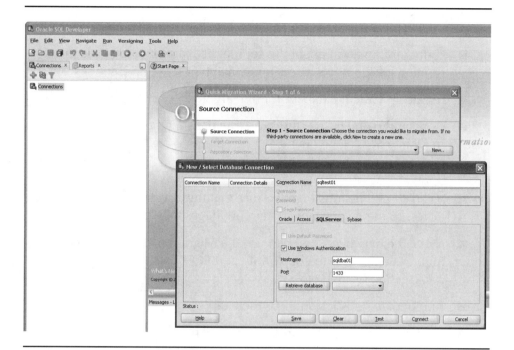

FIGURE 1-2.   *Migration Wizard in Oracle SQL Developer*

the SQL Server database is now available in Oracle doesn't mean that all of the indexes, statistics, and types of stored procedures are the best for use in Oracle and will perform optimally. Testing and more testing are needed to validate that the new structures and datatypes match those in the stored procedures, tables, and views.

Validation of the data should include looking at the timestamps and verifying that times as well as dates match up as needed. Indexes and referential integrity need to be verified. The stored procedures need to be checked to ensure they can return expected results. Jobs will need to be scheduled using DBMS_SCHEDULER. Permissions need to be examined to confirm that the security configured for access by the users is present.

As these pieces get validated for the application, you can look at the areas that would benefit from different standards or from using some new features in Oracle. You can see how you did it in SQL Server and consider the best way to do it in Oracle. The rest of this book will help guide you along that path.

Library Resource Center
Renton Technical College
3000 N.E. 4th Street
Renton, WA 98056

Here's a checklist of common migration tasks:

- Gather information about the source database, including size, running jobs, objects, and strange datatypes.
- Create an Oracle database for the target.
- Convert the object structures to Oracle, using the Migration Wizard in Oracle SQL Developer.
- Validate indexes, triggers, and stored procedures.
- Validate permissions to make sure that the new users in Oracle have access to the objects and system privileges they need.
- Move the data over. You can use the Migration Wizard in Oracle SQL Developer, or the bcp utility and SQL*Loader or an SSIS package in SQL Server.
- Run update statistics on the Oracle tables.
- Review the indexes and referential integrity.
- Recompile all of the objects, and make sure there are no invalid objects.
- Validate the data and application. Following a plan for testing pieces of the application would be the best route here. It might be a test plan that was used for a previous upgrade or a new one, but you need a way to confirm that the results in the application are as expected.
- Look for performance issues.
- Look for areas that might benefit from changing to an Oracle feature.
- Adjust any of the stored procedures and indexes.
- Schedule jobs in DBMS_SCHEDULER.
- Run maintenance jobs against the Oracle database to perform backups and update statistics.
- Run through the test plan again.

These steps would be executed first in a development environment to work through any issues and make a couple of these adjustment steps. In production, you could just make the changes to any of the stored procedures or indexes. Of course, validation of performance as well as the application in production is highly recommended.

The tools are useful for making this a more consistent process. You'll need to know more about Oracle to work through the rest of the conversion, such as to develop the scheduled jobs (Chapter 7) and validate indexes (Chapter 8) and stored procedures (Chapter 9).

Summary

As a DBA, you perform several tasks on a daily basis. You have skills that you use for managing projects and troubleshooting issues. These general skills, along with the knowledge you've gained through your experience managing databases on SQL Server, can be leveraged to learn Oracle.

For example, maintenance and monitoring are tasks that are needed on any database system. Having an existing list of these jobs on SQL Server will help you develop the list for Oracle. In later chapters, we will look at some of the syntax for these jobs and how to perform tasks such as performing backups and gathering statistics. You also will want to look at the best practices for maintaining the database environment. SQL Server and Oracle handle various components, such as transaction logs, in different ways, which will require a different approach to maintaining and monitoring them.

If you are converting an existing SQL Server database to Oracle, Oracle provides a useful tool to assist with the migration: Oracle SQL Developer. Being able to convert the database is only part of the battle, however. The rest involves configuring the database and application to run well and taking advantage of existing features in Oracle. Even though some areas are similar and may just use different terms, there are actual differences. Also, each platform has its own ways to use these features of the database for performance, security, high availability, and manageability.

Knowing that you can leverage what you already understand in the SQL Server world will make it easier to develop your knowledge of Oracle databases. In the next chapter, we'll begin with a look at Oracle internals.

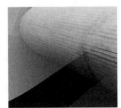

CHAPTER
2

Oracle Internals

nother name for this chapter could be "The Guts of Oracle." What is it doing in there? It is obvious that the inside workings of SQL Server and Oracle are not the same, or they wouldn't be two different database platforms. Understanding how the internal and system structures are set up in Oracle will give you insight into some of the best practices for Oracle.

In this chapter, we will focus on configurations and how the memory and system areas are organized. There are also Oracle processes or services to get to know. Then we will take a look at some of the knobs that can be turned for options of the database. Finally, we will examine how changes and transactions are handled by the logs and processes.

Memory Structures

Databases use memory to cache data blocks for fast access. They have some processes that use memory for sorting or calculations, and other processes that use the memory allocated to cache results.

SQL Server has minimum and maximum values for the memory available for the server. Memory it uses is limited to the memory available on the server. The minimum value does not affect how much memory SQL Server will start with, but rather up to what point it will give back memory to the operating system if the memory isn't being used. Planning the memory for a SQL Server system is based on how many database instances and application processes will be running on the server.

Oracle also uses the memory available on the server. Oracle can dynamically allocate memory between the different memory structures under the server and process area, and with Oracle Database 11g, even between the server and user process areas. There are parameter settings for maximum values, dynamic allocation, and configuring the operating system to have shared memory available for Oracle to use. As with SQL Server, planning for memory is based on how many database instances and application processes will be running on the server.

For either database system, it is not good practice to allocate all of the memory available on the server to the database. The operating system also needs space for its operations.

Oracle Memory Parameters

With Oracle Database 11*g*'s Automatic Shared Memory Management (ASMM) feature, the management of Oracle's various memory parameters has essentially come down to setting one parameter. And if there were no more 9*i* or 10*g* databases out there, or if all applications used memory in the optimal way, memory management would be simple. However, just as some SQL Server 2000 and 2005 servers are still in use, earlier versions of Oracle remain in service. So, you do need an understanding of how Oracle uses memory.

The two main memory areas for Oracle are the System Global Area (SGA) and the Program Global Area (PGA). Under the SGA, the memory is divided into other areas for handling the SQL statements, data blocks, and log buffers. The PGA is the workload area for server processes. Figure 2-1 shows the memory parameters for the SGA and PGA.

In Oracle9*i* Database and Oracle Database 10*g*, the dynamic memory parameters allow the memory to adjust within the SGA. The `SGA_MAX_SIZE` and `SGA_TARGET` parameters are set, and then memory is adjusted between `DB_CACHE_SIZE`, `SHARED_POOL_SIZE`, and the other pools (such as `LARGE_POOL_SIZE` and `JAVA_POOL_SIZE`). This helps for systems that might have different types of workload at different times. Without manual intervention, the allocations could adjust based on the memory needs of the

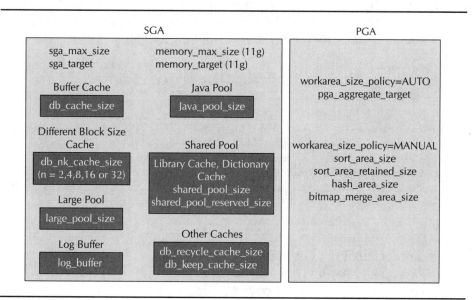

FIGURE 2-1. *Memory parameters for the SGA and PGA*

different areas. Of course, in setting the SGA_MAX_SIZE and SGA_TARGET parameters, the statistics must be at the *typical* level for the correct information to be collected to provide the details required to adjust the memory areas. But why not just set SGA_TARGET and SGA_MAX_SIZE to the same values, if you are allocating a maximum value of memory to Oracle? And, in that case, why not have just one parameter to set?

In Oracle Database 11*g* using ASMM, you can simply set MEMORY_TARGET and let Oracle handle the rest. In this version, the memory allocation on the operating system side is divided into smaller chunks. Shared memory segments are available for Oracle to use for the SGA.

NOTE
Oracle Database 11g also has the parameter MEMORY_MAX_TARGET, which allows you to specify the maximum setting for the MEMORY_TARGET parameter. However, when you set MEMORY_TARGET, the MEMORY_MAX_TARGET parameter will be set to the same value automatically, so you don't need to set MEMORY_MAX_TARGET directly.

On the Linux platform, Oracle uses shared memory in /dev/shm. Here is a typical error message that will come up if the operating system doesn't have enough memory to mount the /dev/shm file system:

```
SQL> startup
ORA-00845: MEMORY_TARGET not supported on this system
In the alert log:
Starting ORACLE instance (normal)
WARNING: You are trying to use the MEMORY_TARGET feature. This
feature requires the /dev/shm file system to be mounted for at
least 4294967296 bytes. /dev/shm is either not mounted or is
mounted with available space less than this size. Please fix this
so that MEMORY_TARGET can work as expected. Current available is 0
and used is 0 bytes.
```

NOTE
I'm using Linux in this example just to give you an idea about running Oracle on another operating system. Chapter 3 covers using Oracle on a Linux platform.

Using operating system memory in this way is a new shift in the Oracle Database 11*g* approach. Earlier versions used the System V-style shared memory, and you could verify the size of the shared memory used by Oracle using the operating system command `ipcs -b` which shows what semaphores have been allocated. To be able to view the memory allocated to Oracle with the POSIX-style shared memory, the OS commands for checking the space used in the file system are used, as in the following example.

```
$df -k /dev/shm
Filesystem 1K-blocks   Used      Available   Use%   Mounted on
           32486028     180068    32305960    1%     /dev/shm
```

Using the memory in Windows for Oracle is similar to using it for SQL Server. Address Windowing Extensions (AWE) and the Windows 4GB RAM Tuning feature are options available for the Oracle database, too. Using a Very Large Memory (VLM) configuration has been available for Oracle on Windows since Oracle8*i*.

Oracle Database 11*g* on Windows can take advantage of AWE to use more than 3GB of memory. Also, setting the /3GB switch in the boot.ini file will at least allow for using about 3GB of memory for Oracle. To use up to 64GB of memory, the /PAE switch needs to be enabled. Physical Address Extension (PAE) allows for mapping of a virtual addressable space above the 4GB of memory. Having both the /3GB and /PAE switches enabled at the same time will allow only 16GB of memory to be available, so the /3GB switch should be disabled to allow for more memory to be used by the PAE. The memory limitations are really applicable only on 32-bit Windows systems. With 64-bit systems, the limitations are measured in terabytes.

Windows supports the use of large pages for systems using a large amount of memory. The parameter in the Oracle key of the registry needs to be set as `ORA_LPENABLE=1` to enable the large pages. In order to use VLM on Windows, the `oracle` user needs the "Lock memory pages" privilege. The `USE_INDIRECT_DAT_BUFFERS=TRUE` parameter must be set in the parameter file for Oracle. Also, the `DB_BLOCK_BUFFERS` parameter must be set for the database cache.

The dynamic SGA parameters are not available for the very large memory settings. If the system doesn't need more than the 3GB of memory for the SGA, you should consider just using the 4GB RAM Tuning feature, so the dynamic parameters are available.

Again, with Oracle Database 11*g*, you can simply set the MEMORY_TARGET parameter and have Oracle manage the rest. However, adjusting some of the other memory parameters may improve the performance of particular applications. When used in combination with ASMM, the settings of the individual parameters are implemented as minimum values.

Sizing the SGA and PGA

As discussed in the previous section, with the new features of Oracle Database 11*g*, the configuration of each individual parameter for memory has become less important. Setting the MEMORY_TARGET is a simple way to manage the memory, even between the SGA and PGA. However, appropriately sizing the SGA and PGA memory remains important for Oracle database performance.

SGA Considerations

Several views provide SGA information. To look at the current sizing of the SGA, use v$sga and v$sgainfo. The v$sgainfo view shows the current sizes and which areas can be resized. The resizeable areas make up the variable size with the database buffers in v$sga.

```
SQL> select * from v$sga;
NAME                      VALUE
-------------------- ----------
Fixed Size              2086288
Variable Size         939526768
Database Buffers     1677721600
Redo Buffers           14688256

SQL> select * from v$sgainfo;
NAME                                 BYTES    RESIZEABLE
Fixed SGA Size                     2086288    No
Redo Buffers                      14688256    No
Buffer Cache Size               1677721600    Yes
Shared Pool Size                 889192448    Yes
Large Pool Size                   16777216    Yes
Java Pool Size                    16777216    Yes
Streams Pool Size                 16777216    Yes
Granule Size                      16777216    No
Maximum SGA Size                2634022912    No
Startup overhead in Shared Pool  201326592    No
Free SGA Memory Available                0
```

To see which objects are using the current memory areas, use the
v$sgastat view.

To get assistance in sizing the database cache, use the v$db_cache_advice view.

```
SQLPLUS> select size_for_estimate, buffers_for_estimate,
estd_physical_read_factor, estd_physical_reads
from v$db_cache_advice
where name = 'DEFAULT' and block_size = (select value from v$parameter
where name='db_block_size')
and advice_status = 'ON';
```

Size_for_est	buffer_for_est	estd_physical_read_factor	estd_physical_reads
160	19790	1.8477	38053244
320	39580	1.3063	26904159
480	59370	1.2169	25061732
640	79160	1.2016	24746320
800	98950	1.1884	24474411
960	118740	1.1792	24284735
1120	138530	1.1762	24223738
1280	158320	1.042	21459758
1440	178110	1.0379	21376570
1600	197900	1	20595061
1760	217690	.9959	20510626
1920	237480	.9938	20466583
2080	257270	.9921	20431565
2240	277060	.9908	20405971
2400	296850	.9902	20393666
2560	316640	.9895	20379145
2720	336430	.9884	20356415
2880	356220	.9848	20281604
3040	376010	.9808	20199710
3200	395800	.972	20018812

As you can see in this example, there is a point of diminishing returns for the amount of memory set and the reduction of physical reads. Even though there is a decrease in physical reads with settings higher than 1600, the decrease is not that significant. Just throwing memory at the database cache may not help the performance of the database.

Since block reads from memory are normally faster than going to disk to get the data block, why don't we size the memory to hold the whole database? Well, for large databases (talking well into terabytes), this isn't normally cost-effective. Of course, with different types of hardware, solid-state disks and flash memory cards could be used as part of a solution. For smaller databases—say, one that might be 20GB—you could have 20GB of memory allocated to the SGA, but that wouldn't necessarily keep all of the data blocks in memory, because the database needs memory for other processes.

Also, think about the data being accessed. Is all of the data always being read? And if it is, what about growth? It will be hard to keep up with supplying memory to the server as the size of the database grows. Full scans of tables will flush some of the blocks out of memory, and when code pulls more data than expected, having everything in memory might prove difficult. Tuning queries to pull just the data that is needed might avoid some of these larger scans, at least minimizing the physical reads.

Blocks that are read into the buffer cache are ordered from most recently used (MRU) to least recently used (LRU). Blocks that are read as part of a full-table scan are put on the LRU end. If the buffer cache is full, the LRU blocks will be flushed out of the cache. The goal is to keep the most frequently used data in memory for quicker access. This also includes the code (SQL statements) in the library cache. So, you will want to size the SGA to follow these guidelines, and then tune it as the database changes and grows.

PGA Considerations

The PGA is used for the program or user processes. As shown earlier in Figure 2-1, there are manual and automatic options for managing the PGA. Setting the `WORKAREA_SIZE_POLICY=AUTO` parameter has Oracle use the `PGA_AGGREGATE_TARGET` parameter for sizing the user processes for SQL that use memory, such as for sorts, group by, hash joins, and bitmaps. You can find information about PGA usage in the `v$pgastat` view, and also by looking at the maximum values of the `pga_used_mem`, `pga_alloc_mem`, and `pga_max_mem` columns in the `v$process` view. There is also an advice table for PGA, `v$pga_target_advice`, to help determine a good setting for `PGA_AGGREGATE_TARGET`.

Where Are the master, msdb, and tempdb Databases?

The SQL Server `master`, `msdb`, and `tempdb` databases do not exist in the Oracle world. In Oracle, other areas keep the system information, provide a way to schedule jobs, and maintain a temporary space for sorting and temporary tables.

System-level Information

For SQL Server databases and logins, the `master` database has the details. The `master` database contains the system information and server configurations. So, where is the `master` database information in Oracle?

In Oracle, the system-level information for the database instance is in the *data dictionary*, which is stored in the `SYSTEM` tablespace under the `SYS` schema. You can query views to retrieve this information about the database and objects contained in the databases and schemas. Here is a small sampling of the information stored and where it can be found on SQL Server and Oracle systems:

	SQL Server Master Database	**Oracle Data Dictionary**
Users	`syslogins`	`dba_users`
Objects	`sys.objects`	`dba_objects`
Tables	`sys.tables`	`dba_tables`
Datafiles	`sys.databases`	`dba_data_files`

NOTE
Some of the system tables are new to version SQL Server 2008. There are also system tables at the database level.

There are many more tables in both the SQL Server `master` database and Oracle data dictionary.

The Oracle catalog also contains system information. The catalog is created when a database is created, and it is updated with upgrades and patches. The catalog.sql and catproc.sql scripts run as part of the Oracle installation, and they create the data dictionary. The `GRANT SELECT ANY CATALOG to USER` role can be granted to a user to allow read access to the catalog views. This role can have three different levels of permissions: `USER_` for those objects owned by the user, `ALL_` for any objects for which the user has permissions, and `DBA_` for any catalog. As you probably noticed, `SYS` isn't included to qualify the name. This is because the public synonyms are set up to allow just using the name of the view.

As an example, let's see how we can get information about the database objects on each platform. Here's the SQL Server query to discover which objects are in the databases:

```
Select type_desc, count(1) from sys.all_objects
Group by type_desc
Order by type_desc;
RESULTS
CLR_STORED_PROCEDURE                            3
DEFAULT_CONSTRAINT                              1
EXTENDED_STORED_PROCEDURE                     149
INTERNAL_TABLE                                  3
PRIMARY_KEY_CONSTRAINT                         80
SERVICE_QUEUE                                   3
SQL_INLINE_TABLE_VALUED_FUNCTION               19
SQL_SCALAR_FUNCTION                            27
SQL_STORED_PROCEDURE                         1275
SQL_TABLE_VALUED_FUNCTION                      12
SYSTEM_TABLE                                   41
USER_TABLE                                     82
VIEW                                          286
```

In Oracle, we query `dba_objects` to get information about the database objects:

```
SQLPLUS> select owner, object_type, count(1) from dba_objects
Group by owner, object_type
Order by owner, object_type;
OWNER                           OBJECT_TYPE            COUNT(1)
------------------------------- --------------------  ----------
MMALCHER                        FUNCTION                      6
MMALCHER                        INDEX                       149
MMALCHER                        LOB                          14
MMALCHER                        PACKAGE                     310
MMALCHER                        PACKAGE BODY                236
MMALCHER                        PROCEDURE                     6
MMALCHER                        SEQUENCE                     60
MMALCHER                        SYNONYM                       1
MMALCHER                        TABLE                       133
MMALCHER                        TRIGGER                     158
MMALCHER                        TYPE                          2
PUBLIC                          SYNONYM                   20066
SYS                             CLUSTER                      10
SYS                             CONSUMER GROUP                5
SYS                             CONTEXT                       5
SYS                             DIRECTORY                    25
```

SYS	EVALUATION CONTEXT	10
SYS	FUNCTION	75
SYS	INDEX	718
SYS	INDEX PARTITION	216
SYS	JAVA CLASS	14747
SYS	JAVA DATA	296
SYS	JAVA RESOURCE	704
SYS	JOB	5
SYS	JOB CLASS	2
SYS	LIBRARY	115
SYS	LOB	112
SYS	LOB PARTITION	1
SYS	OPERATOR	6
SYS	PACKAGE	506
SYS	PACKAGE BODY	484
SYS	PROCEDURE	56
SYS	PROGRAM	4
SYS	QUEUE	15
SYS	RESOURCE PLAN	3
SYS	RULE	4
SYS	RULE SET	11
SYS	SCHEDULE	2
SYS	SEQUENCE	81
SYS	SYNONYM	9
SYS	TABLE	727
SYS	TABLE PARTITION	205
SYS	TRIGGER	9
SYS	TYPE	1127
SYS	TYPE BODY	81
SYS	UNDEFINED	6
SYS	VIEW	2958
SYS	WINDOW	2
SYS	WINDOW GROUP	1
SYSMAN	EVALUATION CONTEXT	1
SYSMAN	FUNCTION	8
SYSMAN	INDEX	398
SYSMAN	LOB	28
SYSMAN	PACKAGE	73
SYSMAN	PACKAGE BODY	72
SYSMAN	PROCEDURE	2
SYSMAN	QUEUE	2
SYSMAN	RULE SET	2
SYSMAN	SEQUENCE	5
SYSMAN	TABLE	342
SYSMAN	TRIGGER	48
SYSMAN	TYPE	217
SYSMAN	TYPE BODY	7

SYSMAN	VIEW	136
SYSTEM	INDEX	191
SYSTEM	INDEX PARTITION	32
SYSTEM	LOB	25
SYSTEM	PACKAGE	1
SYSTEM	PACKAGE BODY	1
SYSTEM	PROCEDURE	8
SYSTEM	QUEUE	4
SYSTEM	SEQUENCE	20
SYSTEM	SYNONYM	8

Not only does this query result show the different object types, but it also lists them by schema owner. Here, you see a few different schemas: SYS has the data dictionary, SYSTEM has objects for the database tools, and SYSMAN has the objects for Oracle Enterprise Manager. MMALCHER is just a user schema.

The count of objects will vary by Oracle version and depends on the different components that were installed. Also, the PUBLIC owner has the synonyms available to all users for the queries against the system objects, so they do not need to be fully qualified.

Data Dictionary Views

The Oracle data dictionary views are the place to go to get details about objects and even sizing. Instead of sp_help, you use DESCRIBE or queries that can be run against the dictionary tables. So just as sp_help has been your friend for looking into SQL Server objects, dba_ views will become your new Oracle friend. When I want to know what a table looks like, how many objects are owned by a user, or the name of a particular dba_ view, I run a quick query to find out.

With so many views available, memorizing them is not a good option. Fortunately, it's easy to find the view that contains the information you're seeking. If you know the view has a name that contains segments, tables, stats, or data, you can generate a list of views with that keyword in their name. For example, I know that the dba_ view for data files starts with data, and can use this query to find it:

```
SQLPLUS> select object_name from dba_objects where object_name like 'DBA_DATA%';
OBJECT_NAME
----------------------------
DBA_DATA_FILES          <======
DBA_DATAPUMP_JOBS
DBA_DATAPUMP_SESSIONS
```

```
3 rows selected.
SQLPLUS> DESC DBA_DATA_FILES;
Name                                      Null?    Type
----------------------------------------- -------- ---------------
FILE_NAME                                          VARCHAR2(513)
FILE_ID                                            NUMBER
TABLESPACE_NAME                                    VARCHAR2(30)
BYTES                                              NUMBER
BLOCKS                                             NUMBER
STATUS                                             VARCHAR2(9)
RELATIVE_FNO                                       NUMBER
AUTOEXTENSIBLE                                     VARCHAR2(3)
MAXBYTES                                           NUMBER
MAXBLOCKS                                          NUMBER
INCREMENT_BY                                       NUMBER
USER_BYTES                                         NUMBER
USER_BLOCKS                                        NUMBER
ONLINE_STATUS                                      VARCHAR2(7)
```

Also, some of the v$ views that contain dynamic information are available even when the database is not open. For example, the v$datafile and v$logfile views show information about the datafiles and redo log files, respectively:

```
SQLPLUS> select file#,status, (bytes/1024)/1024 size_MB, name from v$datafile;
FILE# STATUS    SIZE_MB           NAME
----- -------   ----------        -------------------------------------------
    1 SYSTEM       1070           /data/oracle/orcl/system01.dbf
    2 ONLINE       9225           /data/oracle/orcl/undotbs01.dbf
    3 ONLINE       1230           /data/oracle/orcl/sysaux01.dbf
    4 ONLINE    32767.5           /data/oracle/orcl/users01.dbf
    5 ONLINE      14924           /data/oracle/orcl/users02.dbf
    6 ONLINE      12724           /data/oracle/orcl/users03.dbf
select * from v$logfile order by group#;

GROUP# STATUS  TYPE    MEMBER
------ ------- ------- -----------------------------------------
     1         ONLINE  /data/oracle/orcl/redo01.log
     1         ONLINE  /data/oracle/orcl/redo01b.log
     2         ONLINE  /data/oracle/orcl/redo02.log
     2         ONLINE  /data/oracle/orcl/redo02b.log
     3         ONLINE  /data/oracle/orcl/redo03b.log
     3         ONLINE  /data/oracle/orcl/redo03.log
     4         ONLINE  /data/oracle/orcl/redo04b.log
     4         ONLINE  /data/oracle/orcl/redo04.log
```

Now we have found that the type of data in SQL Server's master database type is stored in the Oracle SYS schema. But where are the jobs stored? And what about templates that are used by the model database to create new databases. And do we even look for a tempdb? The information is closer than you might think.

Jobs and Schedules

Scheduling a job is done either via the Oracle Enterprise Manager (OEM) or using the DBMS_SCHEDULER package. If the job is scheduled using DBMS_SCHEDULER, it can be monitored and viewed in OEM. To create a job, a user needs "Select any catalog role" and "Create job" permissions.

There are three main components to a job: schedule, program, and job. The program and job contain the definitions, and the schedule sets regular times for the job to be run. Just as there are maintenance jobs as well as application jobs that can be scheduled in SQL Server, Oracle jobs can be run to take snapshots of the database and gather statistics, as well as create backups. The program can be PL/SQL code or an executable.

The history of jobs and their status is available on the Database Home page of OEM and in DBA_SCHEDULER_JOBS.

```
SQLPLUS> select owner,job_name, schedule_name, last_start_date, next_run_date  from
dba_scheduler_jobs;
OWNER       JOB_NAME                  SCHEDULE_NAME            LAST_START_DATE
SYS         GATHER_STATS_WEEKLY       WEEKLY_MAINTENANCE_JOB   21-DEC-09
SYS         AUTO_SPACE_ADVISOR_JOB    MAINTENANCE_WINDOW       26-DEC-09
SYS         GATHER_STATS_JOB          MAINTENANCE_WINDOW       26-DEC-09
```

Templates and Temporary Tables

The SQL Server model database has the default template for creating new databases. The Oracle database is created once with the use of the Database Configuration Assistant, script, or template. The schemas are created as users, and the templates or creation scripts can be used to set up other servers that are similar for development or new production environments.

The SQL Server model database is also used to create the tempdb database every time the server is shut down and restarted. It sets the tempdb size and growth of the database. Oracle doesn't need to re-create a temporary database each time it is started, because it doesn't have a temporary database. Oracle uses a temporary tablespace with *tempfiles* that act in this capacity. The temporary area is used for sorting, join operations, and global temporary tables. Similar to the tempdb database, the temporary tablespace cannot store permanent objects, so it doesn't need to be backed up.

The tempfiles are not fully initialized and are sparse files. Only the header information and last block of the file are created, so sizing on the file system might be off, because the tempfile might not be using all of the space that could be allocated to the file. The tempfiles are also not included in the control files. But there is a dictionary view for the tempfiles:

```
SQLPLUS> select file_name,tablespace_name,bytes, status from dba_temp_files;
FILE_NAME                       tablespace_name      BYTES            STATUS
/data/oracle/orcl/temp01.dbf    TEMP                 5368709120       AVAILABLE
```

A database has a default `TEMP` tablespace, and a database can also have more than one temporary tablespace. So, users can fill up their own temporary space only if they have a different one set as their default for sorting and temporary tables. Even with the default temporary tablespace set as `TEMP1`, for example, `user1` might have `TEMP2` as the default and will use only the `TEMP2` tablespace for the temporary space. It is a nice way to isolate some of the areas that are normally shared among different users or different applications.

How Oracle handles temporary tables demonstrates how application coding would be different between the two platforms. Oracle temporary tables are either transaction- or session-specific tables. It doesn't open the temporary or work tables available to other users or sessions. Some of the temporary tables in SQL Server are available for other sessions and processes until the server is restarted, and they are cleaned up at the end of the transaction or session, whether or not there were issues with the transaction or session.

Now that we've covered where to find the information that SQL Server stores in its `master`, `msdb`, and `tempdb` databases in Oracle, let's look at the Oracle services and processes.

Services and Processes

Various processes and services start up with Oracle, just as there are services for the SQL Server instance and SQL Server Agent. On Windows, an Oracle service needs to be started for the database. There is also a listener in the service list for Oracle—the TNS Listener service must be running for remote sessions to connect to the Oracle database. Along with these services, background processes are running on Windows. These processes run on any database server, no matter which operating system hosts it.

When looking at the sessions in the database, you will see a list of other system processes that are started. These take care of writing, logging, jobs, gathering statistics, and monitoring.

The SMON background process performs the system monitoring functions. It takes care of the recovery of transactions after restarting the database. For example, if the database crashes, the SMON process uses the undo tablespace to detect and recover any transactions that were interrupted. If you see the SMON process using up more than the normal amount of CPU, Oracle might not have shut down nicely, and this process could be cleaning up the transactions.

The PMON background process is for the user processes. It will clean up after a failed or killed user process.

When the Oracle database is started, the SMON and PMON processes are always running. You can use this information as a quick check to see which Oracle databases are available on a server. Here is an example that shows two databases (orcl and DBA1) are running on the server:

```
> ps -ef | grep smon
oracle    4889    1   0 Dec26 ?        00:00:04 ora_smon_orcl
oracle    8168    1   0 Dec26 ?        00:00:02 ora_smon_DBA1
> ps -ef | grep pmon
oracle    4877    1   0 Dec26 ?        00:00:01 ora_pmon_orcl
oracle    8154    1   0 Dec26 ?        00:00:00 ora_pmon_DBA1
```

The number of background processes can vary depending on components and how slaves for certain processes might be available. Here is a typical list of processes you will see running in the database:

- **SMON** System monitor process

- **PMON** Process monitor process

- **ARC0** Archiver process for writing out archive logs from the redo logs

- **MMON** Memory monitor gathering memory statistics

- **MMAN** Memory manager for resizing the SGA areas

- **DBW0** Database writer process writing blocks from the buffer cache to datafiles

- **LGWR** Log writer process for flushing the redo log buffer

- **CKPT** Checkpoint process to timestamp the datafiles and control files when checkpoints occur

- **MMNL** Process to assist the MMON process

- **RECO**   Recoverer background process for distributed transactions for two-phase commits

- **CJQ0**   Job queue process for batch processing (slave processes may be spawned)

- **PSP0**   Process spawner, to spawn slave processes for Oracle

- **J000**   Job queue slave process

Other background processes depend on which components are installed. For example, the ASMB and RBAL background processes run for Automatic Storage Management (ASM), and the QMN0 process runs for Oracle Streams. For Data Guard, the DMON and MRP0 processes run. In Real Application Clusters (RAC) environments, you will see the MS0, LMON, LMD, LCK, and DIAG processes.

You can see which background processes are running by listing the processes running as `oracle` on a server, and they are also visible in the `v$sessions` view. OEM also shows the processes under session activity, as shown in Figure 2-2.

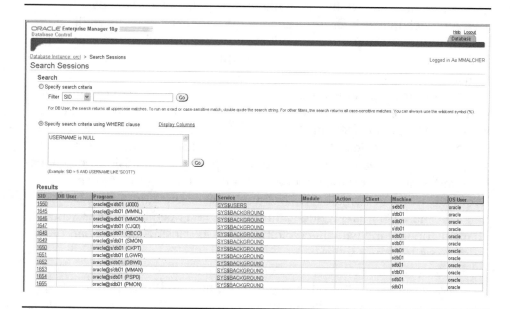

FIGURE 2-2.   *OEM view of background processes*

As you can see, there are quite a few background processes running with Oracle. Depending on how many slaves are spawned and which different components are installed, more processes may be running. Let me just say that there are definitely more than ten background processes! The fact that particular processes are running on the database system can give you more information about the database, such as which components are installed or if the database is in ARCHIVELOG mode.

sp_configure Options and Parameters

Those who say database administration is getting easier are not looking at all of the knobs that can be turned. More options and parameters are released with each new version of Oracle. I think that you will agree that more configurable parameters have been added to SQL Server as well. But setting the parameters is actually not the tricky part. The challenge is knowing which parameters might be related or impacted when you adjust a particular parameter.

As discussed earlier, Oracle has overall parameters, such as MEMORY_ TARGET, which manage the other underlying parameters dynamically. This approach makes it easier to change the parameters, but you still need to know which settings are appropriate—for example, which ones are for online transaction processing (OLTP) and which ones are for data warehouse systems.

I think of these parameters and options like a stereo tuner or soundboard. Preconfigured settings for different types of music can be used, and they will work for most people listening to the music. But then there are trained ears that need more of a definition of the tones or mixes of the music to make it sound exactly the way they want it. What happens if the music type changes or an instrument affects the volume? What if it is playing in the orchestra hall? How about in a small car? For these cases, more adjustments are needed. And when making such adjustments, you need to consider whether changing one setting will affect another, such as causing another part of the music to be louder or softer.

Similarly, the default database configurations may work for several database applications, but other applications need to be top performers and tuned specifically to get the desired results. This does take some understanding of the different settings and how they might affect other settings. On the other hand, a DBA can spend too much time trying to configure and set values without getting much of a return, especially if the environment is changing rapidly. Balance is important here. You need to know which options are available, and how to validate that the dynamic settings are performing as they should, so they can be left alone (giving you time to deal with other administration tasks!).

Viewing and Setting Parameters

In Oracle, you can view all of the parameter settings in OEM, or you can run a quick show query in SQL*Plus. Table 2-1 compares the SQL Server and Oracle commands for retrieving the values of parameters and options.

NOTE
In SQL Server, to see all of the advanced parameters, enable show advanced option *first with* sp_configure. *Oracle has hidden parameters that begin with an underscore. These are normally not configured except internally by Oracle or when working on an issue with Oracle support.*

	SQL Server	Oracle
List all parameters	sp_configure	show parameter
List a parameter	sp_configure 'remote access'	show parameter db_block_buffers
List parameters with a keyword (all parameters that have the keyword in their name)	sp_configure remote	show parameter buffers

TABLE 2-1. *Viewing Parameters*

For SQL Server, the options can be set at the server and database level. For Oracle, the parameters are normally configured at the server level, but some can be modified for a user session, so there are system- and session-level options.

```
SQLPLUS> alter system set parameter = X scope=both;
SQLPLUS> alter session set parameter = X;
```

Oracle parameters are maintained in the init.ora (known as the pfile) or spfile.ora file. The pfile is a text file (initSID.ora) that can be edited directly. The spfile has some binary information so it cannot be edited directly. It is updated through the following `alter` statements:

```
alter system set parameter=x scope=spfile
alter system set parameter=x scope=both
```

The spfile allows for the dynamic parameter changes; you can run `alter` statements against the running database, spfile, or both.

An spfile can be created from a pfile, and a pfile from an spfile. You can change a parameter by editing the pfile, and restart the database with the pfile instead of the spfile. Then create an spfile from the edited pfile to have the spfile file updated with the parameters, if you normally start up using the spfile.

```
SQLPLUS> startup pfile='/u01/oracle/product/11.0.1/dbs/initDBA1.ora'
SQLPLUS> create spfile from pfile; /*can also use create spfile from memory */
SQLPLUS>shutdown immediate;
SQLPLUS>startup /* as long as the spfile parameter is set in the parameter it
will start up using the spfile */
```

Getting Started with Some Parameters

How many knobs are available to adjust? In Oracle Database 10g, there are about 259 configurable parameters, with well over 1100 hidden parameters. In Oracle Database 11g, there are around 342 configurable parameters, and even more hidden parameters. Here, we will take a quick look at just some of these parameters.

Transaction Log Parameters

In SQL Server, transaction logs are handled with the SIMPLE or FULL option. In Oracle, ARCHIVELOG mode is similar to FULL. Archiving will write out the redo logs to a file for backing up, and allow for hot backups and point-in-time recovery. The default is NOARCHIVELOG mode, which is good for creating the database, but after the database is created and started it should be changed to ARCHIVELOG mode to be able to run the hot backups and have the full recovery options.

Versions prior to Oracle Database 10g included a parameter to start archiving. Now just the parameter for the location of the archive logs is needed: LOG_ARCHIVE_DEST.

Database Creation Parameters

The database name (DB_NAME) and character set are some of the parameters set up when a database is created. Parameters also set the location of control files, alert logs, and trace files.

The MAXDATAFILES and MAXLOGFILES parameters are limits that are set to size the control file when creating the database. MAXDATAFILES sets the total number of datafiles you can have in the database. If you reach the limit of MAXDATAFILES, you not only need to adjust the parameter, but also to re-create the control files to allow for the larger limit. MAXLOGFILES sets the total number of redo log files. The DB_FILES parameter is more of the soft limit that can be adjusted, but it needs a restart of the database to be put into effect.

Some Basic Parameters

The following are some basic parameters that are normally adjusted in some way. These parameters deal with system size, the database version, and resources available on the server.

- **DB_BLOCK_SIZE**   Size of the database block in bytes.

- **PROCESSES**   Number of allowable user processes. You need to restart the database to change this value, so plan for the number of users accessing the server.

- **SESSIONS**   Number of allowable sessions. You need to restart the database to change this value, so plan for the number of users accessing the server. This setting is similar to the maximum number of connections for SQL Server.

- **COMPATIBLE**   Database compatible with this software version. The current version would be ideal, but you can also allow for upgrades and still have Oracle behave as a different version. This setting is similar to the compatibility level in SQL Server.

- **PGA_AGGREGATE_TARGET** PGA memory, user process area.

- **SGA_TARGET** SGA memory.

- **MEMORY_TARGET** SGA memory (Oracle Database 11*g*).

- **UNDO_MANAGEMENT** Automatic undo management when TRUE.

- **UNDO_TABLESPACE** Tablespace for undo management.

Location and Destination Parameters

The following parameters will probably be different for every system, as they set the location of files for a database, and they tend to have a database name somewhere in a directory for separation of these locations.

- **CONTROL_FILES** Directory and file names of the control files.

- **BACKGROUND_DUMP_DEST** Directory for the alert log.

- **USER_DUMP_DEST** Directory for the user trace files.

- **AUDIT_FILE_DEST** Directory for audit logs.

- **LOG_ARCHIVE_DEST** Directory for archive logs.

Optimizer and Performance Parameters

Optimizer parameters set different behaviors of the optimizer. These parameters are available to assist with performance and adjust settings to deal with applications in particular ways. They help Oracle to choose a good path for execution plans.

- **OPTIMIZER_MODE** FIRST_ROW or ALL_ROWS (also CHOOSE and RULE in Oracle Database 10*g*). This is the setting for the default behavior of the optimizer for cost-based query plans. The default for Oracle Database 11*g* is ALL_ROWS.

- **CURSOR_SHARING** FORCE, EXACT, or SIMILAR. This setting is used to help reuse SQL statements in the library cache. FORCE and SIMILAR are good for use with code that uses literal values to force the optimizer to use a similar plan if the plan can't be matched because of the literal value.

- **QUERY_REWRITE_ENABLED** Allow rewrite of queries using materialized views.

- **SESSION_CACHED_CURSORS** Number of cursors to place in the cache for a session.

Other Parameters

Let's round off the list with a couple more parameters that should be mentioned here. These parameters will normally use the default setting, but if you're wondering where all of the slave job processes come from, they are probably run by the following parameters.

- **STATISTICS_LEVEL** ALL, BASIC, or TYPICAL. TYPICAL will collect the major statistics needed for automatic parameters like memory and gathering information for workload repository. BASIC will disable automated optimizer statistics and advisory components for memory settings. SQL Server has an auto-update statistics for a database, which gathers only the table statistics. This setting for Oracle gathers database, table, and operating system statistics.

- **RECYCLEBIN** ON or OFF. ON is the default. With this setting, dropped objects are collected in the recycle bin, and objects can be retrieved from the recycle bin if needed (unless it has been cleared).

- **SPFILE** Use of the spfile, file name, and location.

- **JOB_QUEUE_PROCESSES** Number of job slave processes. This setting is used by replication and user jobs through DBMS_JOBS. If it is set to 0, DBMS_JOBS is disabled.

- **MAX_JOB_SLAVE_PROCESSES** Limits the number of job slaves and user jobs scheduled through DBMS_SCHEDULER. You can use DBMS_JOBS and DBMS_SCHEDULER to create jobs, and these two parameters will set the maximum number of job slave processes.

- **DB_WRITER_PROCESSES** Number for database writer processes for background proceses. This is useful for an environment with a large amount of writes. The default is CPU_COUNT/8.

■ **REMOTE_LOGIN_PASSWORDFILE** `EXCLUSIVE`, `SHARED`, or `NONE`. When `SHARED` or `EXCLUSIVE`, a password file must be available; normally used for `SYS`, but can be for other users as well. `NONE` means it will be using operating system authentication. The password file is needed to be able to log in to the database remotely from SQL*Plus or another remote client as `SYSDBA`.

I believe that you have now seen more than enough parameters and options to have fun with. In later chapters, we will look at a couple more that affect performance and high-availability features. Our next topic is automatic undo management.

Undo, Redo, and Logs

Undo versus redo—this almost sounds like the start of a bad joke. Undo and redo were in a boat. Undo jumps out. Who is left on the boat? Redo! In all seriousness, understanding the purpose of the redo logs and undo tablespace will also help explain read consistency and why `SELECT` statements do not block writers and writers do not block readers in Oracle databases.

Transaction Logs Versus Redo Logs

In SQL Server, transactions and changes are written out to the transaction log, which is used by SQL Server to either commit the changes or roll back changes. There is also a save point that can be used for larger transactions, to basically commit the changes up to this point and continue with the transaction. The logs can either be overwritten if the database is in simple mode, or backed up to provide full backup and point-in-time restores. This is the basic flow of transactions through SQL Server and how it uses the transaction logs.

Oracle, with the undo and redo logs, handles transaction flow differently. However, some comparisons can be made between the Oracle redo logs and the SQL Server transaction logs. Like the SQL Server transaction logs, the redo logs record all of the transactions and changes made to the database.

When the database is in ARCHIVELOG mode, the archiver process will write off the redo logs for backing up and keeping these changes. When in

NOARCHIVELOG mode, the transactions that are committed will continue to be overwritten in the redo logs. In NOARCHIVELOG mode, the overwriting of the logs happens only once the changes have been recorded in the datafiles, and the changes can be committed or uncommitted transactions. There is enough information in the redo logs to roll back the transactions that might be rolled back, but Oracle is pulling the information from the datafiles.

The database will hang (or appear to hang) if it's waiting for the redo log to be available after writing the changes to the datafiles, and if in ARCHIVELOG mode writing to the archive log. If there are no other logs available to use, it will wait until these writes are complete to be able to reuse the redo log. If you're getting several waits here, you can increase either the number or size of the redo logs.

The redo logs are only one piece of the puzzle. Next, let's look how undo fits into Oracle processing.

Undo and Beyond

In the parameters section, you saw the LOG_BUFFERS, UNDO_MANAGEMENT, and UNDO_TABLESPACE parameters. The background processes have log writers (LGWR) and archiver processes (ARCn). The redo logs are created with a fixed size during database creation, normally in at least pairs, and there can be several groups. You saw an example of a redo log in the v$logfile view in the discussion of data dictionary views earlier in this chapter. See how nicely that all fits together?

Undo Sizing and Retention

The undo area provides read consistency to the users. Readers get consistent data, not dirty block reads, and at the same time, they are not blocked from anyone updating the data. Not only does the undo area provide concurrency for users, but it also rolls back transactions for rollback statements, provides the details to recover the database from logical corruptions, and allows for analyzing the data for flashback query operations. For all of these cases, the undo tablespace must have a before image of the data.

The undo tablespace should be sized to hold the larger transactions and be able to keep them for a period of time. The UNDO_RETENTION parameter is the setting for Oracle to attempt to keep the changes in the undo segments. If there are committed transactions, and there is more space needed in the undo tablespace, they will be overwritten, even if the time set by the UNDO_ RETENTION period has not passed.

To view the statistics for the undo area, use the v$undostat view. To see undo history, use dba_hist_undostat. This information, along with knowledge of what is running against the database and the undo advisor information, will help you to size the undo tablespace and set the retention period. The package DBMS_UNDO_ADV and the functions available from this package provide the advisory information. For example dbms_undo_ adv.required_retention will help with setting the retention.

Another good practice is to keep transactions small enough to be handled efficiently. Larger transactions run into issues for space, and if they fail (whether because of a transaction issue or a system outage), the rollback time can be significant. Reading through 20GB of undo segments will take time, and making the changes to the before image of the data will also take time.

Overwriting the committed change of the same block in one transaction that was being used in a longer running batch transaction can cause the transaction to fail with an "ORA-1555: snapshot too old" error. Receiving this error doesn't necessarily mean you need to resize the undo tablespace. You may be able to handle the problem by changing the transaction size or by improving the performance of the transaction. In the newer releases, Oracle automatically manages the undo segments, and these errors are less likely to occur. (With the manual configuration of the rollback segments, you risk creating rollback segments that might be too small.)

Transaction Process Flow

Transactions are performed against the database. The log buffer, which is in memory, caches the transaction details. The blocks that are pulled into the buffer cache now have before and after images in the undo segments. The log buffer is flushed out to the redo logs by the log writer. Since the log buffer may not be as big as the transaction, the log writer is continuously writing to the redo logs, not just on commit. So, the redo logs contain committed as well as uncommitted transactions. The redo logs contain the replay SQL, which can be used for other systems, such as a standby database, which we will discuss in Chapter 10.

The redo logs are a fixed size; they are not set to autogrow as are some datafiles. There can be several groups of redo logs. Once a redo log group is full or a switch log file occurs, the archiver process writes the redo log out to an archive file to be picked up by a backup process.

If all of the redo logs are full and have not yet been archived completely, the transaction will wait until that archive process is finished. The alert log will contain the message "checkpoint not complete." This means Oracle was unable to overwrite the redo log the first time and waited until it could overwrite the redo log. To address this issue, you could increase the size of the redo logs, but this is not always the best solution. You might instead add another group of redo logs to give the archiver more time to write out the log to the archive log. Log switching through the redo logs is important so that you have archive logs to back up, because the redo logs are not backed up during the hot backups. You can check how many times the log is switching per hour, through the v$log_history view or the alert log. If it is too many times per hour, make the logs bigger. If not, just add more groups of logs.

Figure 2-3 shows a view how this process flows when transactions are performed against the database. The transaction is not showing as being committed or rolled back. At the point of being committed or when

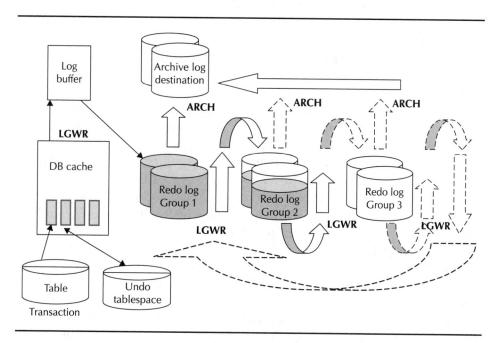

FIGURE 2-3. *Transaction process flow*

checkpoints run, the database writers would join into the process to write the changed database blocks back to the datafiles.

Understanding how Oracle handles transactions will help you in sizing the memory, undo tablespaces, and redo logs. Being able to have consistent reads in the database and provide a way to access the data without being blocked or needing to wait for transactions to complete is also key in the performance of queries against the database.

Summary

SQL Server has system databases, such as `master`, `msdb`, `model`, and `tempdb`. Even though Oracle does not have individual system databases that match the ones in SQL Server, the platforms share some similar concepts. There is a need for system information, there are parameters and options that can be configured and viewed, and transaction logging keeps track of changes.

Oracle has memory structures for supplying memory to server processes and user processes. There are individual parameters to manually configure memory, or dynamic settings that are available in Oracle Database 11 g by setting one parameter. Data dictionary views show the system information, including the values of the parameters. Oracle offers quite a few parameters for tuning and adjusting to provide the best performance options. We went over only a small portion of them in this chapter, but you have a starting point for common requirements.

Temporary and undo tablespaces are distinctive features of Oracle. It is able to have more than one temporary area that can be assigned to different users to isolate their sorting and temporary table processing. The undo tablespace keeps track of the before and after copies to provide consistent reads for concurrent users and be able to roll back changes if needed.

Changes are written to redo logs and kept in the undo segments to handle transactions. There is also a memory cache for the logs to buffer the log for the log writer to be able to process the changes to the redo logs and then off to the archive logs.

The server configurations and background processes offer just a glimpse into the internal workings of Oracle. There are several other system views available to see how Oracle is performing and gathering statistics to be able to process the requests and changes in the database. Some of them will be discussed in the following chapters as needed for more details, and the complete list is provided in the Oracle documentation.

CHAPTER
3

Oracle Installation

ven a basic database system installation requires some planning and preparation. You need to plan for both the hardware and software, including which components you will install. You need to prepare by validating that the prerequisites are in place, creating the users, and determining the required steps. You must consider the operating system version as well as platform. Oracle supports Windows and various flavors of Unix and Linux, so you have several operating system options.

Having checklists and using available scripts to check prerequisites will make the installation process more consistent and repeatable. The Oracle installer does run a check, but it is easier to have this check pass than to wait for this step in the installation to fail and then need to start over.

For SQL Server installation, you have probably planned for various requirements, such as having the logs default to a different file system than where the datafiles are stored, and placing the system databases on a drive other than C:. You may have decided which patches to apply and which version of the operating system to use.

Just as with SQL Server, you'll need to decide where to install the software, where to create the databases, and whether to use the default installation (probably for a test environment) or a custom installation (for a production environment).

This chapter covers Oracle installation, beginning with the operating system preparations. Along the way, we will look at some scripts that you can use to make the rollout to other environments a repeatable process.

Operating Systems

The installation of the Oracle software is very similar on the different operating systems. Some of the types of checks are also the same, such as making sure the version of the operating system is compatible with the version of the database. A 64-bit Linux version of Oracle will not install on a 32-bit Linux or Windows 64-bit system, for example.

The Oracle release notes provide information about where to find the compatibility matrix and the system requirements for the server. As shown in Table 3-1, the requirements listed are minimum values; they might not be adequate for some systems to perform as needed. The additional Oracle components may have some requirements outside the database lists. So, the

	Windows 32-Bit	Windows 64-Bit	Linux 32-Bit	Linux 64-Bit
RAM	1GB	1GB	1GB	1GB
Virtual memory	2 × RAM	2 × RAM	1GB RAM = 1.5GB swap 2 to 16 GB = 2 to 16GB swap > 16 GB RAM = 16GB swap*	
Disk space	4.7GB	5.2GB	3.5–5GB	3.5–5GB
Processor*	550 MHz	AMD64 or Intel (EM64T)	32-bit supported	64-bit supported

*For Linux, the swap space should be the same as the RAM up to 16GB.

TABLE 3-1. *Hardware Requirements (Minimum Values)*

components you plan to install will also determine what is needed for the server. The disk space requirements depend on the components installed, but the base product alone does require more disk space for 64-bit operating systems. Also note that newer processors that are not listed could meet or exceed the minimum requirements.

You can use the following command-line option to run the installer with parameters to perform just the system prerequisites checks, without continuing to install Oracle:

```
E:\Oracle11gR2\database> setup.exe -executeSysPrereqs
```

The results can be viewed in the prerequisite_results.xml file, which will be in the oraInventory/logs directory.

NOTE
Checking for prerequisites does not quite work as expected in Oracle Database 11g Release 1, but it does work in Release 2. In Release 1, the check will be performed during the install process, so you may need to start over if one of the checks fails.

Since SQL Server DBAs are familiar with the Windows platform, we will first discuss the Windows setup for Oracle. Then we will cover Linux, which is a popular platform on which to run Oracle databases. For those who are considering the move from a Windows-based to a Linux-based database system, I will review some useful Linux commands and point out where to find the information to validate the configuration and prerequisites.

Windows Setup

There are advantages to installing Oracle on the Windows platform. One is that as a SQL Server administrator, you are already working with a Windows system. Another is that some tasks that must be done manually on the Linux platform are taken care of automatically on Windows. For example, the environment variables are set up for you, and Windows handles the startup and shutdown of services.

Oracle Homes

SQL Server tends to have a default location for the binaries, and Oracle will set up a default as well: the Oracle home directory. This directory location can be set during the installation process, or it can be specified by setting the ORACLE_HOME environment variable before running the installer.

Although the environment variables are set by the Oracle installer for Windows, there might be more than one Oracle home on a server. If this is the case, when using a command line, you will need to set the variable ORACLE_HOME first, or fully qualify the path to the correct Oracle home.

```
C:\> set ORACLE_HOME=d:\oracle\product\11.2.0\db_1
C:\> set ORACLE_SID=orcl
C:\> sqlplus
```

The release might be different for the Oracle homes, so looking at the set environment variables will be one way of noticing what homes are available, and what the locations of the Oracle homes are. Also, with more than one database on the server, you might get an "ORA-12560: TNS:protocol adapter" error when the ORACLE_SID (database instance name) isn't specified. Using the set commands in Windows or setting the environment variables for both the Oracle home and Oracle SID are important for being able to connect to the database.

User Account for Installation

The installer creates the ORA_DBA group automatically on the Windows platform. A standard practice with SQL Server is to create another user that has administrator privileges to install the software and be the owner of the SQL Server services. This is also a recommended practice with Oracle, even though you can log in as administrator and do not need a separate account.

By default, the Oracle services will use the Local Service account. By having a separate domain account to manage these services and perform the installation, you may even be able to match a standard that is already being used in your current SQL Server environment.

File System

The database software should be installed on the NTFS file system because of the security available for the Oracle home directory, which will contain trace files and database files. You need to plan the Oracle home directory location and on which file system the datafiles should reside. These locations will be needed for the installation.

Network Connectivity

One more minor detail is that, considering that the database is not really meant to be a stand-alone machine, it needs network connectivity. Clustering will have different requirements, but the database server needs to have a primary IP address that is accessible (it doesn't need to be a static IP, unless your environment requires that).

If you are using a dynamic configuration (DHCP), a test conducted during the Oracle installer's prerequisite check will fail if Microsoft Loopback Adapter is not the primary network adapter on the system. Here is a quick check for this adapter:

```
C:\> ipconfig /all
Ethernet adapter Local Area Connection 2:
Connection-specific DBS Suffix . . . . :
Description . . . . . . . . . . . . . .: Microsoft Loopback Adapter
Physical Address . . . . . . . . . . . : 7A-80-4C-9F-57-5D
DHCP Enabled . . . . . . . . . . . . .: Yes
Autoconfiguration Enabled . . . . . . .: Yes
```

If Microsoft Loopback Adapter is not configured, you can set it up through Add/Remove Hardware in the Control Panel. Select Network Adapters, and add it as a new network adapter.

Windows Platform Checklist

Here's a quick checklist for Windows installations:

■ Check that the operating system version and Oracle version and edition are correct.

■ Verify that the hardware requirements are met.

■ Create an Oracle account with administrator permissions to perform the installation.

■ Run the prerequisite check and correct any issues found.

Useful Linux/Unix Commands

Linux might be a new operating system for you. If so, you will be happy to learn that there are graphical user interface (GUI) tools as well as simple commands that will help you navigate through the Linux environment. Here, I'll introduce some commonly used Linux commands. If you're already familiar with Linux, you can skip to the next section, which covers Linux setup for Oracle installation.

Table 3-2 compares some of the command-line commands for Windows and Linux. As you can see, several are the same or similar.

CAUTION
When you are dealing with files from the command line, you should be aware that files removed with rm do not go to a recycle bin. To get these files back after removal, you will need to restore them. Be particularly careful in using rm with a wildcard.

The following are some other useful Linux commands:

■ pwd   Shows the current directory.

■ echo $ORACLE_HOME   Shows the value of the variable.

Task	Windows	Linux
List files and directories	Dir	ls
Change directory	Cd	cd
Copy file	Copy	cp
Move the file to another name or location	Move	mv
Delete a file	Del	rm
View contents of a file	Type	cat or more
Make a directory	Mkdir	mkdir
Remove a directory	Del	rm -r
View the current environment variables	Set	env

TABLE 3-2. *Command-Line Commands in Windows and Linux*

- whoami   Shows the current user.
- ps -ef   Shows the list of current processes running on the server.
- grep   Searches for a name or value in a file or list or process.
- chmod   Changes permissions for a file or directory.
- chgrp   Changes the group for permissions of a file or directory.
- chown   Changes the owner of a file or directory.

The manual pages (man pages) provide parameter options and examples of how to use the commands. To access the man page for a command, just type man and the command at the prompt, as in this example:

```
> man grep
```

When you download files for a Linux system, such as patches or software, they might come in a couple of formats, with file names ending in .Z, .gz, .zip, .cpio, or .tar. These are compressed files. You'll need to uncompress these files so that they are usable. The following are sample commands to uncompress the various formats:

```
> uncompress *.Z
> unzip *.zip
> gunzip *.gz
> tar -xvf file.tar
> cpio -idmv < file_name
```

Again, you can view the man page for help with the options available and other examples by entering `man` followed by the command at the command line.

Linux Setup

For a Linux system, you need to set up users, adjust permissions and kernel parameters, and make sure the required packages are installed.

Users and Groups

Although you can install Oracle and own the services for Oracle as the administrator on the server, this is not recommended, particularly for Linux systems, where the administrator account is the root account. You should create a user and group for the Oracle installation. The Oracle processes will also run under this user. Additionally, if you will be installing certain Oracle components, such as Automatic Storage Management and Clusterware, you should create separate users and groups to own the different pieces of software.

The following example demonstrates creating the `oinstall` (Oracle installation), `dba` (database administrator), `asmdba` (Automatic Storage Management administrator), and `crs` (Clusterware) groups:

```
# /usr/sbin/groupadd  g 501 oinstall
# /usr/sbin/groupadd  g 502 dba
# /usr/sbin/groupadd  g 504 asmdba
# /usr/sbin/groupadd  g 505 crs
```

The users for this example are added as follows:

```
# /usr/sbin/useradd  u 502  g oinstall  G dba     oracle
# /usr/sbin/useradd  u 503  g oinstall  G asmdba  osasm
# /usr/sbin/useradd  u 504  g oinstall  G crs     crs
```

Figure 3-1 shows these users listed in User Manager, which is a Linux tool for managing user permissions and group associations.

As you can see in User Manager, for each user, there is also an associated /home directory. You can browse through the directories and look at the file systems using the GUI, by clicking the Computer or Oracle's Home icon on the desktop (also shown in Figure 3-1).

The `oracle` user is not normally created in Linux with full administration permissions, but certain rights are needed for resources for the software to run properly. The /etc/security/limits.conf file has the resources for `nproc` and `nofile`, which allow a certain number of processes and number of files to be open by the user, and possibly memory limits. Session permissions are in the /etc/pam.d/login file. View these files

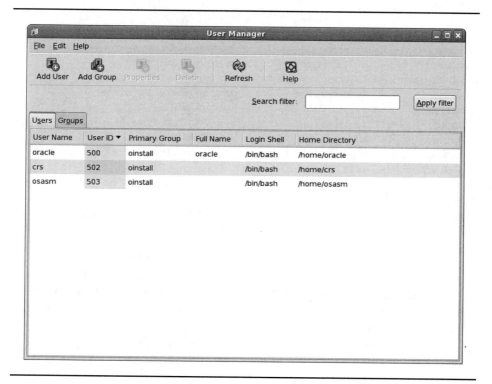

FIGURE 3-1.   *Linux User Manager*

to check that the `oracle` user has been added and to verify permissions. You can edit the files with the vi editor or another text editor.

```
> cat /etc/security/limits.conf
#<domain>              <type>          <item>          <value>
#
oracle                 soft            nproc              2047
oracle                 hard            nproc             16384
oracle                 soft            nofile             1024
oracle                 hard            nofile            65536
# End of file

> cat /etc/pam.d/login
#%PAM-1.0
auth [user_unknown=ignore success=ok ignore=ignore default=bad]
pam_security.so
auth                   include         system-auth
account                required        pam_nologin.so
account                include         system-auth
password               include         system-auth
# pam_selinux.so close should be the first session rule
session                required        pam_selinux.so close
session                include         system-auth
session                required        pam_loginuid.so
session                optional        pam_console.so
# pam_selinux.so open should only be followed by sessions to be
executed in the user context
session                required        pam_selinux.so open
session                optional        pam_keyinit.so force revoke
session                required        /lib/security/pam-limits.so
session                required        pam_limits.so
```

Some system areas, such as those listed for the parameter and option settings, can normally be viewed but not modified. Administrator permissions (root access) might be needed to make changes to these files. If sharing the server with another application, it's important to make sure that changes to these system areas are communicated, or discussed first. Even without write permissions, having access to this information is helpful for doing a comparison of what is needed and being able to communicate what configuration changes are needed to the server administrator.

Other Linux Considerations

Filling up some shared areas, such as /tmp, will cause issues with running or installing Oracle software. You should be careful about placing files in these areas and be sure to purge any old installation logs that are placed there.

Required Packages

The Oracle installation guide lists the required packages for the various Linux flavors. Some of the packages will already exist on your system, since they are included in the Linux installation. You should verify that they were installed by using the command `rpm -q package_name`. You will need to install any of the required packages that have not been installed by default.

As an example, for Red Hat or Oracle Enterprise Linux 5.2 and Oracle Database 11*g* Release 2 (R2), the following required packages are included in the Linux installation by default (verified by using `rpm` with the `-q` option):

```
binutils-2.17.50.0.6-6.el5 (x86_64)
compat-libstdc++-33-3.2.3-61 (x86_64)
compat-libstdc++33-3.2.3.61 (i386)
elfutils-libelf-9.125-3.el5 (x86_64)
glibc-2.5-24 (x86_64)
glibc-2.5-24 (i686)
glibc-common-2.5-24 (x86_64)
ksh-20060214-1.7 (x86_64)
libaio-0.3.106-3.2 (x86_64)
libaio-0.3.106-3.2 (i386)
libgcc-4.1.2-42.el5 (i386)
libgcc-4.1.2-42.el5 (x86_64)
libstdc++-4.1.2-42.el5 (x86_64)
libstdc++-4.1.2-42.el5 (i386)
make-3.81-3.el5 (x86_64)
```

If there are 32-bit and 64-bit versions listed, it doesn't matter whether you are running on a 32-bit or 64-bit version—both must be installed.

Continuing with the same example, the following required packages are not installed by default and will need to be added:

```
elfutils-libelf-devel-0.125-3.el5.x86_64.rpm
elfutils-libelf-devel-static-0.125-3.el5.x86_64.rpm
elfutils-libelf-devel and elfutils-libelf-devel-static
static-0.125-3.el5.x86_64.rpm
glibc-headers-2.5-24.x86_64.rpm
kernel-headers-2.6.18-92.el5.x86_64.rpm
glibc-devel-2.5-24.x86_64.rpm
```

```
glibc-devel-2.5-24.i386.rpm
gcc-4.1.2-42.el5.x86_64.rpm
libgomp-4.1.2-42.el5.x86_64.rpm
libstdc++-devel-4.1.2-42.el5.x86_64.rpm
gcc-c++-4.1.2-42.el5.x86_64.rpm
libaio-devel-0.3.106-3.2.x86_64.rpm
libaio-devel-0.3.106-3.2.i386.rpm
sysstat-7.0.2-1.el5.x86_64.rpm
unixODBC-2.2.11-7.1.x86_64.rpm
unixODBC-2.2.11-7.1.i386.rpm
unixODBC-devel-2.2.11-7.1.x86_64.rpm
unixODBC-devel-2.2.11-7.1.i386.rpm
```

The first three packages listed need to be installed together:

```
> rpm -ivh elfutils-libelf-devel-0.125-3.el5.x86_64.rpm elfutils-libelf-devel
```

To install the unixODBC-devel-2 packages, enter the following at the Linux prompt:

```
>rpm -ivh unixODBC-devel-2*rpm
```

Once again, use `rpm` with the `-q` option to verify that a package is installed:

```
>rpm -q unixODBC-devel-2.2.11
```

The installation guide provided by Oracle will have the most up-to-date information for your versions of Oracle and Linux, and point out any dependencies with certain packages and if there are any issues.

Kernel Parameters

You may need to adjust the kernel parameters if your Oracle system will have high memory needs. Recall from Chapter 2 the example of the error message that appears when the operating system doesn't have enough memory to mount the /dev/shm file system. Kernel parameters are in the /etc/sysctl.conf file, which can be edited to make the necessary modifications.

```
kernel.shmall = physical RAM size / pagesize
kernel.shmmax = ½ of physical RAM, but < 4GB
kernel.shmmni =4096
```

```
kernel.sem = 250 32000 100 128
fs.file-max = 512 x processes
fs.aio-max-nr = 1048576
net.ipv4.ip_local_port_range = 9000 65500
net.core.rmem_default = 262144
net.core.mem_max = 4194304
net.core.wmem_default = 262144
net.core_wmem_max = 1048576
```

After this file is edited, you must activate the changes by running the following at the command prompt as root:

```
sysctl -p
```

Use the following command to view the current settings for a kernel parameter:

```
> /sbin/sysctl -a | grep <param-name>
```

This was a quick overview of the setup for the Linux operating system. The Oracle installation guide will have the details for your specific environment.

Storage Requirements

Now we need to look at where the database is going to live. There are many storage options available with hardware, configurations, and file systems, and with new hardware developments, even more options may be coming soon. However, we do want to eventually get to actually installing Oracle, so this will not be an all-inclusive discussion about storage, but enough to cover the basics.

If you don't have enough memory in which to store the database—whether it's SQL Server or Oracle—fast read access is great. For backing up data and applications that are heavy on the transactions, fast writing to the disk is another bonus. In designing the storage layout, striping and mirroring play a definite part. The databases need to be highly available, and the users will always be happier with faster access, so building in fault-tolerant systems at the storage level is a necessity. Making it fast is even better. Chapter 10 will cover some I/O tuning and possible issues. Here, we'll first examine what disk storage is needed, and then look at Oracle Automatic Storage Management (ASM), which can simplify your work by handling much of the storage for you. We'll also review the types of Oracle files.

Disk Storage

You will need storage for datafiles and log files, as well as disk space for installing the software, but what other disk storage is required? You will need space for server logs and backups, and possibly a scratch area for exports and working with files.

Although you could use certain storage solutions, such as striping, to make your database system work with just two disk drives or one file system, such a setup isn't ideal. With Linux, it's possible to just have one mount point and place everything there under different directories. To set up storage for a particular system properly, the DBA needs to understand the different pieces: files, I/O events, and backups. You need to know which are typical events for databases and which are not, and which databases are heavy on read and writes of disk, and how each of these can affect the disk storage needed.

Under Windows, you would at least hope for two additional drives besides the C: drive. For example, you might set up disk storage on Windows as follows:

- **D:\oracle**   Base directory for software and server logs

- **D:\oradata**   For datafiles and one control file

- **E:\orabackup**   For backups

- **E:\oraarch**   For archive logs

- **E:\oraexp**   For data dump files and exports

- **E:\oradata**   Another location for control files

Control files contain information about the datafiles that can be used for recovery, as discussed in the "Oracle Files" section a little later in the chapter. You should place the control files in different directories and have multiple copies available in case they are needed.

Under Linux, you might set up your disk storage as follows (/u0*n* is a typical naming convention):

- **/u01/oracle**   Base directory for software, server logs, and control files

- **/u02/oracle/SID**   For exports, archives, backups, and control files

- **/u03/oracle/SID**   For datafiles (numbers can continue to increase) and control files

Alternatively, you could use another naming convention such as /ora0*n*, and this type of setup:

- **/ora01/oracle**   Base directory for software

- **/ora01/SID**   For datafiles and control files

- **/ora02 and subdirectories**   For export, backups, control files, and so on

These are just some examples, intended to demonstrate how you might break up the software, datafiles, and backup files.

Storage Management with ASM

ASM makes managing datafiles simple. With Oracle Database 11*g* R2, ASM can manage all of the files—database files, nonstructured binary files, and external files including text files.

This means that all of the discussion in the previous section could actually be ignored. ASM handles managing the disk, adding disk storage, and tuning I/O performance with rebalancing while the storage is up and available to the Oracle databases on that server. The discussion then just comes down to how many disk groups you will create. ASM will take care of mirroring and striping. Different levels of redundancy are available for the disk groups: normal, high, and external. With external, ASM doesn't provide the redundancy, but it can take advantage of external hardware mirroring.

With Oracle Database 10*g* and even 11*g* R2, the ASM installation was part of the database software installation routine. Starting with Oracle Database 11*g* R2, ASM is a separate installation using the Grid Infrastructure. Use a different home directory than the database home directory for the installation of ASM, and perform the installation as another user, such as `asmadm` user. The home directory for ASM contains other pieces, such as Clusterware, which are part of the ASM installation.

If you are installing a version of Oracle earlier than 11*g* R2, start the installation process of the database software. After you set the home to install the software, an option will come up for choosing which type of install to do, as shown in Figure 3-2.

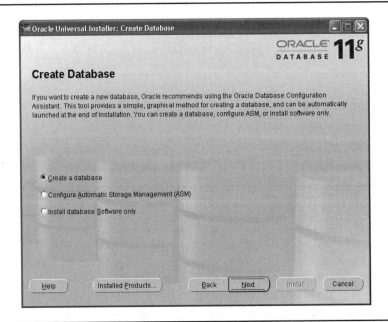

FIGURE 3-2. *Choose to install ASM in Oracle Database 11g R1 or earlier versions*

After you choose the ASM installation, the Database Configuration Assistant will start to create the instance that is used by ASM. In Figure 3-3, the password is set for the system user, and the parameters to discover the disk groups can be set here as well.

Next, create the disk groups. You can also add disk groups later. You should see a list of devices available for the disk groups; if not, the parameter for disk discovery might not be set. Figure 3-4 shows how to set this discovery path, and then select the disks to be part of the disk group. Here is where the redundancy for the disk group is selected. This is just the setup of the ASM instance. In Chapter 10, we will look at how this plays into a highly available database environment.

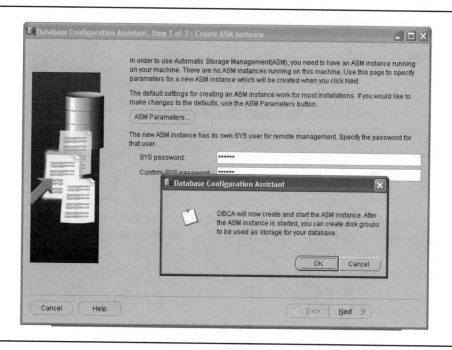

FIGURE 3-3.   *ASM instance creation*

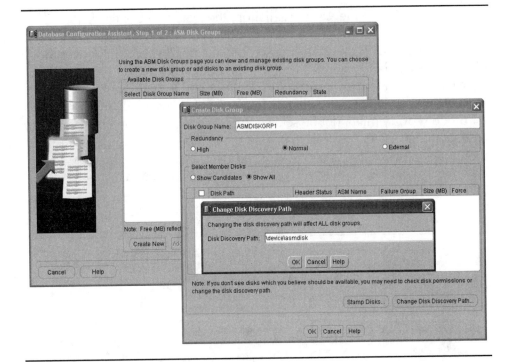

FIGURE 3-4. *ASM disk groups*

If you are installing Oracle Database 11*g* R2, ASM is a Grid Infrastructure installation. As shown in Figure 3-5, you can install Clusterware and the Grid Infrastructure. With this installation, the creation of the ASM instance, disk groups, and volumes is done by the ASM Configuration Assistant instead of the Database Configuration Assistant.

You can also use the ASM command-line utilities ASMCMD and ACFSUTIL to create and manage the disks. Here's an example of creating a volume group from the operating system command line:

```
ASMCMD > volcreate -d DISKGRPDATA -s 20G volume1
```

ASMCMD can help manage the instance, with startup and shutdown, disk group, and disk failure management.

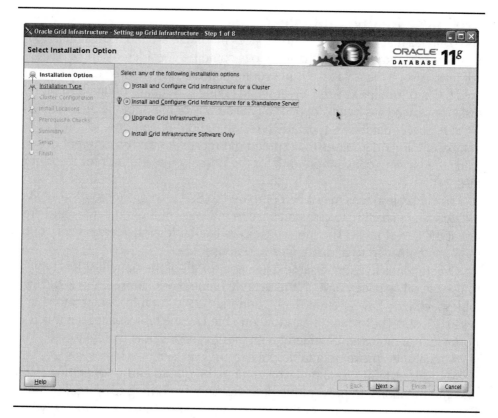

FIGURE 3-5. *ASM installation on Oracle Database 11g R2*

The setup of the ASM disks needs to be done before even installing ASM instance. The disk groups can be created so that they are available for the software install. If using the file manager for the regular files, such as create scripts and parameter files, as well as the datafiles for the database, these disks and storage areas will need to be available for installation.

We have just scratched the surface of ASM. It has many more features and options, and is an important piece of a stable database environment.

Oracle Files

Various types of files are part of the Oracle system. Understanding what these files contain will help you to plan for storage and disk space.

Are These Really .mdf Files?

The datafiles that make up the tablespaces in Oracle are the most similar to SQL Server's .mdf files, and the redo logs could be considered similar to the .ldf files. Also, if the database is not running, these files can be copied for a cold backup, similar to SQL Server when taking a database offline or if the instance service has been stopped to take a copy of the .mdf file and .ldf files.

SQL Server databases typically have one .mdf file and one .ldf file per database. Larger databases may spread out more files across different drives, using the naming convention .mdf for the primary file and .ndf for the other files.

Oracle tablespaces might be compared to SQL Server filegroups, but the filegroups are specific to one database to manage multiple datafiles and are not at the server level. The tablespaces are available at the server level, but might be managed to allocate files to one user.

Oracle tends to use the same extension for all of the datafiles. It is typical to use the tablespace name in the datafile name. For example, the SYSTEM tablespace may have system01.dbf, and the SYSAUX tablespace may have sysaux01.dbf. These examples show one file for one tablespace, but this is normally not the case. Especially with older versions, it is typical to see several datafiles make up a tablespace.

Multiple datafiles for a tablespace might be due to earlier operating system limitations, to prevent the datafiles from becoming too large. Balancing the need for fewer files to manage against being able to easily restore datafiles is one of the fun tasks of a DBA. It's nice to be able to turn over this task to ASM. If faced with an application that has been around for a couple of versions of Oracle, and the tablespaces seem a little on the unmanageable side, it might be time to convert to ASM.

More Files to Manage

Datafiles are just some of the files needed by the Oracle database. Then there are control files, parameter files, password files, and log files. Each file type has a specific purpose in the Oracle environment, and these files are key pieces for being able to restore systems, configure parameters dynamically, and allow access for privileged users.

The control files are critical for database operation. They contain information about the change numbers in the redo logs; records of the datafiles with checkpoints, file names, database name, and creation timestamp; and backup information. With all of these details in the file, you can see that it's important to have several copies, as noted in the earlier section on disk storage.

The location of the control files is set at database creation, and the parameter CONTROL_FILES has the values for the location:

```
CONTROL_FILES = (/u02/oracle/SID/control01.ctl,
 /u03/oracle/SID/control02.ctl,/u04/oracle/SID/control03.ctl)
```

Oracle Database Components

The Oracle system is made up of database components. Many are included as options with the database installation. Other components—such as client tools and client connectivity pieces, Grid Infrastructure, gateways, and examples with schemas—are available as separate downloads. For Windows and earlier releases of Linux, Clusterware is a separate installation. Oracle Database 11*g* R2 has Clusterware as part of the Linux database main installation. (Clusterware is discussed in Chapter 10.) You can install the client from the server media, but if you are installing only the client, separate downloads are available.

The default installation will not install all of the components. You will need to decide which ones you need for your environment. Also, you should understand the licensing impact before installing everything available. Installing only the components you will use and have licensed will keep the environment simple and is a first step to a secure configuration. Note that even some of the components that are installed by default may require additional licensing for use in the environment.

The following are some of the components that are part of the database installation:

Oracle Advanced Security	Oracle Partitioning
Oracle Spatial	Oracle Label Security
Oracle OLAP	COM Automation Feature
Data Mining RDBMS	Database Extensions for .NET
Database Vault	Real Application Testing
Oracle Net Services	Oracle Net Listener
Oracle Connection Manager	Oracle Call Interface
Oracle Programmer	XML Development Kit
Oracle Configuration Manager	

Also, as part of the Windows installation, the following components are available:

- Services for Microsoft Transaction Server

- Administration Assistant for Windows

- Counters for Windows Performance Monitor

- OLE, ODBC, and .NET drivers

NOTE
Oracle Configuration Manager is available without additional licensing. It hooks into My Oracle Support, which allows for health checks and provides details on patches that are available based on the release of the database.

You can add and remove components as necessary after the initial installation. This means that the software can be installed in pieces, such as first some components like Clusterware and ASM, and then the binaries for the database system. The database creation can be done as part of the installation. Taking this approach allows you to make sure each component is working properly before moving on to the next one. It also means that if the prerequisites are not met, you just need to take a quick step back, rather than completely starting over.

Oracle Software Installation

Operating system configurations—check; storage—check; users—check. You're ready to install the software. With the planning and setup completed, the installation of the Oracle software is the easy part. I recommend that you install just the software first, and then run the assistants separately to create a database and configure other required components.

On Windows, start the installation by executing setup.exe to run the Oracle Universal Installer (OUI).

On Linux, a couple of environment variables need to be set up first, and then the installer program can run.

```
> export DISPLAY = ip address:0.0
> export ORACLE_BASE = /u01/oracle
> export ORACLE_HOME = /u01/oracle/product/11.2.0
> export PATH = $PATH:$ORACLE_HOME/bin
> export LD_LIBRARY_PATH=$LD_LIBRARY_PATH:$ORACLE_HOME/lib
> cd ../oracle/Disk1
>./runInstaller
```

When setting up the variables in Linux, they will appear as the selected values in the install screen (similar to Figure 3-6).

After the opening welcome screen, you will be asked to choose between basic and advanced installation, as shown in Figure 3-6. Notice that the Oracle home location is already filled in by default. This is where the software will be installed, as well as the datafile for the sample database. Note that you can choose the advanced installation and change the Oracle home directory.

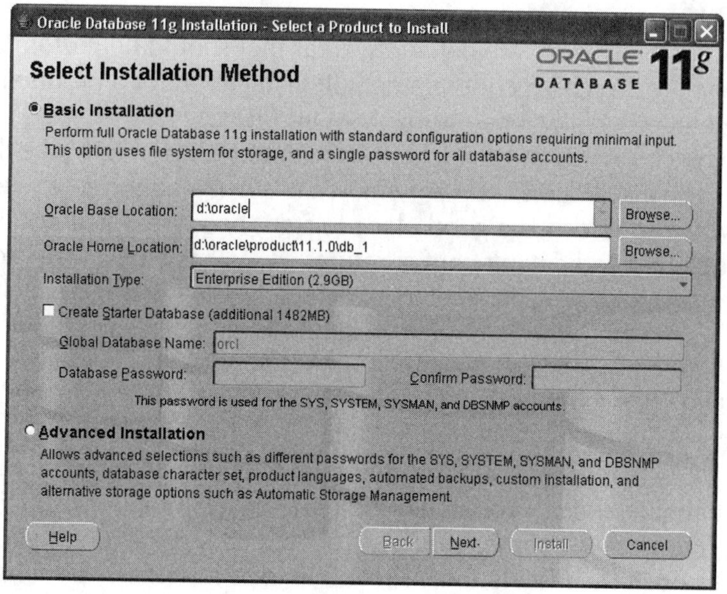

FIGURE 3-6. *Selecting basic or advanced installation*

The advanced installation allows for the following:

- Install the software first without creating any databases.

- Choose which software components to install. As noted earlier, this is part of a secure configuration for the environment. Also, knowing which pieces have been installed will help with patching and upgrading.

- Configure the passwords for the system users differently for each user.

- Install RAC.

- Configure ASM.

- Use a different template or configuration for the database.

- Select a character set.

- Upgrade an existing database.

- Use a different file system for the database files to separate them from the Oracle home.

As you can see, these are definitely areas that should be customized. It would not be typical to choose a default installation for a production environment, especially when using ASM and RAC.

So, why choose the basic (default) installation? You might take this route for testing the installation and verifying what is installed for new releases. With new versions, this is a good place to start, because it will install some of the recommended default configurations as well as a database. You will be able to check for new parameters or default behaviors that have changed. Another reason to choose a basic installation would be to see the flow of the installation process and the checks that it makes. You could see where it sets up the alert logs, control files, and other files.

The components that are installed with the basic installation are the some as those that are already selected for the advanced installation—you just can't change them if you chose the basic installation. Figure 3-7 shows the screen to choose components in an advanced installation. If you're walking through the installation a second time to install one or more components, you will see Installed as the state of the components you have already installed.

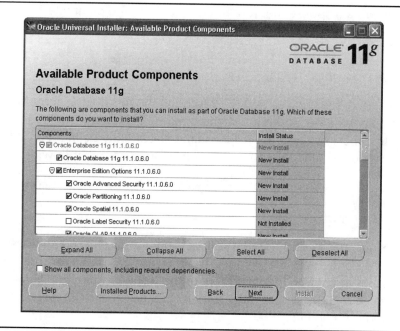

FIGURE 3-7.   *Choosing Oracle components for installation*

As you go through the rest of the installation process, the screens provide information and details about the current step of the process; they are not just a place where you blindly hit the Next button. The installation screens have information about where the logs are for the installation, if there are errors or issues, and other configurations. During the installation, make sure the default directories match the planned directories and file systems.

Using a Response File

When installing one server, going through the screens and responding is not that bad. But the option to silently install and have the same responses is useful to ensure consistent environments. You can do this with a response file. A response file can be recorded, or a template can be used and edited. Response files are not just for the server level, but also for the client installation. Having a noninteractive mode for installing the client piece is probably even more valuable.

To record a response file, run the installer with the parameters of `-record` and the destination of the response file:

```
E:\oracle\Disk1> setup -record -destinationFile
d:\oracle\response\install_oracle11.rsp
```

Select all of the choices and walk through the installation screens. On the summary window of the installation, either finish the installation or choose to cancel because the response file has already been recorded.

To run the installation with the response file, enter the following:

```
E:\oracle\Disk1> setup -silent -nowelcome -noconfig –nowait
    -responseFile
d:\oracle\response\install_oracle11.rsp
```

The `noconfig` option does a software-only installation, and doesn't go through the configuration assistants. There is also an option for passing in the variables instead of updating them in the response file. The `nowelcome` and `nowait` options suppress the startup screen and exit the installer when installation is complete.

Removing Software

Even though you can add and remove components after installing Oracle, it might take a couple of attempts to get everything right. You may need to deinstall the software or components to develop a clean installation. The OUI can handle this step as well.

After opening the OUI, click Installed Products. You will see a list of Oracle homes and installed software, as shown in Figure 3-8. Select a home or component to remove. This will remove the software, but some of the file structures will remain. They can be removed manually. On Windows, information is written to the registry, which could be cleaned up, depending on if you want to reuse an Oracle home. Services can also be removed.

Upgrading the Database

As part of the installation, if an Oracle database already exists on the server, there will be an option to upgrade the database. The Oracle Database Upgrade Assistant (DBUA) is also available after the installation of the software to perform upgrades.

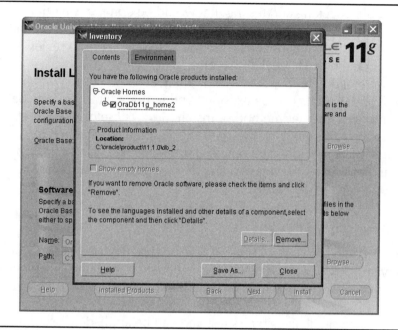

FIGURE 3-8. *Installed products*

The DBUA will do an in-place upgrade of the database under the new version of the database. But there is work to be done before the DBUA runs. As discussed earlier, installing the database software so you can review the new features and parameters that come with the new release is an excellent way to prepare for this upgrade. You may want to create a test database first to look at which defaults have changed and see which parameters should be adjusted for the upgraded database. This information can be used after the DBUA runs to modify the parameters and validate if there are configuration issues or if there are areas that will benefit from the new features.

Getting help in planning and looking at some of the pitfalls of an upgrade are extremely useful for a DBA. The Oracle Database Upgrade Guide and the Upgrade Companion provide some guidance for a successful upgrade. The Upgrade Companion, which is a part of My Oracle Support, isn't an automatic tool for testing, and even if it were, there would still be some double-checking and testing that would be done. It is partially automated, however, which helps speed the process for upgrades and provides some recommendations, but the DBA still needs to review the recommendations and tweak as needed.

A couple of different upgrade paths are available. The software can be installed, and the data can be exported and imported into the new database environment as another method of installation. These different methods provide ways to test and develop a back-out plan to roll back changes if necessary. There are also extra options for the database to do real application testing and easy ways to do versioning to develop a safer and more consistent way to upgrade the databases.

Applying Patches

Patches are nothing new to DBAs. SQL Server has hot fixes, security updates, and service packs for patching the base release. The patches have one-off fixes for bugs or a group of fixes or security releases. Oracle also has different types of patches.

Patches are single fixes for issues, and can be applied as issues are discovered. The patches are rolled up into *patchsets*. As with managing any database environment, testing and planning are required before applying patchsets.

The Critical Patch Update (CPU) has the latest security updates for the database. These are released on a quarterly basis, and applying them in a regular fashion reduces the risks for security vulnerabilities. The Patch Set Update (PSU) includes the security patches and the recommended and proactive patches. These are also released quarterly. Only one patching path can be chosen for the environment. If applying the PSUs, then the CPUs cannot be used going forward, and the PSUs will be the way to implement the security updates.

The Oracle Configuration Manager component provides help in managing the patches through My Oracle Support, as shown in the example in Figure 3-9. The support tools make recommendations for the patches and issue alerts for security patching to proactively maintain the environment.

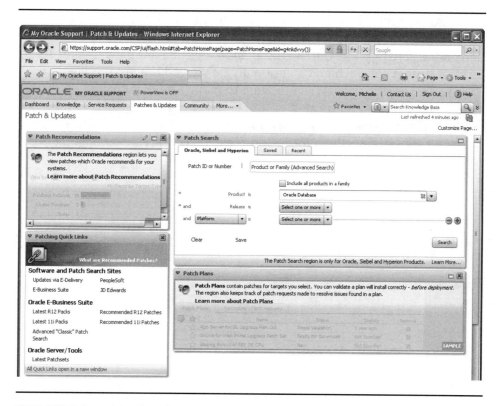

FIGURE 3-9. *My Oracle Support, Patches & Updates tab*

Summary

This chapter walked through the preparations and procedures for installing Oracle. It covered the operating system setup for both Windows and Linux, storage planning, an introduction to ASM, and other preinstallation considerations. As you saw, with proper planning and preparation, the actual installation of Oracle is straightforward.

Several options and configurations are possible with the Oracle database. Getting it installed is just a first step. Setting up a database environment that is easy to maintain, secure, stable, and robust comes next.

There are some shared areas such as /tmp that will cause issues to running or installing Oracle software if they fill up. So carefully place files here, or be sure to purge out old installation logs that are placed here. There are also system areas which can normally be viewed but not modified. If sharing the server it would be important to make sure that changes to these system areas are communicated, or discussed first. The Oracle user does not need full permissions or root access to view the configuration information, but being able to view the information is useful to verify the configurations.

CHAPTER
4

Database Definitions
and Setup

I n the previous chapter, we walked through installing the Oracle software. The server should now be configured for Oracle, and the required components installed. The advantage of installing the software by itself first is that if there are any issues with the configuration, the database doesn't need to be dropped and re-created each time. It is very easy to launch the Oracle configuration assistants after the installation.

This chapter covers the next steps after the software is installed. The Database Configuration Assistant will guide you through the creation of the database. We will look at some of the configuration options, as well as how to use templates and scripts.

Security is a big part of database setup. We already talked about security at the operating system level, and there will be more at the application level. Here, we will look at server and schema security. These various levels of security will help you to achieve a more secure system.

Before we get into the details of database setup, let's clarify some of the terminology, which also will reveal some of the differences between the SQL Server and Oracle platforms.

Servers, Databases, Instances, and Schemas

As a DBA, you are certainly familiar with database terminology. The problem is that on different database platforms, the terms don't always mean the same thing. Consider that even general terms can take on various meanings. A generic definition of *database* is "data and information that is collected together for the ability to access and manage." The term *server* could refer to the actual server hardware or to the database server.

A SQL Server database is not the same as an Oracle database. The SQL Server database has users allocated to it, its own system objects, and its own datafiles. In Oracle, the term *schema* is more closely related to the SQL Server database. Schemas can own the objects in both environments. In SQL Server, there could be several databases for the instance, so there can be several different schemas in a database. In Oracle, there are multiple schemas in a database, including the system schemas.

The Oracle schema is a collection of objects, and it could have its own tablespace allocated to it on the datafiles for the database. The user schema usually does not contain system objects, because the system objects are in their own schema. There is only one set of system objects for each database server, unlike with SQL Server, which has different layers of system objects at the server level and the database level. Also, there are no users inside the Oracle schemas, because they are only at the server level.

The Oracle database is almost like the instance level for SQL Server. The Oracle database is the overall group of datafiles and system information. The Oracle software, memory structures, and processes make up an instance. There is one Oracle database for the instance. In a clustered environment, there can be multiple instances that all point to one database on a shared disk.

Database owner is another term that doesn't really exist in Oracle. Typically, the term *schema owner* is used.

Figure 4-1 shows some of these terms and how they apply in the different database environments. Understanding the differences will help you to see where the services, processes, and datafiles play their parts, and how the different levels interact and handle processes within the various structures.

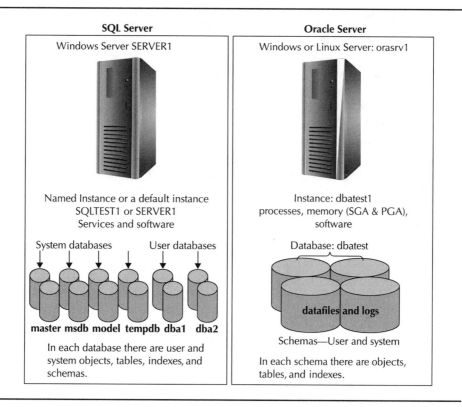

FIGURE 4-1.   *Comparing SQL Server and Oracle terminology*

Database Name Definitions

The following are used to identify Oracle databases:

- **SID** System identifier—database or instance name. The SID and hostname uniquely identify an Oracle database (similar to a SQL Server instance name).

- **Database name** Unique name, normally the same as a SID.

- **Global database name** Database name plus the domain (such as us.demo.com).

- **DBID** Unique database identifier that is assigned by the system. This information is found in `v$database`.

The SQL Server SID and Oracle SID are two very different animals. A SQL Server SID is a security identifier, which is the system-assigned key to a login, as seen in the `syslogins` table. The Oracle SID is the database name that the database creator chooses for the database or instance.

To clarify how these terms are used in the different database systems, let's look at some naming examples. We'll use the domain us.demo.com and a server intended to support a human resources (HR) application, with information about payroll, benefits, employees, and so on. Table 4-1 shows the names for a single server, and Table 4-2 shows the names for a clustered environment.

NOTE
It is helpful to name a server with a department or functional name, so that it's easy to recognize the purpose of the server.

Name	SQL Server	Oracle
Server (Windows or Linux)	`sqlsrvhr01.us .demo.com`	`orasrvhr01.us .demo.com`
Instance	Local server or named instance: `PRODHR`	`PRODHR (SID)`
Database	`payroll_db, benefits_db, hr_db, employee_db`	`PRODHR` (global database name `PRODHR.us.demo.com`)
Schema	`dbo`	`PAYROLL, BENEFITS, HR, EMPLOYEE`
Database server	`sqlsrvhr01\PRODHR`	`orasrvhr01\PRODHR`

TABLE 4-1. *Database Server Naming Examples*

Name	SQL Server	Oracle
Server	`sqlsrvhr01v, sqlsrvhr02v`	`orasrvhr01v, orasrvhr02v`
Instance	`PRODHR`	`PRODHR01, PRODHR02 (SID)`
Database	`payroll_db, benefits_db, hr_db, employee_db`	`PRODHR`

TABLE 4-2. *Clustered Environment Naming Examples*

SQL Server Setup Versus Oracle Setup

With SQL Server, we tend to install an instance with the software, which creates the service and allocates the memory. The system databases are also created, with some of the defaults being set up in the `model` database for other databases. SQL Server databases can be a different collation and a different version than the server. For example, a server can have the collation of SQL_Latin1_General_CP1_CI_AS, and a new database can be created with a collation of French_CI_AI.

```
SELECT
SERVERPROPERTY('ProductVersion') AS ProductVersion,
 SERVERPROPERTY('Collation') AS Collation;
ProductVersion        Collation
10.0.1600.22              SQL_Latin1_General_CP1_CI_AS
Create database Example1
collate French_CI_AI;
select name, collation_name, compatibility_level
from sys.databases;
name          collation_name                        compatibility_level
master        SQL_Latin1_General_CP1_CI_AS                  100
tempdb        SQL_Latin1_General_CP1_CI_AS                  100
model         SQL_Latin1_General_CP1_CI_AS                  100
msdb          SQL_Latin1_General_CP1_CI_AS                  100
test1         SQL_Latin1_General_CP1_CI_AS                  100
example1      French_CI_AI                                  100
```

A SQL Server database gets a different version by attaching a database from a different version. The upgrade of the database can be done after attaching it to the server, but it can also exist as a different version than the server version. The following example shows the compatibility level from SQL Server 2005 on a SQL Server 2008 instance.

```
select name, collation_name, compatibility_level
from sys.databases;
name          collation_name                        compatibility_level
master        SQL_Latin1_General_CP1_CI_AS                  100
tempdb        SQL_Latin1_General_CP1_CI_AS                  100
model         SQL_Latin1_General_CP1_CI_AS                  100
msdb          SQL_Latin1_General_CP1_CI_AS                  100
mmtest        SQL_Latin1_General_CP1_CI_AS                   90
```

With Oracle, the software is installed, and then we set up the database with character sets, system information, and version. The database and instance have the same character set. The Oracle schemas do not have the option for changing the character set. The software components installed are the versions that are used for the database server. This demonstrates that the Oracle database has the system objects and keeps the system-level options at the database level.

Creating Databases

Oracle provides the Database Configuration Assistant (DBCA) to help you create new databases. Other assistants are available for configuring upgrades (DBUA) and Oracle Enterprise Manager (EMCA). You can also use database scripts and templates to re-create databases with the same configuration. We'll start by walking through the DBCA.

Using the DBCA

The DBCA will create the instance parts, which are the processes and the datafiles for the database. It will set up the memory structures.

Launch the DBCA from the ORACLE_HOME\bin directory. Figure 4-2 shows step 1 of the assistant, where you select to create a database.

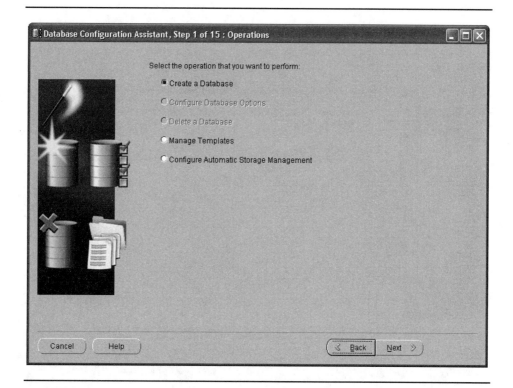

FIGURE 4-2. *Selecting to create a database with the DBCA*

As you step through the assistant, you name the database and accept default values or change them as necessary. Here are some points to keep in mind:

■ Choose a unique name for the database. It is possible to create a database with the same name as an existing database if it is on another server. You might do this if you are planning a move or an upgrade that is not in place. The global name just includes the domain name for the environment.

■ The generic templates are good starting points for creating a database. You can choose from a data warehousing template, a general transaction database, or a custom shell to start, as shown in Figure 4-3. The transaction processing and data warehouse templates have the option to set up the datafiles. The custom template starts without the datafiles, which can be added later.

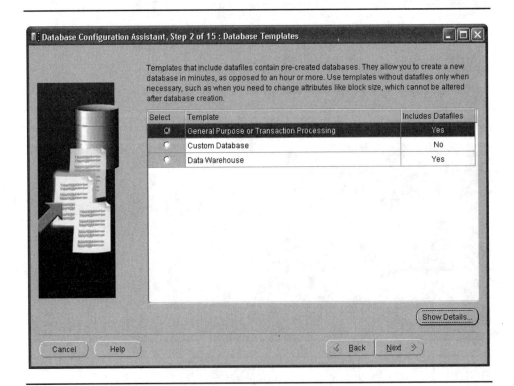

FIGURE 4-3. *Choosing a database template*

■ Oracle Enterprise Manager (OEM) and the dbconsole process will be set up to manage a couple of the regular maintenance jobs. Having these steps here is just a convenience, as these can be set up separately at another time.

■ The variables set for ORACLE_HOME and ORACLE_BASE will be used for where the datafiles and various alert log directories are set up.

■ You can select ASM and add disk groups for this database or for using the file systems, and changes can be made to where the files are created.

■ As part of the database creation, the SYSTEM, UNDO, and TEMP tablespaces are created. A user tablespace can also be configured.

■ You can specify locations for the database files, as shown in Figure 4-4.

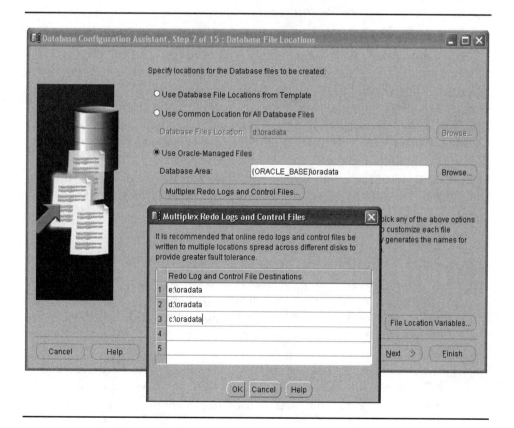

FIGURE 4-4. *Choosing database file locations with the DBCA*

- The flash recovery area is a valuable location for being able to flashback the database. The sizing of this area may need to change based on the size of the transactions and database, but it is a dynamic change that can be made as needed. The key to sizing this area is to have the disk space available. This will be the area where the backup files can be stored, and based on retention, should be estimated appropriately.

You can also remove databases with the DBCA. The Delete a Database option (see Figure 4-2) takes care of removing the services and datafiles.

CAUTION
Even though the DBCA will ask "Are you sure?"
when you choose to delete a database, without
a backup of the database, the only parts that
can be re-created are the structures.

So what is created with the database? The redo logs and log groups, SYSTEM tablespace, SYSAUX tablespace, temporary tablespace, undo tablespace, and control files will be created. The catalog.sql and catproc.sql construct the data dictionary with the views, tables, and stored procedures. SYS, SYSTEM, and a couple more users are added as well.

The job scheduler is set up with background processes, because it is the default setting for parameters to have job slave processes. The parameter JOB_QUEUE_PROCESSES in Oracle Database 11*g* has a default of 1000, and the job coordinator starts only as many processes as requested.

Database Templates = model Database?

Are the Oracle templates really like SQL Server's model database?

The templates are the basic building blocks for the database creation. They have defaults for the files, parameters, and some basic configuration. In that respect, they have the same kind of information that is stored in the model database.

However, only one database is created for an Oracle server; there is no need for templates to be used over and over again to create the databases, as the model database is used in SQL Server.

Duplicating Databases with Templates and Scripts

Oracle template files can be used to duplicate and rebuild databases. You can use a template you saved to create another database in the same Oracle home or copy the template file to another server for use. This obviously makes it easy to duplicate a database without having to go through the setup and configure all the options. You can reuse previously defined values and make adjustments as needed. The database can be created easily, similar to using a response file, but without having to go through all of the steps.

Database scripts provide another way to duplicate or re-create databases. Using a script is really the manual way to create the database. It has the advantage that you can take a database script from an older version, make a couple of modifications if you want to use any new features, and then use it to create the database in a new Oracle version.

When you use a script, setting up the external operating system and Oracle environment is more critical than with the DBCA. This is because nothing is set up to take the defaults. All the environment variables are empty, and you need to make sure they are set up properly before you create the database.

For scripts, a parameter file must be available with the parameters set for control files. This parameter file can be copied from another database and modified with the new database name and file directories. Also, all of the directories need to be created before running the script. Otherwise, the script will fail with the "ORA-27040: file create" error. The following code shows the command-line steps for manual database creation in a Windows environment.

```
set ORACLE_SID=dba01
set ORACLE_HOME=d:\oracle\app\product\11.2
## Create service
ORADIM -NEW -SID dba01 -STARTMODE auto
Instance created.
sqlplus /nolog
sqlplus> connect / as sysdba
Connected to an idle instance
sqlplus> startup nomount
```

```
pfile='d:\oracle\app\product\11.2.\database\initdba01.ora'
sqlplus> create database dba01;
Database created.
## create tablespace for Temp, users
>sqlplus> create temporary tablespace TEMP1 TEMPFILE
'e:\oracle\oradata\dba01\temp01.dbf'
Tablespace created.
sqlplus> alter database default temporary tablespace TEMP1;
Database altered.
## Run scripts for dictionary views
sqlplus> %ORACLE_HOME%\rdbms\admin\catalog.sql
sqlplus> %ORACLE_HOME%\rdbms\admin\catproc.sql
sqlplus> %ORACLE_HOME%\sqlplus\admin\pupbld.sql
## Create server parameter file
sqlplus> create spfile from pfile;
## Shutdown and startup the database
sqlplus> shutdown immediate;
Database closed.
Database dismounted.
ORACLE instance shut down.
sqlplus> startup
ORACLE instance started.
Total System Global Area  535662592 bytes
Fixed Size                  1334380 bytes
Variable Size             234881940 bytes
Database Buffers          293601280 bytes
Redo Buffers                5844992 bytes
Database mounted.
Database opened.
sqlplus>
```

The creation of the instance starts with the service on the Windows platform. When logging in to the database and doing a `startup nomount`, the background processes actually get started and services are running, so that the database can be created.

You can use additional scripts to continue the configuration, including to create other tablespaces, set up the server parameter file, and then build the dictionary views, synonyms, and PL/SQL packages.

Shutdown Options

Several options are available for how the database is shut down:

■ Shutdown *normal* will not allow any new connections, but will wait until all current connections disconnect from the database. This is obviously the cleanest shutdown process, but can also take a long time if users do not disconnect from the database, and large transactions haven't completed.

■ Shutdown *immediate* will not allow any new connections, but will not wait for users to disconnect. Any active transactions will be rolled backed. Long, uncommitted transactions still might take a while to roll back with this option, but there is no recovery needed on startup.

■ Shutdown *transactional* will wait for the currently running transactions to complete. There are no new connections allowed, and connected users that are inactive are disconnected. Current transactions are not rolled backed because of shutdown, and there is no recovery needed on startup.

■ Shutdown *abort* is a last resort. It will bring the database down fast, but it will abort the current transactions, and uncommitted transactions are not rolled back before shutting down. A media recovery on startup will be required to roll back the terminated transactions and clean up these connections.

Creating the Listener

A listener is needed on the database server in order for clients to connect to the database. The listener can be created via another creation assistant: the Net Configuration Assistant (NETCA), as shown in Figure 4-5.

The listener can retain the default name of `LISTENER`, or be renamed, perhaps to indicate the Oracle version or database service that it is listening for, as shown in the example in Figure 4-6.

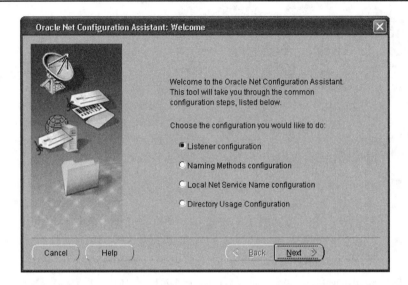

FIGURE 4-5. *Creating a listener with the Net Configuration Assistant*

FIGURE 4-6. *Naming the listener*

One listener can listen for all of the databases on the server, so you do not need a listener for every database. However, depending on your upgrade plans or maintenance downtime considerations, it might be useful to have more than one listener. Each listener will need a different port number.

The listener must be started before connections from other clients can be made. On Windows, the listener is a service, which can be started and stopped via the Administration panel. On both Windows and Linux, the lsnrctl utility can be used to script the startup and shutdown of the listener, as in the following example.

```
####TO START####
>lsnrctl start LISTENER
LSNRCTL for 32-bit Windows: Version 11.1.0.6.0 - Production
on 07-FEB-2010 13:49:33
Copyright (c) 1991, 2007, Oracle.  All rights reserved.
Starting tnslsnr: please wait...
TNSLSNR for 32-bit Windows: Version 11.1.0.6.0 – Production
System parameter file is
d:\oracle\product\11.1.0\db_1\network\admin\listener.ora
Log messages written to
d:\oracle\tnslsnr\MMTEST\listener\alert\log.xml
Listening on: (DESCRIPTION=(ADDRESS=(PROTOCOL=tcp)
(HOST=MMTEST.US.demo.com)(PORT=1521)))
Connecting to (DESCRIPTION=(ADDRESS=(PROTOCOL=TCP)
(HOST=MMTEST.US.demo.com)(PORT=1521)))
STATUS of the LISTENER
------------------------
Alias                   LISTENER
Version                 TNSLSNR for 32-bit Windows:
Version 11.1.0.6.0 – Production
Start Date              07-FEB-2010 13:49:35
Uptime                  0 days 0 hr. 0 min. 3 sec
Trace Level             off
Security                ON: Local OS Authentication
SNMP                    OFF
Listener Parameter File
D:\oracle\product\11.1.0\db_1\network\admin\listener.ora
Listener Log File
D:\oracle\tnslsnr\MMTEST\listener\alert\log.xml
Listening Endpoints Summary... (DESCRIPTION=(ADDRESS=
(PROTOCOL=tcp)(HOST=MMTEST.US.demo.com)(PORT=1521)))
The listener supports no services
The command completed successfully
```

```
####CHECK STATUS####
>lsnrctl status listener_name
LSNRCTL for 32-bit Windows: Version 11.1.0.6.0 - Production
 on 07-FEB-2010 13:50:00
Copyright (c) 1991, 2007, Oracle.  All rights reserved.
Connecting to (DESCRIPTION=(ADDRESS=(PROTOCOL=TCP)
(HOST=MMTEST.US.demo.com)(PORT=1521)))
STATUS of the LISTENER
------------------------
Alias                   LISTENER
Version                 TNSLSNR for 32-bit Windows:
Version 11.1.0.6.0 - Production
Start Date              07-FEB-2010 13:49:35
Uptime                  0 days 0 hr. 0 min. 25 sec
Trace Level             off
Security                ON: Local OS Authentication
SNMP                    OFF
Listener Parameter File
D:\oracle\product\11.1.0\db_1\network\admin\listener.ora
Listener Log File
D:\oracle\tnslsnr\MMTEST\listener\alert\log.xml
Listening Endpoints Summary...
  (DESCRIPTION=(ADDRESS=(PROTOCOL=tcp)
(HOST=MMTEST.US.demo.com)(PORT=1521)))
Services Summary...
Service "+ASM" has 1 instance(s).
  Instance "+ASM", status READY, has 1 handler(s)
for this service...
Service "MMDEV" has 1 instance(s).
  Instance "MMDEV", status READY, has 1 handler(s)
for this service...
The command completed successfully

####TO STOP####
>lsnrctl stop listener_name
LSNRCTL for 32-bit Windows: Version 11.1.0.6.0 - Production
 on 07-FEB-2010 14:13:08
Copyright (c) 1991, 2007, Oracle.  All rights reserved.
Connecting to (DESCRIPTION=(ADDRESS=(PROTOCOL=TCP)
(HOST=MMTEST.US.demo.com)(PORT=1521)))
The command completed successfully
```

There is also a client piece for the listener, which we will look at in the next chapter.

The database is now ready to use, but it might still need some user tablespaces. User objects should not be in the SYSTEM tablespaces or owned be the SYSTEM schema. You might develop scripts to add some regular users, schemas, and tablespaces.

Next, we'll look at choosing a character set for your Oracle database.

Choosing a Character Set

An important consideration for your Oracle database is the character set it uses. Before just accepting the default character set, you should do some research about globalization and the options available, as well as the application requirements for the character set of the database.

For SQL Server, collations are available at the server level and can be configured down to the column level of a table. The SQL Server collations are not only for international characters, but also affect whether the database is case-sensitive and the sort order.

NLS Parameters

In Oracle, the character set choice is governed by which languages the database needs to support, and separate parameters deal with sort order and case sensitivity: NLS_SORT and NLS_COMP. As of Oracle Database 10*g*, the CI value appended to the NLS_SORT parameter setting will determine if the sort is case-sensitive. The NLS_SORT default value is BINARY, and with a case-insensitive sort setting, it is BINARY_CI. Here is a quick sort example using NLS_SORT, which shows the default behavior:

```
sqlplus> select first_name, last_name from cust1
order by last_name;
first_name            last_name
-------------------- --------------------
RANDY                 EASTWOOD
Laura                 Eastwood
danimal               Johnson
BO                    MEYERS
henry                 johnson
sqlplus> select first_name, last_name from cust1
order by nlssort(last_name,'NLS_SORT=BINARY_CI');
first_name            last_name
-------------------- --------------------
Laura                 Eastwood
RANDY                 EASTWOOD
henry                 johnson
danimal               Johnson
BO                    MEYERS
```

NLS_SORT can also be set at the server or session level, instead of including it in the sort of the query.

The client and the database can even have different character set settings based on the NLS_LANGUAGE (NLS_LANG) parameter, which has three parts: the language, territory, and character set. Here are a few examples:

```
NLS_LANG=AMERICAN_AMERICA.AL32UTF8
NLS_LANG=GERMAN_GERMANY.WE8ISO8859P1
NLS_LANG=FRENCH_CANADA.WE8ISO8859P1
```

The NLS (National Language Support) parameters are also modifiable at a session level, so that the sorting and language can be changed by altering the session. Here is a quick look at the NLS parameter list:

```
SQL> select parameter from v$nls_parameters;
PARAMETER
--------------------------------------------
NLS_CALENDAR
NLS_CHARACTERSET
NLS_COMP
NLS_CURRENCY
NLS_DATE_FORMAT
NLS_DATE_LANGUAGE
NLS_DUAL_CURRENCY
NLS_ISO_CURRENCY
NLS_LANGUAGE
NLS_LENGTH_SEMANTICS
NLS_NCHAR_CHARACTERSET
NLS_NCHAR_CONV_EXCP
NLS_NUMERIC_CHARACTERS
NLS_SORT
NLS_TERRITORY
NLS_TIME_FORMAT
NLS_TIMESTAMP_FORMAT
NLS_TIMESTAMP_TZ_FORMAT
NLS_TIME_TZ_FORMAT
```

These parameters are useful for globalization and allow you to adjust sorting and languages. This is similar to collations on columns and databases with SQL Server. However, the Oracle database is created with the chosen character set. It is possible to change a database character set, but it isn't always an easy process.

If different languages need to be supported in the database, the character set needs to be able to handle storing and retrieving the characters for the language. That is also why a Unicode character set, AL32UTF8, is normally selected for databases that must support international languages. There is also a national character setting for NCHAR, NVARCHAR2, and NCLOB. This recommended value is AL16UTF16.

At this point, you might be thinking, "NLS this and that, sorting, case-sensitive with Unicode character sets—does this all really mean SQL_Latin1_General_CPI_CI_AS?" An example might make things clearer. First, to handle international characters and support other client character sets, such as WE8ISO8859P1, the AL32UTF8 character set is recommended. Using AL32UTF8, the database will hold multibyte characters. Let's look at the type definition of two columns:

```
last_name       varchar2(20 BYTE),
last_name2      varchar2(20 CHAR)
```

The last_name column will hold international characters, but it will hold only 20 bytes. So, if any characters are 2 or more bytes, the column will hold fewer than 20 characters. The last_name2 column will hold 20 characters, no matter how many bytes are involved. The NLS_LENGTH_SEMANTICS parameter can be set to BYTE or CHAR for the database level, or the datatypes can be defined on the column level.

For an example for sorting and case sensitivity, consider the following table, which has some columns for first name, last name, and an updated date. The character set for the database was created as AL32UTF8, and the NLS_LANG parameter was set to AMERICAN_AMERICA.UTF8 on the server side.

```
SQL> select first_name, last_name, entered_date
from mmalcher.example_sort;
FIRST_NAME                LAST_NAME                 ENTERED_D
------------------------- ------------------------- ----------
LAURA                     EASTWOOD                  02-JAN-10
D'Animal                  Eastwood                  17-JAN-10
Henry                     Johnson                   23-JAN-10
RANDY                     JOHNSON                   28-JAN-10
Bo                        Meyers                    29-JAN-10
SQL> select customer_id,last_name,entered_date
from example_sort where last_name='JOHNSON';
```

```
CUSTOMER_ID LAST_NAME                       ENTERED_D
----------- ------------------------------- ---------
       1487 JOHNSON                         28-JAN-10
--Change the NLS parameters for sort and case
SQL> alter session set NLS_COMP='LINGUISTIC';
SQL> alter session set NLS_SORT=GERMAN_CI;
SQL> select customer_id,last_name, entered_date
from example_sort where last_name='JOHNSON;
CUSTOMER_ID LAST_NAME                       ENTERED_D
----------- ------------------------------- ---------
       1032 Johnson                         23.01.10
       1487 JOHNSON                         28.01.10
--The date is also now changed because of the client
connection was set as NLS_LANG=GERMAN_GERMANY.UTF8 and
date format is also set as German standard.
```

Of course, the application itself can ensure consistent data by allowing only certain formats to even make it into the database. These examples were just intended to demonstrate the use of the NLS parameters for language. The character set allows for the international characters to be stored and the base for globalization of the database, and the other parameters help with region and understanding how data is being retrieved to adjust sorts, dates, and other formats accordingly.

Setting the Environment Variable for NLS_LANG

The NLS_LANG parameter should be part of the environment variable setup, and on the database server, you want to set the value to be the same as the character set. When you are exporting or importing files that require character set conversions, the utilities may not be able to import the records because the records in a different character set might not fit in the datatype length for the database character set.

```
## Example error message value too large
## Some rows will import, only those that don't fit will fail
ORA-02374: conversion error loading table "TBL1"
ORA-12899: value too large for column COL1 (actual: 263,
maximum: 255)
```

Data Pump jobs will use the NLS_CHARACTERSET parameter, but non-English parameter files will use NLS_LANG, so setting this variable correctly is important for character set conversions.

```
>export NLS_LANG=AMERICAN_AMERICA.US7ASCII
>exp  FULL=Y file=Exp_test.dmp log=Exp_test.log
```

```
Export done in US7ASCII character set and AL16UTF16 NCHAR
character set server uses WE8MSWIN1252 character set (possible
charset conversion)
...
#Using NLS_LANG=AMERICAN_AMERICA.WE8MSWIN1252 will avoid the
charset conversion
```

Changing the Character Set

Even with the best planning, you might need to change the character set after the database has been created. This is possible, but there are some hoops to go through. There is no simple "alter database" command for changing the character set.

One approach is to just start over and create a new database, export out the current one, and import that data into the new database with a new character set. However, that might not be possible, so you might need to instead use a tool to do the character set conversion.

The csscan utility is one tool you can use for character set conversion. It will list areas that are issues and also create a script to change the character set after the issues are handled. Exporting a couple of tables and importing them back in might be easier than re-creating the database. The following example shows the steps involved in changing the character set and gives an idea of what will need to be planned.

```
>csscan FULL=Y TONCHAR=UTF8 LOG=check CAPTURE=Y ARRAY=1000000
PROCESS=2
csscan> sys as sysdba
--Use the sys password to login and get the output of the scan
-- Now log into the database via sqlplus and shutdown database
-- and startup in restrict mode
SQL>shutdown immediate;
SQL>startup restrict
SQL> alter system set aq_tm_processes=0;
SQL> alter system set job_queue_processes=0;
SQL> alter database CHARACTER SET new_characterset;
-- National character can be set here
SQL> %ORACLE_HOME%/rdbms/admin/csalter.plb
--set the aq_tm_processes and job_queue_processes back
to their initial settings and restart the database
```

This example demonstrates some of the issues that will need to be resolved to change the character set. For more details, see the Oracle documentation on csscan.

Security

As a DBA, you have probably dealt with plenty of compliance and security considerations. Protecting the company assets that are stored in the database is one of the main focuses of a DBA. Compliance and tracking of who has permissions to update and change data or systems and security can become a DBA nightmare if not planned for and handled properly.

Maintaining a security standard—whether it includes some security tools, password policies, or highly privileged accounts—is a key component here as well. With SQL Server, you might have a policy to use Windows authenticated logins where possible, and when using database logins, have the same password policies as the operating system. For managing permissions, the policy might be to use the system-provided roles with limited permissions and use roles to grant permissions to users.

With Oracle Database 11g, several new features focus on security and being able to secure Oracle by default:

- Strong passwords are enforced, and the default policies are 10 failed login attempts, 180 days for password lifetime, and case-sensitive passwords.

- Sensitive packages that allow access to more than what is needed by most users are no longer available for nonprivileged users.

- Auditing is turned on by default. Many auditing options are available. The performance of auditing can be improved by using an XML format.

NOTE
When creating a new database, it is great to have a more secure configuration by default. When upgrading, some of these security features will need to be tested to verify their functionality. Also, just upgrading doesn't turn on the auditing or password policies.

After creating a database using the DBCA, you are offered the option of having different passwords for the system users, which is the recommended configuration. In Oracle Database 11g, the DBCA expires and locks most default accounts. If you're using an earlier release or created the database

Security Considerations

The following are some points to keep in mind for a secure configuration:

- Install only what is needed.
- Ensure strong password authentication.
- Protect sensitive database resources with permissions and access.
- Expire and lock out old users.
- Use sample schemas only in test environments.
- Use the principle of least privileges.
- Use DBA permissions only when needed.
- Take advantage of new security features and defaults.

manually, any users that were created as a part of features that were installed but are not being used should be expired and locked.

Here, we will focus on the database security and look at the permissions for highly privileged accounts, as well as schema permissions.

Permissions for the Server

As discussed in the previous chapter, the `oracle` user for the operating system is the owner of the software and directories, and normally owns the processes and services. You can create other operating system users to restrict access to these directories but still allow access to different parts of Oracle software, if desired. Operating system users can also get access to the database. Just as with using Windows authentication for SQL Server, a user can be granted access by external authentication.

The permissions on the operating system don't carry through to the database. The user must be added to the database and granted database permissions. For example, the `oracle` user on Linux can be added to the database and granted permissions and login from the same server.

```
sqlplus>create user ops$oracle identified externally;
sqlplus>grant create session to ops$oracle;
sqlplus>exit
. . .
>whoami
oracle
>sqlplus
enter user-name: /
## The / will use the OS user to login
sqlplus> select sysdate from dual;
SYSDATE
--------
27-FEB-10
```

What permissions are needed as a DBA? A simple answer would be all the permissions to be able to do your job to maintain, back up, and support the database environment. Are all of these permissions needed all of the time? Probably not. For example, being able to shut down a database or change system configurations any time isn't normally needed for day-to-day tasks. There are several different ways to grant access at different times or audit when someone logs in to a database as `SYSDBA`.

NOTE
Oracle Database Vault is an extra security tool that will prevent access as a full-privileged user to sensitive data areas. It creates realms around parts of the database that are based on roles to allow super users the access they need.

Table 4-3 lists some of the server roles of SQL Server and Oracle. Realize that these are not exactly equal, but the roles do have similar permissions. To see the underlying permissions for the roles, select against the `dba_sys_privs` view. Obviously, the `DBA` and `SYSDBA` roles have several permissions granted. `RESOURCE` is another role that receives more permissions than might be expected. To limit permissions, you can create another role and grant only those permissions needed.

SQL Server	Oracle
sa	DBA
sysadmin	SYSDBA
bulkadmin	EXP/IMP_FULL_DATABASE
db_ddladmin	RESOURCE
Processadmin	SCHEDULER_ADMIN
db_datawriter	UPDATE, INSERT, DELETE grants
db_datareader	SELECT grants (select ANY table)

TABLE 4-3. *Server Roles in SQL Server and Oracle*

Oracle includes some other roles that are needed for users to log in that are not typical in SQL Server. For example, the CONNECT role has the CREATE SESSION permission.

 NOTE
The CONNECT role has changed over time and across many versions of Oracle. In Oracle Database 10g and later, it has only the CREATE SESSION permission to allow a user to log in directly to the database. In previous versions, it had more rights.

The sysadmin role has full system privileges for SQL Server—from being able to shut down a server to backing up a database or even creating a user and granting any permission. In Oracle, SYSDBA is similar to sysadmin. If you need to do anything to the database, the SYSDBA role would be the one place to go. The SYS account normally gets the role of SYSDBA granted for these permissions. Both roles are created with Oracle installation. The SYS user has the SYSDBA role granted, but SYS needs to log in as SYSDBA to use the permissions.

NOTE
SYSDBA can also be granted to other users, but with that many permissions, it should be granted with caution and its use very limited.

Other system roles can be used to grant some of the permissions of SYSDBA without granting everything. For example, the SYSOPER role is used for granting operations, such as shutdown and startup, but does not give full access to the database. SYSASM is a new role in Oracle Database 11*g* that allows for management of the ASM instance, separating storage management from database management.

In SQL Server, sa used to be the main login, but now it is recommended that you avoid the use of the sa account and revoke some of the permissions or lock the account. Since SQL Server has Windows authentication for the other SQL Server logins, it provides the needed security by having the sysadmin role available to people who need to perform server administration. In Oracle, the SYSTEM user has this lesser role.

The SYSTEM user in Oracle owns some of the objects for the data dictionary and system information, but it does not have the SYSDBA role granted to it. It's a scaled-down version of SYS, because it doesn't have all of the privileges of SYS but still has the DBA role. It is even a better practice to create another user account for the DBAs, and then grant the DBA role to these accounts. It makes it easier to audit these logins and activities, rather than keeping track of several users using the SYSTEM account.

Permissions for Schemas

With SQL Server, the user is added to the database, and then permissions can be granted to either roles or different schemas. Users can create their own objects in their own schemas in the database, or just get permissions on another user's schema.

With Oracle, the user is added to the database server. With the appropriate permissions, users can create their own schema objects. Users may just have read or other types of permissions to execute parts of the application, and permissions are even needed to connect to the database directly with the CONNECT role or CREATE SESSION. The application could validate the permissions and user in the Oracle database, but that user is not allowed direct access to the database; it is the application account that is logging in to the database.

```
SQL> create user mmtest identified by "passwd1";
User created.
SQL> connect mmtest
Enter password:
ERROR:
ORA-01045: user MMTEST lacks CREATE SESSION privilege; logon denied
Warning: You are no longer connected to ORACLE.
```

Setting up users takes some planning and decisions on server roles and user-defined roles for a schema. For example, for schema users, you might set up one role with read-only permissions, a second role for a super user type with the ability to execute procedures, and a third role to create views from tables.

Now let's take a look at what permissions might be needed for SQL Server database owners compared to Oracle schema owners.

Database Owners

In SQL Server, if you are the database owner, you have permissions to everything in the database, but not necessarily all of the server roles. Grant dbo to another user, and that user has all of the permissions in the database.

Oracle database owners are the system users, and SYS and SYSTEM serve in this role. They own the server objects, services, and data dictionary. These users also are the ones to shut down and start up the database.

Since the Oracle database owner is more of the system owner, there are server roles that can be granted to a user. However, it is recommended that you do not create any user objects in the SYS or SYSTEM schemas, or in the SYSTEM or SYSAUX tablespaces. Even if the user has the DBA and SYSDBA roles, that user is still not really considered the database owner; if there were to be an "owner," it would be the user that is running the processes.

The DBAs should also be the system owners for several of their activities. They would have the DBA role, which will allow for backing up the database, creating new users and objects, running maintenance jobs, and managing the database server.

Schema Owners

If a user is granted dbo in SQL Server, that user has permissions to create the different objects in the database. As we discussed, a database in SQL Server is similar to the schema in Oracle, so the SQL Server database owner is similar to the Oracle schema owner.

Each of the users in Oracle could potentially be a schema owner and create objects. Permissions would need to be granted to create and alter certain objects. Other objects that should be maintained by another role or by the DBAs can be restricted. The RESOURCE role grants most of the typical permissions for creating objects.

```
SQL> select grantee,privilege from dba_sys_privs
where grantee='RESOURCE';
GRANTEE                          PRIVILEGE
------------------------------   ------------------------
RESOURCE                         CREATE TRIGGER
RESOURCE                         CREATE SEQUENCE
RESOURCE                         CREATE TYPE
RESOURCE                         CREATE PROCEDURE
RESOURCE                         CREATE CLUSTER
RESOURCE                         CREATE OPERATOR
RESOURCE                         CREATE INDEXTYPE
RESOURCE                         CREATE TABLE
8 rows selected.
```

CREATE PROCEDURE includes packages, package bodies, and functions, and the owner of the objects can also change and alter the objects. Additional object permissions, such as for creating views and synonyms, would need to be granted outside this role if needed.

Access to the tablespace is needed for the schema owner to be able to create objects on a tablespace. Granting an unlimited quota on a specific tablespace is recommended, as opposed to granting the UNLIMITED TABLESPACE role, which would also allow access to the system tablespaces.

```
SQL> alter user ABC123 quota 4000M on USERS;
SQL> alter user DEF123 quota unlimited on USERS;
```

In this example, the ABC123 user would be allowed to use only a total of 4GB of space on the USERS tablespace. The DEF123 user would be able to use all of the available space on USERS, but this access applies only to the USERS tablespace.

Another way to secure a schema is to not give out the password for access to the schema. This would allow for auditing of the schema changes or setting up a change process to have only the access needed. The other users could still have access for read and write permissions, but other actions, such as altering the objects, would be handled in other ways. The session can be altered to change the current user, which is an action that can be audited and allow for logging in as a schema owner without knowing the password to do selected activities.

```
SQL> grant alter session to MMTEST;
SQL> alter session set current_schema=SCHEMA_OWNER;
```

This example is intended to give you an idea of how to change to a different user and the permissions needed for the schema owner. Triggers and other auditing would need to be set up to track these types of changes if required for compliance.

As the schema owner creates objects, grants to execute or access those objects need to be passed on to the other roles or users.

DBA Roles and Responsibilities Revisited

In Chapter 1, we looked at various DBA responsibilities and roles, such as system DBA, application DBA, development DBA, and architecture DBA. Now that we've discussed database security, we can explore some ways to divide privileges among these roles.

The DBA has the responsibility to create the database and create users. Depending on the access to the production environment, the application DBA might be the only one with the schema password to make changes to tables or objects. The application and development DBAs might have these roles in a test environment, and the application code should be what is running against the data to perform the updates and changes, rather than via direct loads to the database or ad hoc queries that directly make data changes. This sounds like a typical database environment.

The system DBA would have the roles of SYSOPER and EXP/IMP_FULL_DATABASE to be able to maintain and back up the database. The architecture DBA may have access only to a development machine or a lab machine. Granting SELECT ANY CATALOG provides a higher-access privilege, but less than SYSDBA or DBA, and that would allow any of these DBAs to look at performance and see what is running against the database.

A new role with the select permissions could be created for each of the represented DBA roles, which would limit full access to the database based on responsibility. Even if there is only one DBA, creating a different user with some of the basic permissions for a DBA would be better than always logging in as SYSDBA.

Summary

In this chapter, we first looked at some database terminology used by the different platforms. You saw that the SQL Server database is more similar to the Oracle schema than to the Oracle database. Since there is one Oracle database server for an Oracle instance, creating an Oracle database requires a good bit of configuration and planning.

Several assistants are available to create a database, upgrade a database, create a listener, create scripts and templates for the database, and set up the OEM. The assistants provide an interface to be able to walk through the different steps, and allow for configuration and customizations along the way.

Database scripts and templates can be used to re-create the same database or to clone the database in another environment. The scripts can also be modified to create a new database with similar characteristics. The DBCA is a good tool for creating a database for a new Oracle version and taking the defaults to see what some of the new default parameters and configurations might be. This could help in planning upgrades and acceptance of new features.

Security is another important topic when it comes to databases, and setting up permissions for least privilege is a database standard. Users are added only to the Oracle database server, and then granted permissions to create objects in their schemas or have access to other schema objects. There are some system roles for just the DBAs to use with caution.

Access to the database can be handled in several different ways. Also, determining who has permissions to create objects and manipulate data can be based on application security and other security policies and standards.

In discussing the creation assistants in this chapter, we have already started to look at some of the Oracle tools. In the next chapter, we'll continue to explore the tools that are provided to aid DBAs in an Oracle environment.

CHAPTER
5

DBA Tools

n the previous chapters, we've covered installing Oracle and creating the database. The next chapters will move on to specific Oracle database administration tasks. Here, we will take a look at the tools available for performing these tasks.

What do I mean by "tool"? It's true that even a simple SQL statement that is saved to be reused can be considered a tool. And, yes, we could be writing Perl and shell scripts to manage everything. But we'll focus on some of the Oracle-provided tools that make the job a little easier, and some good checks and verification steps to do when using these tools. Note that tools from third-party vendors are available, and although they are not included in this discussion, some are also quite useful for DBAs.

Overview of Tools for Typical Database Tasks

Table 5-1 shows the main tools in SQL Server and Oracle for performing some common DBA tasks.

Task	SQL Server	Oracle
Get an overview of objects and database activity	SQL Server Management Studio	Oracle Enterprise Manager
Run queries	SQL Server Management Studio, Query Analyzer	SQL Developer, SQL*Plus, SQL Worksheet
Trace sessions	Profiler	Oracle Enterprise Manager, v$ views
Back up databases	Maintenance Plans, SQL Server Management Studio	Oracle Recovery Manager, Oracle Enterprise Manager
Monitor	SQL Server Management Studio	Oracle Enterprise Manager, v$ views
Schedule	SQL Server Agent, SQL Server Management Studio	Oracle Scheduler, Oracle Enterprise Manager

TABLE 5-1. *DBA Tools for Common Tasks*

You can see from the table that both SQL Server and Oracle provide a main tool for database administration: SQL Server Management Studio and Oracle Enterprise Manager (OEM). Let's start with a look at OEM.

Oracle Enterprise Manager

OEM is similar to SQL Server Management Studio in that it gives you a look at the server information, error logs, scheduled tasks, and object information. OEM also provides some operating system information and performance statistics. OEM offers an easy view into a database and provides the ability to manage the database in a GUI.

 NOTE
Managing multiple databases in an enterprise environment is better left to the Grid Control, rather than the single instance of the Database Control. However, the Database Control for a single database is a good starting point for understanding the templates and setup for monitoring.

OEM Navigation

OEM has come a long way since it was first introduced. With the improvements in OEM, there have been many changes to where things appear within the tool. Even from OEM 11*g* R1 to R2, a few categories have been rearranged. Some of these changes come directly from recommendations by users, based on how they use features. So change is good, but explaining where to find different options and administration tasks is more difficult, since it depends on the version. However, although a tool may be in a different place in the various versions, its header or description will be very similar.

The first page that appears after logon provides some basic information about the system being up and available, any new alerts in the error log, the server name and listener, and if using ASM, the ASM instance information. The tabs and categories changed from Oracle Database 10*g* to 11*g*, but you can still navigate from this home page to the areas to manage the server and perform administration tasks.

The tabs do a good job of describing the areas that are available:

■ **Performance** The Performance tab has some graphs that show the active sessions, CPU utilization, and throughput statistics. It has links to drill down into the top sessions, currently running SQL, and a view to check if there is any blocking. These areas will allow for some tuning of queries and the current activity.

■ **Availability** The Availability tab has the backup and recovery tasks. We will look at these options and settings in the next chapter.

■ **Server** The Server tab contains tasks such as scheduling jobs, setting up security, configuring parameters, and managing storage and statistics. This area is probably the closest to the information in properties for a SQL Server instance, as well as the database properties that are seen in SQL Server Management Studio.

■ **Schema** The Schema tab provides a view into the objects in the schemas. The tables, indexes, views, packages, procedures, triggers, materialized views, defined types, and other objects are available to view by schema. After drilling down to an object, such as a table, the object can be edited or new objects of that type can be created. The Schema tab is similar to the Object Explorer for SQL Server Management Studio, but it also offers the functionality to walk through the tasks, step by step. Additionally, you can view the SQL statements to perform the tasks, which can be executed in other tools.

■ **Data Movement** As the name suggests, the Data Movement tab has steps for exporting and importing data. There is also a Streams category, which is for the setup and management of replication.

■ **Software and Support** The Software and Support tab includes details on the host configuration and the Oracle Inventory, including the version of the installed Oracle software. There is a section for patching, with a way to stage and apply patches. The Real Application Testing option allows for replay of the database activity to test a patch rollout, upgrade, or new deployment of configurations.

In SQL Server, after installation of an instance, you launch SQL Server Management Studio to verify and adjust settings, create users, and configure the instance for the needed databases. The options and configurations available in properties of the SQL Server instance correspond to the properties that are available in the Server tab of OEM, as shown in Figure 5-1. After creating the database, the Server tab of OEM is a good place to start to add users, create user tablespaces, and verify the parameter settings. Most of the server setup and configurations are under the Server tab, and by exploring the categories, you can learn how to navigate through the OEM to perform the needed tasks. So, let's take a closer look at the Server tab.

Storage Management

Under the Storage category, the Tablespaces section will list the system tablespaces that have been created: SYSTEM, SYSAUX, TEMP, UNDO, and

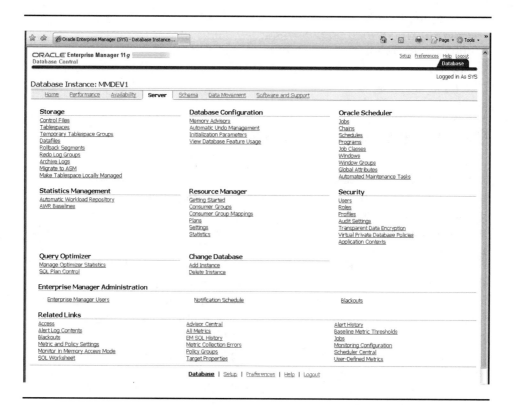

FIGURE 5-1. *OEM Server tab*

probably USER as well. You can adjust the defaults for sizing the tablespaces and add new tablespaces, for an application or for a schema. Having different tablespaces helps to organize the objects in the database. This organization used to be mainly by tables and indexes, but now it can be more about usage and how and when the tablespaces are being accessed. You can size the tablespaces based on initial estimates when you create them, and then use OEM to watch their growth and see if more disk is needed.

From the Control Files section under Storage, you can back up the control file, which is part of a backup strategy, as discussed in the next chapter. The last change number is here with the database ID, which is important information about the database, particularly if you need to recover the database.

Redo logs can be managed from here as well. The Redo Log Groups section shows the current log file. Here, you can add groups or add members to the groups.

NOTE
It is good practice to name redo logs with an extension other than .log, even though that is the Oracle default. Use something like .rdo or .ldf to make sure that these are treated like critical database files, rather than output logs.

Database Configuration

Under the Database Configuration category, the Initialization Parameters section lists the database parameters. You can verify and adjust these parameters as needed. You can also modify the way that the parameters are listed, so that they are divided by basic, dynamic, or categories (such as memory) to give a more meaningful grouping of the parameters—the whole listing of all the parameters can be overwhelming.

The View Database Feature Usage section shows the installed components. After the database is up and running, it will show which components are actually being used. This is useful information for patching and testing the areas in use. If some installed components are not being used, you may want to consider disabling those components.

The Memory Advisors section is the place to go to view how memory is being allocated and managed. It shows statistics about the memory. Obviously, viewing this section after there is load on the database will provide more valuable information than looking at it immediately after database startup.

Oracle Scheduler

The Oracle Scheduler category provides information similar to what you find in the SQL Server Agent and Job Activity Monitor in SQL Server Management Studio.

The Jobs section lists all of the jobs that run against the database. You can view and edit the job description and properties. The jobs can also be run from here, and you can view the history of the job and the schedule.

The Automated Maintenance Tasks section lists tasks such as statistics gathering and possibly backups. This is different from how these tasks are handled in SQL Server, which has the Maintenance Plans feature for setting up backups and statistics gathering. This feature is found under Management, rather than with the jobs and schedules.

Statistics and Resource Management

The Statistics Management category offers a view into the workload repository. These are statistics that are collected for sessions and processes running against the database. The repository pulls together the information to help assess the database performance, with top wait events, top SQL sessions, cache hit ratios, and several other statistics.

SQL Server 2008 introduced a new Resource Governor, under the Management folder. In Oracle, Resource Manager has been around for a few versions. The Resource Manager category on the Server tab has sections for setting up consumer groups and plans.

Security

The Security category provides access to security-related areas. Under Users, all of the system users are listed, and the list might be longer than expected, depending on the components and examples installed. Many of the users might be locked and expired, which is the default security for the components. You can activate the user accounts you need and change their passwords. You can also create new users, either as a copy of an existing user or as a completely new user.

When creating users that will be allowed to create tables and indexes, keep in mind that they will need a quota on a tablespace—just setting a default tablespace will not be enough. Even with the permissions to create a table or index, without access to a tablespace, users will receive an error when they try to create the object:

```
SQL> create table example1
(object_id        number,
object_desc       varchar2(20));
create table example1
*
ERROR at line 1:
ORA-01950: no privileges on tablespace 'USERS'
```

Figure 5-2 shows an example of a USER tablespace quota being set for a new user. The quota can be a specific value or be set to unlimited. You can also edit an existing account to set the quota.

Even though the UNDO and TEMP tablespaces are listed as options here, you cannot grant a quota on these tablespaces, as they are used for transactions and available to all of the users. If you try, you will get an "ORA-30041: Cannot grant quota on the tablespace" error. You can grant quotas on the SYSTEM and SYSAUX tablespaces, but this is not recommended, because those areas should be used for system objects.

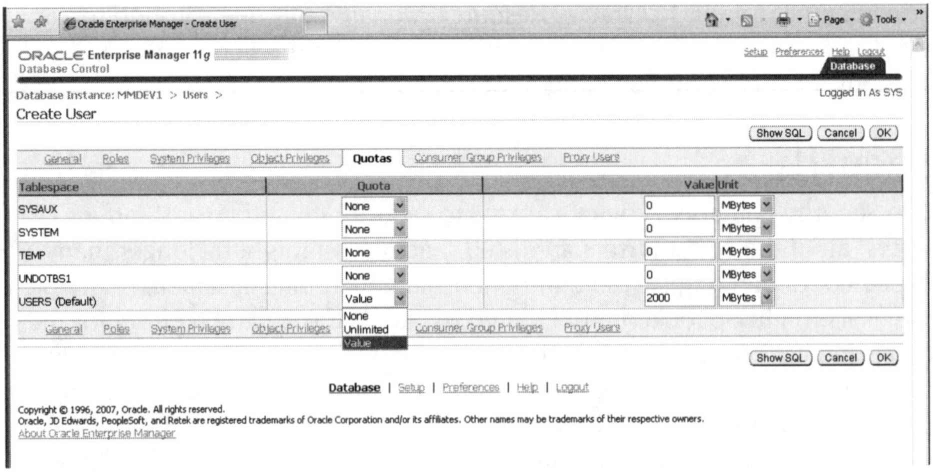

FIGURE 5-2. *Setting a USER tablespace quota*

When Do You Need Quotas?

You do not need to set tablespace quotas for users if they will just be performing transactions on that table—selecting, inserting, updating, and deleting. However, if the schema owner had a set quota of 2GB and a user attempted to insert 3GB of data, that user might receive an "exceeded quota" error on the transaction.

Quotas are just needed to create tables or indexes in tablespaces. Procedures and functions do not need tablespaces, so a user that will be creating these objects might not have quotas on tablespaces.

There is a system privilege of unlimited tablespace, which grants a user unlimited access to all of the tablespaces, including system tablespaces. So you can see why it's a good idea to just grant access to the specific tablespaces, instead of opening up the system tablespace for some random object from a user.

Enterprise Manager Configuration

One other area to look at under the Server tab is Enterprise Manager Administration. The agent and dbconsole process were created with the creation of the database. Here, you can configure notifications, set thresholds for monitoring, and set blackouts.

Figure 5-3 shows the Administrators section, which lists the system administrators who can log in to OEM to perform management tasks. A new administrator account can be created outside the system accounts, with fewer privileges, to allow administrators to manage templates, blackouts, and notifications (a good practice to follow for a secure implementation).

The other sections show setup information for OEM. The Management Pack Access section lists some of the database packs which are options and may require additional licensing.

This was just a brief overview of some of the areas of OEM to get you started with this tool. Next, we'll look at SQL*Plus, a tool for managing database objects.

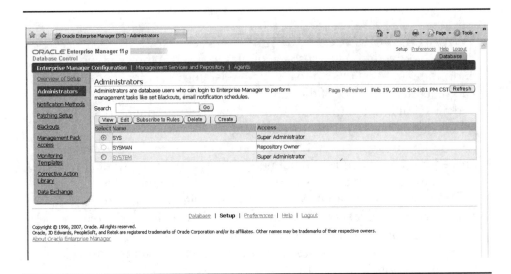

FIGURE 5-3. *Enterprise Manager Configuration, Administrators section*

SQL*Plus

If you created a database in the Linux environment, you have already used SQL*Plus. With Windows versions before Oracle Database 11g, SQL*Plus was a simple graphical interface for entering SQL statements. With 11g, running SQL*Plus opens a command-line window for executing queries. Figure 5-4 shows the new and previous versions.

FIGURE 5-4. *SQL*Plus in Oracle Database 11g (left) and 10g (right)*

You may be thinking, "Oh no—not command line! How can I go from a nice graphical interface to using a command-line tool?" It is not as bad as you might think.

SQL*Plus is handy for queries, such as a quick check or count, and also to incorporate into scripts. Consider how you might use SQL Server `sqlcmd` or `osql` to run a query or for scripting. For example, here's how you would pass in a SQL statement and capture the output of the statement in a log file with `osql`:

```
>osql -U user1  -P userpasswd -i sqltest.sql -o output.log
```

In Oracle, with SQL*Plus, you can do this as follows:

```
>sqlplus user2/userpasswd sqltest.sql > output.log
```

So now you are probably wondering where the `sp_who` and `sp_who2` commands are in Oracle, because they would be useful for a quick check from the command line. Well, there is not really an `sp_who` command, but here's a query that will provide the same results:

```
SQLPLUS> SELECT s.username, s.schemaname, s.status,
s.process, t.sql_text
from v$session s, v$sql t
where t.sql_id(+) = s.sql_id and s.type = 'USER';
USERNAME      SCHEMANAME      STATUS      PROCESS    SQL_TEXT
-------------------------------------------------------------------
MMTEST        MMTEST          INACTIVE    5840:5140  select cust_name,…
...
```

You can put this query in a package or procedure to create your own version.

Using the command line in scripts or batch files is very useful. You can write the results of a query to file, and if you're using the results to create new SQL commands, these files can then be executed. The `spool` command used with a file name will write the results to a file.

```
SQLPLUS> spool c:\temp\results.lst
SQLPLUS> select customer_name, created_date from cust_table;
SQLPLUS> spool off
```

This example will write the results of the query, including the header and verify information. Using the `SET` command, you can suppress the header and verify information from appearing in the output, both on the screen and

Output Option	SET Command
Turn off column headings	`SET HEADING OFF`
Suppress display of the number of records returned	`SET FEEDBACK OFF`
Suppress display of the commands	`SET ECHO OFF`
Suppress display of the command when replacing substitution variables	`SET VERIFY OFF`
Suppress display of the output from a command file (doesn't affect the display of commands entered)	`SET TERMOUT OFF`
Turn on the display of the output from PL/SQL, such as `DBMS_OUTPUT.PUT_LINE`	`SET SERVEROUTPUT ON`
Set the width of the line before wrapping	`SET LINESIZE 200`
Suppress all headings, page breaks, and titles	`SET PAGESIZE 0`
Display the timing statistics for each command or block of PL/SQL	`SET TIMING ON`

TABLE 5-2. *Some SQL*Plus SET Commands*

in files. Table 5-2 shows just some of the SET commands for directing how the output is shown on the screen and in the output files.

Let's look at a few script examples that demonstrate the use of some of the output options shown in Table 5-2. The following script can run in silent mode, process the query, and capture the output to a log file to check if there were errors and validate that things ran correctly.

```
View system information without headers and verification:
SQL> select tablespace_name from dba_tablespaces;
TABLESPACE_NAME
-------------------------------
SYSTEM
SYSAUX
UNDOTBS1
TEMP
```

```
USERS
SQL> set heading off
SQL> set pagesize 0
SQL> select tablespace_name from dba_tablespaces;
SYSTEM
SYSAUX
UNDOTBS1
TEMP
USERS
--without the pagesize 0, there will be a blank line before the
--first result record

-- To be able to view the output from dbms_output, you need
--serveroutput on. Otherwise it does just verify the procedure
--executed.

SQL> exec dbms_output.put_line('testing output');
PL/SQL procedure successfully completed.

SQL> set serveroutput on
SQL> exec dbms_output.put_line('testing output');
testing output
PL/SQL procedure successfully completed.

--To remove the statement that the script ran and just return
--the value
SQL> set feedback off
SQL> exec dbms_output.put_line('testing output');
testing output
```

The next example is just a check to make sure that the database is up and available. It will return an error if there is an issue running queries against the database.

```
Just checking that an instance is up and available:
>$ORACLE_HOME/bin/sqlplus -s > output.log <<EOF_SQL1
$USER/$PASSWORD
select 1 from dual;
exit
EOF_SQL1
>view output.log

         1
----------
         1
```

```
>$ORACLE_HOME/bin/sqlplus -s > output.log <<EOF_SQL1
$USER/$PASSWORD
set feedback off
set heading off
set pagesize 0
select 1 from dual;
exit
EOF_SQL1
>view output.log
        1
--The output log can also scanned for ORA- errors and then message
sent if failures.
```

As a final example, the following script generates SQL statements that can be run against the database.

```
SQL> spool gen_sql.sql
SQL> select 'select count(1) from '||table_name||';'
from user_tables;
select count(1) from TABLE1;
SQL> spool off;
. . .
SQL> show heading
heading ON
SQL> gen_sql.sql
SP2-0734: unknown command beginning "SQL> gen_..."
- rest of line ignored.
  COUNT(1)
----------
        0
SP2-0734: unknown command beginning "SQL> spool..."
- rest of line ignored.
--Errors are because of the commands coming after the spool
--command and they are in the spool file.
> view gen_sql.sql
SQL> select 'select count(1) from '||table_name||';'
from user_tables;
select count(1) from TABLE1;

SQL> spool off
>

--A cleaner way to do this is by having the SQL in a file and
--using termout which doesn't display the output of the
--command file.
> view gen_count.sql
set heading off
```

```
set termout off
set pagesize 0
set feedback off
set echo off
set verify off
spool gen_sql.sql
select 'select count(1) from '||table_name||';'
from user_tables;
spool off
exit;
>sqlplus -S user1/userpass gen_count.sql
>sqlplus
SQL>gen_sql.sql
  COUNT(1)
----------
         0
SQL>
```

These examples should give you an idea of some of the options available with the SQL*Plus command-line tool. Many Oracle DBAs have a set of SQL statements and scripts to generate other statements, and get quick information from the database. The formatting might not matter, depending on what is being executed, but you do have some control over how the output appears.

As you've seen, ad hoc queries, generated SQL, and code extracted from OEM or another place can be run in SQL*Plus. They can be also run in another tool: SQL Developer, which offers a query window and puts you back in a GUI.

SQL Developer

SQL Developer is a free graphical tool that Oracle provides for database development. This tool supports several platforms, so it is useful for managing environments with multiple platforms, such as SQL Server and Oracle. With SQL Developer, you have a tool to work with the database objects, develop code for the database, and even do some unit testing and data modeling in one place.

SQL Server DBAs will find that SQL Developer has a more familiar look and feel than the other Oracle tools. Instead of drilling down to new windows for information, as in OEM, you can right-click on objects to view properties and perform tasks, as shown in the example in Figure 5-5.

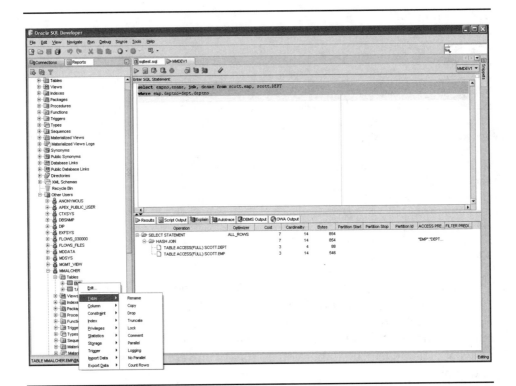

FIGURE 5-5. *SQL Developer*

The first step in using SQL Developer is to create connections. The connections are defined by the user, database name, and other information, including hostname and port. The connections can also be for another database platform.

As you can see in Figure 5-5, in SQL Developer, you can browse the objects by type under the schema you connected as. The other users are the other schemas available, and under each schema there are the different object types.

As also shown in Figure 5-5, right-clicking a table brings up a menu with options to edit, move, rename, drop, get a row count, truncate, and more. You can create indexes, constraints, and triggers, as well as configure privileges and storage. There are also options to export and import the data.

When the view of the object is in the right pane, the SQL statement that created it is available on the SQL tab. The other tabs show the columns, data, constraints, grants, statistics, indexes, and dependencies. Under the Tools menu, there is an option to export the DDL, which will walk through scripting out several objects at one time. Along with the scripts of the objects, there is a filter to pull data.

Take a look at the query in Figure 5-5. Notice that the result set is not listed below it but it has just the explain plan with information about the tables and any indexes used. This brief query plan has full-table scans—thank goodness there are only 14 rows in one table and 4 in the other.

Since SQL Developer is a development tool, it includes features for editing PL/SQL and running, debugging, and formatting code. It provides a command history and version control, which hooks into something like CVS and Subversion, to keep track of the code while developing against the databases. You can copy a schema to another one, as well as compare two schemas or objects (to check for differences in indexes, stored procedures, and so on).

Although SQL Developer is primarily a tool for developers, it definitely has value for DBAs. It will help you understand the different database options and how to use explain plans, and let you pull code out of the database. Don't forget that this is a free tool. And if you're managing multiple database platforms, having all of the connections in one place is very nice.

Client Connections

With all of the tools discussed in this chapter, you need to pass in information about the database. SQL Server has an instance name (or may be local if not named), a server, and a port. The same is true with Oracle. It has the database name (SID), server name, and port. The SID is the instance name, and a service name could be for the database, as in the case of a clustered database.

Just as with SQL Server, the clients and tools need to be able to connect to the database. You can install some sort of client on the client side or use a database driver that can accept the information needed to connect. Table 5-3 compares the connection tools available for SQL Server and Oracle.

Connection Tool	SQL Server	Oracle
Client	Client Tools install	Client install, instant client, runtime client, administrator client
Drivers	ODBC, JDBC, OLE DB, OCI, native, etc.	ODBC, JDBC, OLE DB, OCI, native, etc.
Connection configuration	Client Network Utility	Net Configuration Assistant

TABLE 5-3. *Client Connection Tools*

Several different types of Oracle clients are available for installation:

- **Instant client**   This is a minimal client that doesn't require an Oracle home to be set up and has different drivers for connections. SQL*Plus is not installed with this client, but it can be added.

- **Administrator client**   This type of client installs with the tools needed for DBAs, such as SQL Developer and SQL*Plus. During the installation, the Net Configuration Assistant is executed to set up the information for the connections to the databases.

- **Runtime client**   With this client, the client pieces are installed in an Oracle home. SQL*Plus and some of the basic tools needed to connect to the databases are included.

A custom installation will allow for different parts of the client to be installed.

Client Connection Configuration

Instant client connections do not require extra files or a service definition on the client side. The following is an example of a connection string for a database:

```
connect username/passwordoraserver1:1521/MMDEV1
```

The other types of clients require details on the database connection and the location for the client to connect, which can be handled through a tnsnames.ora file or the Oracle Internet Directory (and LDAP directory).

As discussed in Chapter 4, the listener is configured on the server side with the database. The Net Configuration Assistant sets up the host, port, and database name to listen for. The tnsnames.ora file has the details for the client to connect to the listener on the server. The sqlnet.ora file has information such as domain and if the tnsnames file or the Oracle Internet Directory should be used to look up listeners. These files are created as part of the installation of the administrator client or runtime client, and are found in the ORACLE_HOME/network/admin directory.

So, what is in the tnsnames.ora file? Really, it just lists the server locations and where to find the listener. Here is a sample tnsnames.ora file, including an example for a cluster database.

```
## Connection to a single database server
MMDEV1 =
  (DESCRIPTION =
    (ADDRESS = (PROTOCOL = TCP)(HOST = oraserver1)(PORT = 1521))
    (CONNECT_DATA =
      (SERVER = DEDICATED)
      (SERVICE_NAME = MMDEV1)
    )
  )
## Connect with fail over and load balancing to a RAC database
RACDB =
  (DESCRIPTION_LIST =
   (FAILOVER = true)
   (LOAD_BALANCE = true)
   (DESCRIPTION =
   (ADDRESS = (PROTOCOL = TCP)(HOST = orasrvrac1-vip)(PORT = 1521))
   (ADDRESS = (PROTOCOL = TCP)(HOST = orasrvrac2-vip)(PORT = 1521))
      (CONNECT_DATA =
        (SERVICE_NAME = RACDB)
        (SERVER = dedicated)
        (FAILOVER_MODE = (BACKUP=orasrvrac2)(TYPE=select)(METHOD=BASIC))
        )
    )
  )
```

Depending on the size of the environment, managing the tnsnames.ora file can become cumbersome, unless you have ways to push the file changes out to the application servers and client servers as needed. Oracle Internet Directory is another option. This is a directory for the database servers and locations that can be centrally managed. All that is required on the client side is the information for the Oracle Internet Directory. For the connection to the Oracle Internet Directory to look up the location of the database, an ldap.ora file is needed in the ORACLE_HOME/network/admin directory. Here is an example of an ldap.ora file:

```
DEFAULT_ADMIN_CONTEXT = "ou=databases,dc=company1,dc=com"
DIRECTORY_SERVICES = (ldap_server.company1.com:389:636)
DIRECTORY_SERVER_TYPE = OID
```

The sqlnet.ora file has parameters for using the Oracle Internet Directory, tnsnames.ora, EZCONNECT (easy connection naming method without tnsnames.ora), and the default domain. There is also expiration time of the client connection, and this can be used to trace client sessions. Here is a list of some of these parameters in a sample sqlnet.ora:

```
NAMES.DEFAULT_DOMAIN = (US.COM)
###It will try these connections in this order path first
### LDAP, etc.
NAMES.DIRECTORY_PATH = (LDAP, TNSNAMES, EZCONNECT)

## NTS allows oracle to use current Windows domain credentials to
## authenticate. If Oracle server is not configured for this, errors will
## occur in connecting.But setting NONE first will only disable the local
## support using Windows credentials
SQLNET.AUTHENTICATION_SERVICES = (NONE,NTS)

##These parameters can be uncommented to start the tracing
##TRACE_LEVEL_CLIENT=4
##TRACE_FILE_CLIENT=client_sqlnet.trc
##TRACE_DIRECTORY_CLEINT=D:\oracle\trace

## Time is specified in minutes for the expire time but this
## would be set on the database server
SQLNET.EXPIRE_TIME=30
```

As seen with the NTS setting in this file, the Windows domain credentials would be useful for defining externally authenticated users in the database, and then setting AUTHENTICATION_SERVICES = (NTS) will allow for passing the Windows credentials through to the database. Since the sqlnet.ora file is on both the client and server side, there might be some parameters that are set for the server, but these may still have an effect on the client. For example, EXPIRE_TIME will time out sessions.

The most common issues when setting up a connection to the database stem from incorrect information in the connection string, tnsnames.ora file, or sqlnet.ora file. I have even tried to track down a connection issue, only to discover that there were two different tnsnames.ora files, and the one with the incorrect information was being looked at first because it came up first in the path environment variable.

As you've seen, the sqlnet.ora file also has information on authentication and the domain. If this doesn't match up with your environment, it might be looking for a database in a different domain, or even looking for a tnsnames.ora file when it is set up to use LDAP.

These files can be edited manually, but typing issues may cause trouble if the files were generated by an Oracle configuration tool.

It is also possible that TNS errors will come up if you are logging in to SQL*Plus and the ORACLE_SID variable is not set or you are using *username*ORACLE_SID to define which database the client is attempting to connect to.

JDBC Connections

The applications and clients normally set up the connections, and the details of the host, database name, and port should be all that they need to get started. However, they may sometimes need assistance with connections and using different drivers.

For JDBC drivers, there are thin and thick clients. There is not much difference between the two, except that the thick client has the ability to use the tnsnames.ora file, and the thin client might not have these structures set up because just the drivers were installed.

```
url="jdbc:oracle:thin:host:port:sid"
url="jdbc:oracle:thin:(DESCRIPTION=
(LOAD_BALANCE=on)
   (ADDRESS=(PROTOCOL=TCP)(HOST=orasrvrac1-vip)(PORT=1521))
   (ADDRESS=(PROTOCOL=TCP)(HOST=orasrvrac2-vip)(PORT=1521))
   (COONECT_DATA=(SERVICE_NAME=RACDB)))"
## thick client can use the database name in the tnsnames.ora file
url="jdbc:oracle:orci:MMDEV1"
```

Aliases

A SQL Server instance can have an alias to use a client network utility. Even a local instance with no name can get a different name to use as an alias.

The same is true for Oracle databases. A database alias can be set up in the tnsnames.ora file.

```
DB_ALIAS =
  (DESCRIPTION =
    (ADDRESS = (PROTOCOL = TCP)(HOST = oraserver1)(PORT = 1521))
    (CONNECT_DATA =
      (SERVER = DEDICATED)
      (SERVICE_NAME = MMDEV1)
    )
  )
```

In this example, DB_ALIAS will actually connect to the MMDEV1 database. It is that simple to create an alias, and it obviously doesn't change the actual name of the database.

CAUTION
In the tnsnames.ora file, having the same name listed twice can cause connection issues. Even if the details are the same for both of the listings, duplicates can cause problems connecting.

My Oracle Support

Most of these tools discussed in this chapter are used on a daily basis to manage the database and log in to databases. I consider My Oracle Support a tool, because not only does it have a knowledge base for commands, issues, and possible errors, but it also has the Configuration Manager for assistance in applying patches and upgrades. It also offers a health check monitor that provides some suggestions based on the configurations in the databases.

There is community out there, and through My Oracle Support, you can have discussions with other DBAs. In addition to those you can find through the message areas in My Oracle Support, other Oracle user communities are great resources for information and networking. User groups such as the Independent Oracle User Group (IOUG) have real DBAs performing real tasks, and they are willing to share their experiences and help you to work through issues.

Summary

In this chapter, we have discussed several different tools available to Oracle DBAs. Some of the tools are geared more toward the management of the database servers; others might be more focused on development. Both types are useful for DBAs. There are several areas to explore in OEM and SQL Developer to make you more productive as a DBA. And don't forget that even though it is good to have an easy interface to use, it's also handy to be able to run simple scripts and queries in a regular SQL*Plus session.

However, it's not too useful to have these tools if you cannot connect them to the database. So, we discussed how to get connected and took a look at the pieces that are needed to connect, including the tnsnames.ora and sqlnet.ora files.

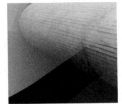

CHAPTER
6

Database Backup, Restore, and Recovery

s a DBA, you already know the importance of database backups. You have probably developed your own backup strategies and disaster recovery plans for the SQL Server databases you support.

You also know that being able to back up a database is just part of the job. You need to manage the backups and know which backup pieces to use to be able to recover quickly and easily. Testing restore procedures validates that you have solid, usable backups, and also lets you develop restore scripts to save for a rainy day.

In this chapter, you will learn about the set of backup and recovery tools available for the Oracle platform. This will help you to develop your backup and recovery strategies for your Oracle databases.

Backing Up Databases

Sometimes your job as a DBA may seem like all you are doing is verifying that backups are running successfully and restoring testing environments with those backups. This is definitely an important task for the system DBA, and backups are key to providing a secure and reliable database environment.

Backup Strategies

As a DBA, no matter which database platform you are administering, you need to plan a backup strategy that makes recovery a simple process and fits the needs of the business. There are several strategies for backing up databases, depending on resources, the importance of the data, and if it is needed for recovery and running the business.

For SQL Server databases, creating maintenance plans sets up some backup strategies. The SQL Server database recovery model setting of either SIMPLE or FULL also determines if log backups are needed. As the database changes or grows, plans to compress, write to tape, and allocate threads to use for the backup are all taken into consideration.

The Oracle DBCA also has a step to set up maintenance plans, which include backup settings. You also have the option to create the database in NOARCHIVELOG mode, which is similar to the SQL Server SIMPLE option, or ARCHIVELOG mode, which is like the FULL option.

It is important to be able to communicate the options for backup and restore strategies to the business owners. Understanding the options, the resources needed (disks, tapes, and so on), and what data loss would mean to the business are key to being able to convey how the restore options would benefit the business. This will help you and the business owners to develop the best plan to balance the resources and protect the data assets.

What are you protecting against? You probably have been setting up backup strategies to protect against hardware failures, data loss, changes that have gone wrong, and disasters. Running backup database and transaction logs, and saving copies to disk and tape with certain retention policies are all part of this plan.

So what options are available in Oracle to protect the data against those "oops" or "oh no" moments? Besides the backups, there are exports, a recycle bin, and a way to flashback queries and even the database. We'll start with some of the commands for backing up the database, and then progress through the other options.

Backup and Restore Commands

The basic commands for backing up and restoring Oracle databases should look familiar to SQL Server DBAs. Let's start with the SQL Server command to back up a database:

```
backup database customer_db to
    disk ='E:\mssql\bkups\customer_db_02022010.bak'
backup log customer_db to
    disk='E:\mssql\bkups\customer_db_log_02022010.trn'
```

This will take care of the SQL Server database and log backups, and write the backup file to disk.

In Oracle, you use a Recovery Manager (RMAN) command, like this:

```
RMAN> run {
allocate channel disk1 device type disk;
backup database plus archivelog;
}
```

This command will back up the database with the archive logs and write the backup file to disk.

Here is the SQL Server command to restore a database:

```
restore database customer_db from
    disk ='E:\mssql\bkups\customer_db_02022010.bak'
```

The Oracle RMAN command is basically the same:

```
RMAN> run {
allocate channel disk1 device type disk;
restore database;
}
```

Both database platforms can perform "hot backups" while the database is up and available, when it's possible that changes are happening as the backup is running. The transaction and archive logs keep these changes, so these logs must be part of the backup set.

NOTE
RMAN puts the database (datafiles and tablespaces) in backup mode when it runs the backups. If you're not using RMAN, you'll need to issue ALTER DATABASE BEGIN BACKUP before being able to do a hot backup of the database.

Typically, 24/7 access to the database is required, so hot backups are made. However, there might be opportunities to take a cold backup when the downtime is available, such as before an upgrade or hardware move. This will get a full backup, so the transaction and archive logs do not need to be handled. In SQL Server, if the instance services are shut down for a cold backup, the files can be copied over. The same is true for Oracle databases. This script runs a cold backup:

```
RMAN> run {
shutdown immediate
startup mount
allocate channel disk1 device type disk;
backup database;
}
```

Looking at the script, you may wonder why there is a startup. The `startup mount` command will allow RMAN to read the control files to know which datafiles need to be backed up. The database server is still not available, so the files can be copied and backed up by RMAN in this "cold" state.

Since the database is down for a cold backup, the datafiles can be copied without using RMAN. Scripts can be written using operating system commands to just copy the datafiles to another location, tape, or another mount point while the database is down. A shell script or batch file can shut down the database, and then `cp/copy` commands can be issued to copy the datafiles, or a file system backup can be done. This type of cold backup would not need the database in mount state, because it wouldn't be using the control file, as RMAN does.

As you can see from the examples, RMAN is a big part of the backup and restore strategies for Oracle databases. RMAN can be used through the command line as well as OEM. We've skipped over a few pieces in these examples. As you'll learn next, RMAN requires some configuration to be able to run backups.

RMAN Configuration for Backups

RMAN is installed with the Oracle software and placed in the ORACLE_ HOME/bin/ directory. RMAN can use a catalog to track and manage the backups, or it can use the control file of the database for this purpose.

A database must be available to be able to create the schema needed for the RMAN catalog. One catalog can manage the backups of several databases, but the catalog should be at the same database version as the databases being backed up.

To configure RMAN, create a user to be catalog owner, and grant that user a quota on the tablespace where the schema is going to live, as well as the `RECOVERY_CATALOG_OWNER` role. Next, create the catalog using the RMAN command line:

```
>rman
RMAN> connect target
connected to target database: DBDEV1 (DBID=280973718)
-- DBDEV1 will be the database that will have the catalog schema.
```

```
    If another database is to have the catalog, the connect
    catalog string will have the database as part of the
    string: rman/rmanpswdRMANCAT
RMAN> connect catalog rman/rmanpswd
connected to recovery catalog database
RMAN> create catalog
recovery catalog created
RMAN> register database;
database registered in recovery catalog
starting full resync of recovery catalog
full resync complete
RMAN>
```

After the catalog is created, the databases can be registered with the catalog. The target database that is connected is the one that is registered with the catalog. Now the target database is ready for backups.

You can configure RMAN for the default backup type, where the backup files should be written, the format of the backup file, retention policies, compression, encryption, and control file autobackup. The tape drivers and encryption options are part of the Oracle Secure Backup product. Other vendors provide drivers to write directly to tape and encryption, and Secure Backup will also integrate directly with RMAN.

Looking at the configuration for RMAN is just like looking at the parameters in the Oracle database, but from the RMAN command line.

```
RMAN> show default device type;

RMAN configuration parameters for database with
db_unique_name MMDEV1 are:
CONFIGURE DEFAULT DEVICE TYPE TO DISK; # default

## Change the default device from disk to tape
RMAN> configure default device type to sbt;

new RMAN configuration parameters:
CONFIGURE DEFAULT DEVICE TYPE TO 'SBT_TAPE';
new RMAN configuration parameters are successfully stored
```

These configuration settings can be part of a script. If they are set in a script, the script settings will overwrite any defaults that are set up for that database in RMAN.

Here are some examples of setting the defaults for the backup directory, file format, type of backup, and retention policy:

```
--example to configure channel to write to disk using
  the diskgroup format
RMAN> configure channel device type disk format '+dgroupbkup1';
-- examples of two different backup types
RMAN> configure device type disk backup type to backupset;
RMAN> configure device type disk backup type to
compressed backupset;
-- example to configure retention policy
RMAN> configure retention policy to recovery window of 7 days;
RMAN> ## use recovery window or redundancy (but not both)
RMAN> ## configure retention policy to redundancy 3;
```

In the example, the disk format is configured to be used with ASM and a disk group that has been set up as a backup disk group. For a regular file system, the format can also be set as /orabkup/ora_d%_%T.bak, which will define the backup with the name of the database and a date in the file system directory.

The example uses the backupset backup type. Another type is copy, which will do an image copy of the database. The copy backup type is allowed only for writing the copy to disk; it does not work for tape backups.

When allocating a channel as type disk in a script, these parameters become part of that allocation. Unless you want to overwrite the defaults, they do not need to be mentioned each time a backup is run.

For the retention policy, the setting of the recovery window sets the number of days between the current time and the earliest point of recovery, which doesn't matter if there are incremental or full backups in between. But those backups will be marked obsolete when they hit the number of days set here. This example sets the window to seven days, which makes sure that the database can be recovered within the past week. The retention policy's redundancy setting indicates the specific number of full backups to be kept. The example sets redundancy to 3, which will keep three full backups; it doesn't matter how many days are in between backups.

The same configurations that were demonstrated here in the command line can be done through OEM's Backup Settings. Figure 6-1 shows the

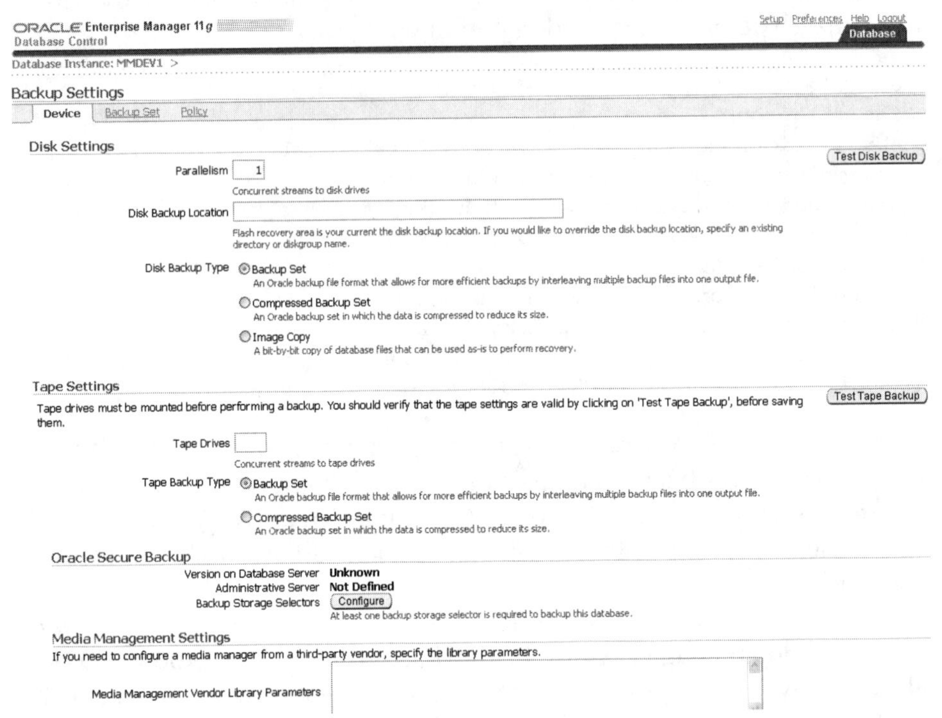

FIGURE 6-1. *OEM Backup Settings, Device tab*

Device tab, where you set the backup location and type. Figure 6-2 shows the Policy tab, where you set the retention policies. As you can see in Figure 6-2, you can set up the retention policies by date or number of backups to be retained. The Policy tab also includes an area to exclude tablespaces from whole backups, which is useful for tablespaces that might be in read-only mode or archived tablespaces that might not need to be included in every full backup.

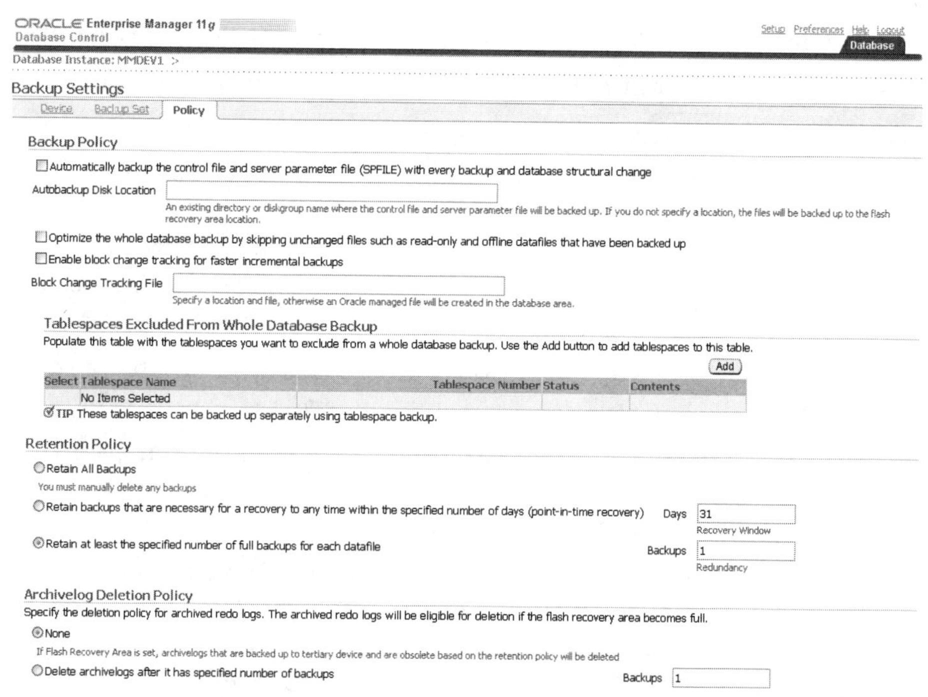

FIGURE 6-2.   *OEM Backup Settings, Policy tab*

Backup Options

Table 6-1 shows some common backup types and how to run them in SQL Server and RMAN.

Your backup strategy should include full and incremental backups. It should also make sure all of the needed pieces are backed up properly.

For incremental backups, a base backup (full backup) is needed first. The cumulative database backup option in RMAN backs up all of the changes since the base, or level 0, backup. The incremental backup backs up the differences between the incremental backups. The advantage of having a cumulative backup is that only the last cumulative backup would need to be restored to recover the database. With incremental backups, all of them need to be available to restore. Of course, an incremental backup will use less disk or tape, and it usually takes less time to run.

Backup Type	SQL Server Command	Oracle (RMAN) Command
FULL	`backup database`	`backup database`
Files or file groups	`backup database db1 filegroup ='db1file1' to disk…`	`backup as backupset datafile '/u01/data/ users01.dbf';`
Tablespaces		`backup tablespace system, users;`
Logs (transaction and archive)	`backup log db1 to disk …`	`backup archivelog all;`
Incremental backups/base backup	`Backup database db1 to disk='S:\bkups\ db1.bak' with init`	`Backup incremental level 0 database;`
Incremental backups/ differential backups	`Backup database db1 to disk='S:\bkups\ db1.bak' with differential`	`Backup incremental level 1 cumulative database;` `Backup incremental level 1 database;`

TABLE 6-1.   *Backup Options in SQL Server and Oracle*

In SQL Server, the system databases, as well as `master`, `msdb`, and `model`, need to be backed up. Similarly, in Oracle, the control files, system datafiles, and parameter files for the Oracle database need to be backed up. In SQL Server, the `tempdb` database is not part of backups; in Oracle, the temporary tablespace is not included. The undo tablespace does contain uncommitted changes, but with the newer versions of RMAN, only the uncommitted changes that haven't been written out to the datafiles are backed up.

Full backups will include all of the datafiles in the Oracle database, including system datafiles, but not the control files. As discussed in Chapter 3, the control files have information about the changes and archive logs needed for recovery. Without a current control file, the recovery up to the latest point could be difficult. You may run backups of the control files outside the full backup, or after backups of the full or transaction logs, you can include the control files to make sure the information is captured. Backups of parameter files might not be as important, but you need to have a copy in case changes must be reverted.

Backup Examples

Allocating more channels is like using multiple devices and writing in parallel. For example, if you have a couple of tape drives available, this would allow you to take full advantage of the multiple drives and speed up the backup.

```
> rman target rman/rmanpwdrmancat
RMAN> run {
RMAN> allocate channel disk1 device type disk;
RMAN> allocate channel disk2 device type disk;
RMAN> backup database plus archivelog;
RMAN> backup current controlfile;
RMAN> }
```

Just as you would run transaction log backups multiple times a day with SQL Server, with Oracle, the archive logs need to be backed up more than once a day. The number of transactions and size of disk space available to hold the logs will determine how often.

```
> rman target rman/rmanpwdrmancat
RMAN> run {
RMAN> allocate channel disk1 device type disk;
RMAN> allocate channel disk2 device type disk;
RMAN> backup archivelog all delete all input;
RMAN> }
```

Running archive log backups helps you to avoid filling up the space allocated to the logs. The preceding example will back up any archive logs and then delete them from this space, because they are now included in a backup set. This will keep the file system to a manageable size for archiving.

OEM Backup Jobs

With OEM, you can configure backups and schedule them as jobs in the database. OEM will generate the RMAN script and display it for your review. This provides a good way to gain a better understanding of the backup options and RMAN commands.

When You Run Out of Archive Space

If the archive log space fills up, the database will just hang, with the error "archiver error connect internal until freed." Knowing the command-line RMAN commands is important in this situation. Chances are that the connection through OEM will not be available because of the limited connections allowed to the database as it is waiting for archive log backup space to be freed up.

Moving archive logs to another location will free up space to allow the archive process to continue to run until the files can be backed up and purged. However, after archive logs are moved or deleted, RMAN may fail to run the backup because expected files are not there. So, before you run the backup, you should perform a cross-check to verify which files are available and what has been backed up. The cross-check will also resynchronize the catalog with the files that are present in the backup directory or tape. It will expire the backups in the catalog that are no longer available.

```
## validate archive logs are available
RMAN> crosscheck archivelog all;
## validate database backupsets available
RMAN> crosscheck database;
```

So, you've moved archive logs to another location to free up the space, completed the cross-check, and then run the backup. But there are still logs in another location that have not been backed up. If there is now space in the archive log directory, you can move those files back, perform a cross-check, back them up, and then delete them. If the archive files are just deleted without being backed up, recovery will not be possible.

All of this bouncing around of the archive files is to prevent the database from being put into a hung state, waiting to be able to archive logs again. A better approach is to plan the available space and make sure that the archive logs are backed up to prevent filling up the space.

Figure 6-3 shows the options for customizing a backup job in OEM. If the database is running in NOARCHIVELOG mode, only the full cold backup is available (as well as any files that might be in the flash/fast recovery area, as discussed later in this chapter). If it's in ARCHIVELOG

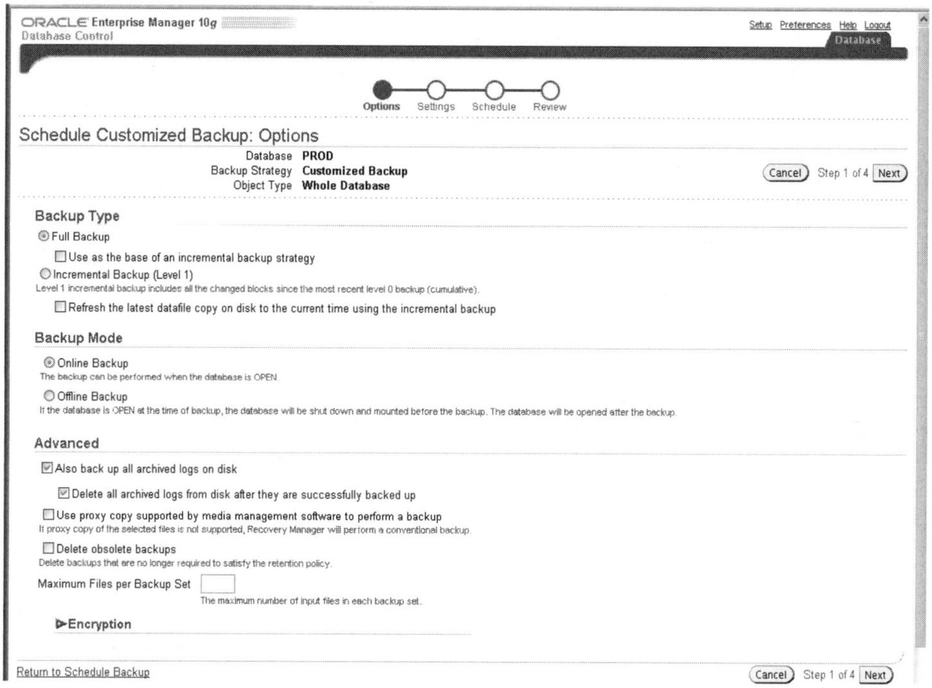

FIGURE 6-3. *Customizing a backup job in OEM*

mode, there are more options, including those to back up tablespaces, datafiles, archive logs, and recovery files.

Next, you set up the schedule for the backup, as shown in Figure 6-4. As typical for other database jobs, you can run the backup as a one-time job immediately or later, or make it a repeating job.

The final step, shown in Figure 6-5, shows the RMAN script and provides an opportunity to edit the script, or even copy it to modify and run outside the scheduler. Submit the job to save and schedule the backup, or run the backup if it's a one-time job.

You can also use OEM to create a restore point, which is useful when you're performing a task against the database for data changes, application upgrades, or even database upgrades. The restore point marks a time to recover to if the upgrade goes awry. Although you could also get the information from the logs and database about the last change or current archive log sequence, having a defined point to roll back to makes the

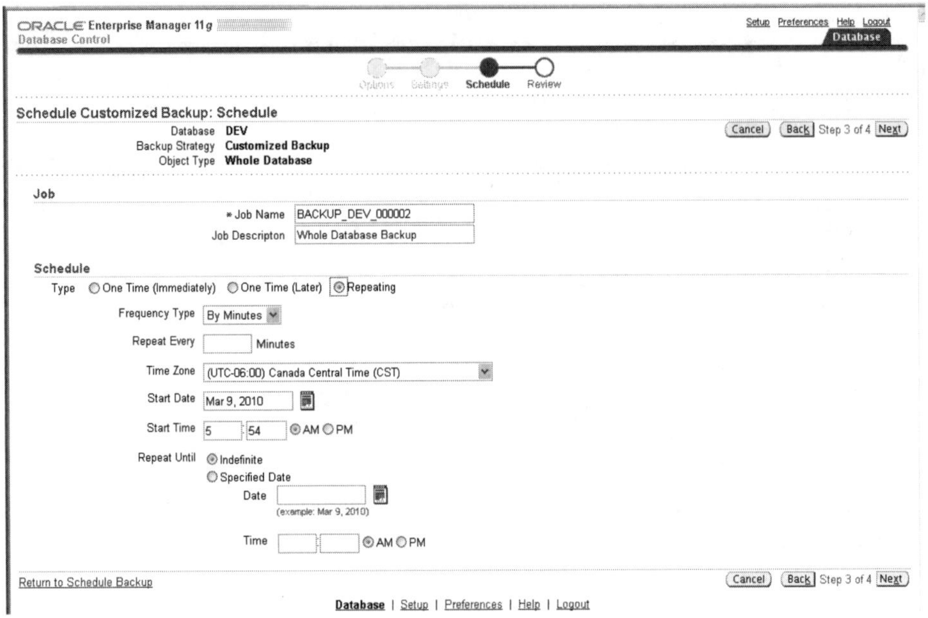

FIGURE 6-4. *Scheduling a backup job in OEM*

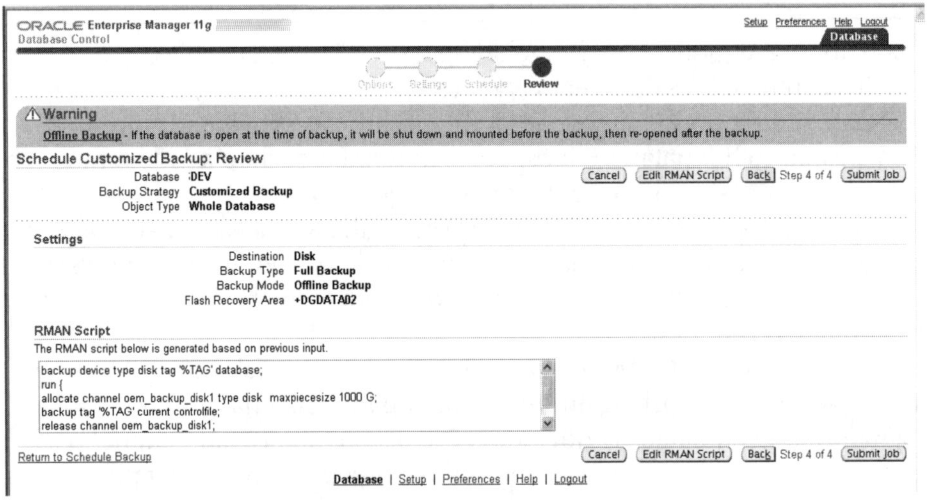

FIGURE 6-5. *Reviewing the RMAN script in OEM*

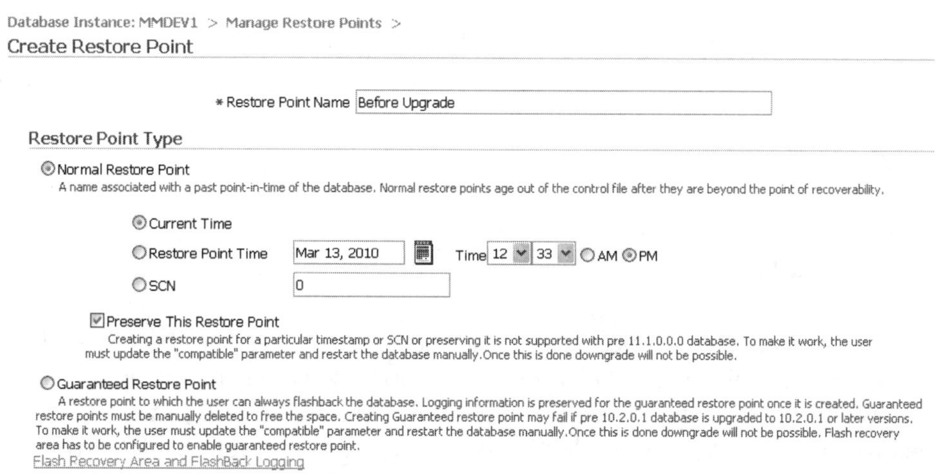

Database Instance: MMDEV1 > Manage Restore Points >
Create Restore Point

* Restore Point Name Before Upgrade

Restore Point Type

⦿ Normal Restore Point
A name associated with a past point-in-time of the database. Normal restore points age out of the control file after they are beyond the point of recoverability.

⦿ Current Time
○ Restore Point Time   Mar 13, 2010   Time 12 ∨ 33 ∨ ○ AM ⦿ PM
○ SCN   0

☑ Preserve This Restore Point
Creating a restore point for a particular timestamp or SCN or preserving it is not supported with pre 11.1.0.0.0 database. To make it work, the user must update the "compatible" parameter and restart the database manually. Once this is done downgrade will not be possible.

○ Guaranteed Restore Point
A restore point to which the user can always flashback the database. Logging information is preserved for the guaranteed restore point once it is created. Guaranteed restore points must be manually deleted to free the space. Creating Guaranteed restore point may fail if pre 10.2.0.1 database is upgraded to 10.2.0.1 or later versions. To make it work, the user must update the "compatible" parameter and restart the database manually. Once this is done downgrade will not be possible. Flash recovery area has to be configured to enable guaranteed restore point.
Flash Recovery Area and FlashBack Logging

FIGURE 6-6.   *Creating a restore point in OEM*

restore process easier. Figure 6-6 shows an example of setting the restore point in OEM.

Restoring and Recovering Databases

What good are backups if you can't use them to restore the database? Oracle provides several ways to restore all or parts of a database. But before we look at the various restore methods, let's consider why you might need to use them. We'll examine some of the failures and consider ways to recover the database. I say "recover," rather than "restore," because in recovery, the system needs to go back to where it was, and this might not mean restoring the entire database.

What Can Go Wrong?

Understanding the different ways a database can fail and reasons for a restore can help in planning a backup strategy. So, what can go wrong?

- ■ Hardware failures/firmware issues
- ■ User error

- Bad code

- Loss of a file, control file, redo log, or datafile

- Corrupt block

- Upgrade issues

- Bad change

- Disaster

A disk or hardware has an issue and the database needs to be restored. Or perhaps a panicked user tells you that an upgrade failed and the application isn't working anymore. As a DBA, you need to really understand the issue before you can develop an effective plan to bring the system back to where it needs to be. For example, a disaster might require a restore in another location. Does the database need to be just read-only to get some information temporarily? Does an application need to be functional at the other location and then moved back when things are cleaned up?

Troubleshooting failures and understanding if there is data corruption or loss of any files are first steps to determine whether individual files need to be restored or if a full recovery is required. Knowing which backups are available will give you different possible solutions. You'll need to consider how long it takes to do the restore, as well as the expected data loss because of the restore.

Suppose the database crashed for some reason, it did a shutdown abort, or the hardware rebooted, and the database came up with an ORA-01113 error saying that a datafile needs recovery. Before heading down the path of restoring the datafile or even the whole database, do a little investigating. If the backup happened to be running when the database crashed, the database might still be in backup mode, which is causing it to think that it needs to be recovered. Looking at the v$database view will show you if it is still in backup mode. If so, you can end the backup (with ALTER DATABASE END BACKUP), and then open the database. This will fix the issue, without having to go through the restore.

Being prepared to do a restore at a critical moment means at least practicing a couple of different restores. Normally, I include testing of restores of databases that I just created, so I have a script that is valid for the database and ready to be used if needed. I also know that the script works, since I just tested it against the database.

Oracle provides various options for recovery, such as rolling back a query or returning to a point before a change. Since we just finished discussing RMAN backups, we'll start with how to restore pieces of the database using RMAN.

Restore and Recover Options

To use RMAN to restore or recover a database, you must first connect to the recovery catalog, and then allocate channels to the tape or disk. The catalog has the information about the database backup and backup set. A control file can be used for the same information. The `restore database` command restores the database files, and the `recover database` command applies any of the changes that are in the archive logs.

```
RMAN> connect target
connected to target database: MMDEV1 (DBID=298473718)
RMAN> connect catalog rman/rmanbkup
connected to recovery catalog database
RMAN> run {
allocate channel disk1 device type disk;
allocate channel disk2 device type disk;
restore database;
recover database;
}
```

Using the control file is the default if you are not connected to the catalog.

```
RMAN> connect target
connected to target database: MMDEV1 (DBID=298473718)
RMAN> restore database;
Starting restore at 12-APR-10
using target database control file instead of recovery catalog
allocated channel: ORA_DISK_1
channel ORA_DISK_1: SID=114 device type=DISK
```

If the current control file is not available, you must restore the control file first before restoring the database.

```
RMAN> connect target
RMAN> run {
allocate channel disk1 device type disk;
restore controlfile;
}
```

How Long Will the Restore Take?

You might find it useful to know how long a restore will take. Here's an example that will provide this information:

```
RMAN> run {
allocate channel tape1 device type sbt;
allocate channel tape2 device type sbt;
debug io;
restore database;
debug off;
}
```

Since the restore is writing the database files from the backup, it will show how much time is left. Here is the output of the preceding example:

```
RMAN> debug io;
DBGIO: channel tape2: blocks=131072 block_size=8192 (rsdf_name)
command restore:7.9% complete, time left 00:24:32
command restore:23.2% complete, time left 00:13:29
command restore:40.6% complete, time left 00:08:55
command restore:57.2% complete, time left 00:06:04
command restore:71.2% complete, time left 00:04:05
channel tape1: restored backup piece 1
```

If you're doing a full restore of the database, and you have already verified that you have a good backup, the restore performs faster if the existing datafiles are not there to be overwritten. If possible, rename the files (if space permits) or remove the files before doing a complete restore for better performance. Later in this chapter, in the "Managing Backups" section, we will look at how to verify that backups are available before removing files that you are not able to restore because of a bad backup.

Recovering to a Specific Point

In SQL Server, you have the options to restore with recovery or with no recovery. With Oracle, you can just restore the database, and then use the `recover database` command with options to define to which point to recover. Along with recovering everything possible, the Oracle RMAN `recover database` command can bring the database to a point in time, to a change number, or to a specific archive log.

You can recover to a system change number (SCN). The current SCN can be seen in the v$database view (select current_scn from v$database;). You can also recover to an "until time" or a sequence from archive logs. If a restore point, such as before_upgrade, has been set for the backup, you can recover the database to that point. Here are some examples of the recovery options:

```
RMAN> run {
allocate channel tape1 device type sbt;
recover database until scn 4059040147;
}
## Other options to set UNTIL, but only one option can be
## used at a time. This just lists the possibilities
RMAN> run {
allocate channel disk1 device type disk;
set until time 'Dec 20 2009 08:23:00';
set until sequence 3421;
set until restore point before_upgrade;
restore database;
recover database;
}
```

With a point-in-time recovery, the database will need to be opened using ALTER DATABASE OPEN RESETLOGS, which will reset all of the redo logs and the SCN for the database. Since the archive logs and backup sets cannot be used after the reset of the logs, this is a good time to take another backup of the database.

As you would expect, you are able to recover only to the point in time when logs and information are available. If you have a SQL Server database in SIMPLE mode, you can recover only to the last backup. If you are using WITH RECOVERY, you must have all of the log backups or have the data needed in the current log file to the point you want to recover. If one of the log backups is missing, you can recover only to that point, even if you have logs available after the missing one. The same is true for Oracle.

With a cold backup and in NOARCHIVE LOG mode, you are rolling back to that last cold backup. In ARCHIVELOG mode, if any of the archive logs are missing or are deleted before being backed up, they will not be in the set, and the restore option will be only to the point before the missing file. This also applies to the redo logs. The options for restoring to an SCN, sequence, or time are valuable to get at least up to the latest point when the needed data was still available.

Restoring Tablespaces, Datafiles, and Blocks

In some cases, just a block is corrupted, or there was an issue with just one of the tablespaces or datafiles. With RMAN, you can recover just these pieces of the database.

A full backup can be used to restore just a tablespace or datafile. It doesn't need to be a tablespace backup to restore a tablespace.

```
## Need to login to SQLPlus to offline the tablespace
SQLPLUS> alter tablespace USERS offline;
## Login to rman for the restore, and notice all of the
## configurations that are set up are being used and not
## scripted out with these commands.
RMAN> connect target
RMAN> restore tablespace users;
RMAN> recover tablespace users;
## Back to SQLPLUS
SQLPLUS> alter tablespace USERS online;
```

This example does a full recovery of the tablespace up to the current database time. If there are more tablespaces in the database, this would be one way to recover with downtime for only the applications or users in the damaged tablespace. To recover a tablespace to a point in time, to before an error occurred or it was corrupted, an auxiliary database or files would be used. After restoring a tablespace, you should run a backup, because recovering the tablespace after the restore is not possible.

With SQL Server, you have DBCC procedures to look for block corruption. In Oracle, the DBVERIFY utility serves this function.

```
Execute DBVERIFY check
### to check file, and dbv help=Y for other options
> dbv file=/u01/oradata/users01.dbf
DBVERIFY - Verification complete
Total Pages Examined          : 1280
Total Pages Processed (Data)  : 151
Total Pages Failing   (Data)  : 0
Total Pages Processed (Index) : 96
Total Pages Failing   (Index) : 0
Total Pages Processed (Other) : 502
Total Pages Processed (Seg)   : 0
Total Pages Failing   (Seg)   : 0
Total Pages Empty             : 531
Total Pages Marked Corrupt    : 0
```

```
Total Pages Influx          : 0
Total Pages Encrypted       : 0
Highest block SCN           : 1647260 (0.1647260)
```

If a block of data is corrupt, DBVERIFY will throw an error and provide some details about the datafile number and block number. The system view `v$database_block_corruption` will confirm the block number. Using RMAN, you can supply the datafile number and block number to recover the blocks.

```
SQLPLUS> alter system switch logfile;
### switching redologs will cause it to write out to the
### archive logs (may need to do a couple of times), which will
### make the redo log information available in the archive logs
### for recovery, and not have the restore in the same redo logs.

login to RMAN connect to target
RMAN> recover
datafile 4 block 23
datafile 3 block 58;
```

Along with tablespace-level restores, there are other options for restoring objects and schemas, which are especially useful when dealing with a database that supports multiple applications. Only one of the applications might have had an issue, and just that object or schema may need to be restored. We will look at some of those other backup and restore options in the "Backing Up and Restoring Objects" section later in this chapter.

OEM Restore and Recovery

As with backups, OEM can walk you through restoring the database. In Figure 6-7, you see the same recovery options we just went through in the RMAN scripts—point-in-time, whole database, datafile, tablespace, block, and so on.

Data Recovery Advisor

If there was an issue with one of the database files, you can use the `LIST FAILURE` command and `ADVISE FAILURE` command to help figure out what to do. Here is an example:

```
RMAN> list failure;
using target database control file instead of recovery catalog
List of Database Failures
=========================
```

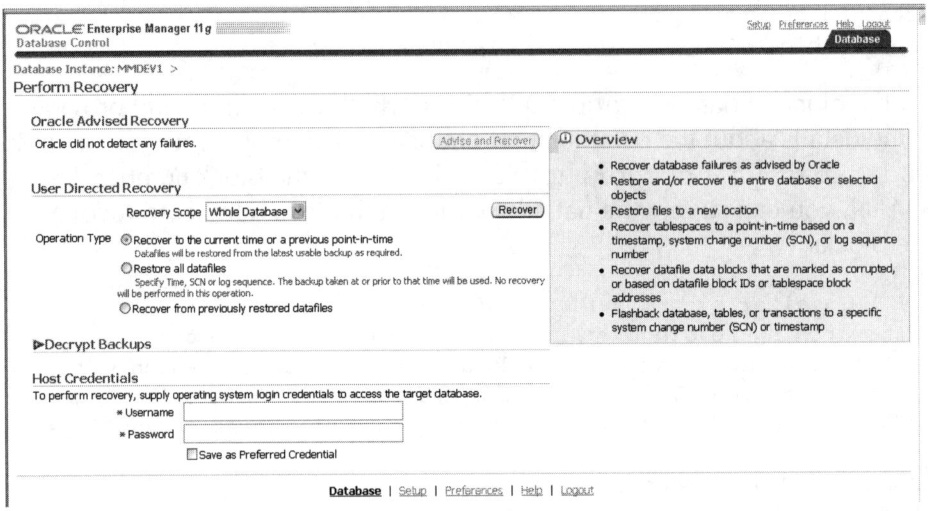

FIGURE 6-7. *Restoring in OEM*

```
Failure ID Priority Status  Time Detected Summary
---------- -------- ------- ------------- -------
582        HIGH     OPEN    13-MAR-10     One or more non-system
                                          datafiles are missing

RMAN> advise failure;
analyzing automatic repair options; this may take some time
allocated channel: ORA_DISK_1
channel ORA_DISK_1: SID=170 device type=DISK
analyzing automatic repair options complete
Mandatory Manual Actions
========================
no manual actions available
Optional Manual Actions
========================
1. If file D:\ORADATA\MMDEV1\USERS01.DBF was unintentionally
renamed or moved, restore it
Automated Repair Options
========================
Option Repair Description
1       Restore and recover datafile 4
  Strategy: The repair includes complete media recovery
  with no data loss
  Repair script:
  d:\app\diag\rdbms\mmdev1\mmdev1\hm\reco_2315272930.hm
```

As you can see, the advisor also provides a repair script and, in this example, says that the recovery is possible without data loss. The script can be run after running the advisor, with `REPAIR FAILURE`. Using `REPAIR FAILURE PREVIEW` will show you the script first, which in this case, just has to restore datafile 4 and recover datafile 4.

The same steps can be taken in OEM. When you perform a recovery (see Figure 6-7), the Oracle Advised Recovery section offers information about the failure and the steps needed to recover.

Copying the Database

So far, we've looked at the options to restore databases back to their original spot, which are useful to recover from failures in a production environment. However, you may want to use backups in other ways, such as to refresh test environments or set up a new database on a different server. For example, you may want to create a test environment for upgrades or patching, providing a production-like environment in development with all of the same permissions, data, and so on. Copying the database can also be useful for troubleshooting. Since you can go back in time, you can look into an issue from a couple of days ago by creating a new database server, doing the research, and then knocking it down after the issue has been resolved.

Using `WITH MOVE` of the datafiles will restore a SQL Server backup to another location. This could be on a different server, such as development, or just to provide another copy. Oracle allows for moving datafiles to another location to either make another copy or to duplicate the database to another server. This is normally accomplished with RMAN's `DUPLICATE` command.

When you duplicate a database to a new host, the files may be in the same place, but chances are that they are under a different database name, and they might have a different file sytem structure. The following RMAN example demonstrates moving the files, which can be used on both a different host or the same host, and if the file structures are the same.

```
RMAN> connect target sysPROD01
RMAN> connect auxiliary sysDEV01
RMAN> connect catalog rmanrmanprod

RMAN> run {
DUPLICATE TARGET DATABASE to DEV01
from active database
```

```
DB_FILE_NAME_CONVERT '/u01/oracle/oradata/PROD01/',
'/u01/oracle/oradata/DEV01'
spfile
NOFILENAMECHECK - needed to restore to a different host
PARAMETER_VALUE_CONVERT '/u01/oracle/oradata/PROD01/',
'/u01/oracle/oradata/DEV01'
set LOG_FILE_NAME_CONVERT ''/u01/oracle/redo/PROD01/',
'/u01/oracle/redo/DEV01';
}

## To use a backup file allocations to a channel to be
## used for pulling the backup file
## Also you can duplicate the database to a previous point in time
## This example will also assume same directory structure for
## the file systems but different host

RMAN> connect target sysPROD01
RMAN> connect auxiliary sysDEV01
RMAN> connect catalog rmanrmanprod

RMAN> run {
allocate channel disk1 device type disk;
allocate auxiliary channel disk2 device type disk;
DUPLICATE TARGET DATABASE to DEV01
SPFILE
NOFILENAMECHECK
UNTIL TIME 'SYSDATE-2'; --restore to two days ago
}
```

You may want to use a duplicate database to migrate to ASM. To do this, first create an ASM instance, and then move from the current database to the new instance and duplicate the database using RMAN. Or if your test environment is also an ASM instance, you might need to duplicate from ASM to ASM for the datafiles. The next two examples show both approaches.

```
## file system migrate to ASM
RMAN> connect target sysPROD01
RMAN> connect auxiliary sysPROD02

RMAN>run{
DUPLICATE target database to PROD02
from active database
spfile
PARAMETER_VALUE_CONVERT '/u01/oracle/oradata/PROD01/','+DG_DATA01'
```

```
set DB_CREATE_FILE_DEST +DG_DATA01;
}

## ASM to ASM
RMAN> connect target sysPROD01
RMAN> connect auxiliary sysDEV01

RMAN>run{
DUPLICATE target database to DEV01
from active database
spfile
PARAMETER_VALUE_CONVERT '+DG_DATA01','+DG_DEV01'
set DB_FILE_NAME_CONVERT '+DG_DATA01','+DG_DEV01'
set LOG_FILE_NAME_CONVERT '+DG_DATA01','+DG_DEV01';
}
```

Again, you can use OEM to make the database copy and review the RMAN script it generates. In OEM, from the Move Data tab, choose the Clone Database option (which uses the RMAN `DUPLICATE` command), as shown in Figure 6-8. In the next steps, it gathers the information about moving the files, database to copy to, and host information.

These duplicates include the whole database, with all of the different users and schemas. So if there is more than one application in the database,

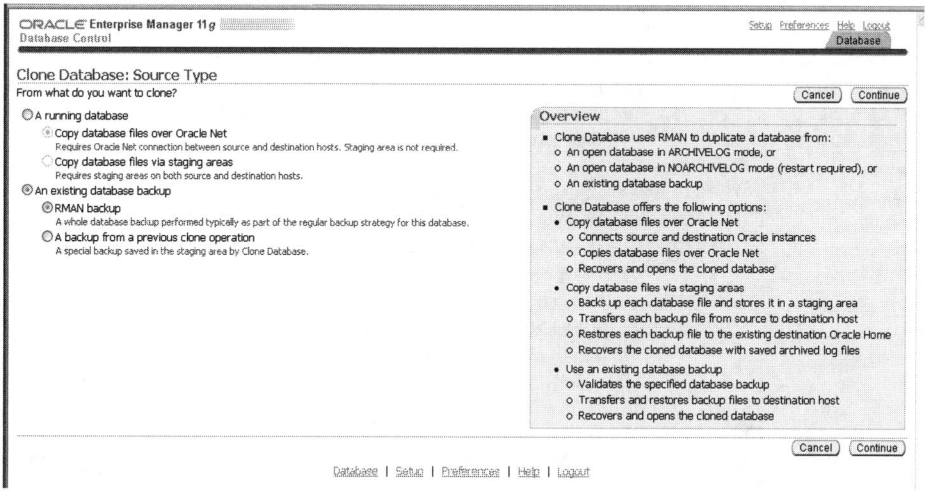

FIGURE 6-8. *Cloning a database in OEM*

this will take all of the application databases and copy them over to the new database server.

Managing Backups

Managing backups is not just about purging and maintaining the retention policy, but also about knowing which backups are available for restores. Oracle provides several ways to get information about backup sets.

Viewing Backups

RMAN has a `LIST` command that will return the backup sets that are present in the catalog or control file. The listing shows the different backup pieces and details, including the checkpointed SCN, the date, full or incremental, and tablespaces that were backed up. In the following example, the archive logs were included as part of the full backup, so they are also listed.

```
RMAN> list backup;
using target database control file instead of recovery catalog
List of Backup Sets
===================
BS Key   Type LV Size       Device Type Elapsed Time Completion Time
------- ---- -- ---------- ----------- ------------ ---------------
13       Full   1.02G      DISK        00:01:20     08-MAR-10
        BP Key: 13    Status: AVAILABLE   Compressed: NO
      Tag: TAG20100308T200144
      Piece Name:
E:\APP\FLASH_RECOVERY_AREA\MMDEV1\BACKUPSET\2010_03_08\
O1_MF_NNNDF_TAG20100308T200144_5SCC0GDZ_.BKP
  List of Datafiles in backup set 13
  File LV Type Ckp SCN    Ckp Time  Name
  ---- -- ---- ---------- --------- ----
    1      Full 1760175    08-MAR-10  D:\ORADATA\MMDEV1\SYSTEM01.DBF
    2      Full 1760175    08-MAR-10  D:\ORADATA\MMDEV1\SYSAUX01.DBF
    3      Full 1760175    08-MAR-10  D:\ORADATA\MMDEV1\UNDOTBS01.DBF
    4      Full 1760175    08-MAR-10  D:\ORADATA\MMDEV1\USERS01.DBF

BS Key   Type LV Size       Device Type Elapsed Time Completion Time
------- ---- -- ---------- ----------- ------------ ---------------
14       Full   9.36M      DISK        00:00:07     08-MAR-10
        BP Key: 14    Status: AVAILABLE   Compressed: NO
      Tag: TAG20100308T200144
        Piece Name: E:\APP\FLASH_RECOVERY_AREA\MMDEV1\BACKUPSET\2010_03_08\
O1_MF_NCSNF_TAG20100308T200144_5SCC2YYM_.BKP
```

```
     SPFILE Included: Modification time: 08-MAR-10
     SPFILE db_unique_name: MMDEV1
     Control File Included: Ckp SCN: 1760265        Ckp time: 08-MAR-10

BS Key   Type LV Size         Device Type Elapsed Time Completion Time
-------  ---- -- ----------   ----------- ------------ ---------------
15       Full   9.36M         DISK         00:00:06     12-MAR-10
         BP Key: 15   Status: AVAILABLE  Compressed: NO
         Tag: TAG20100312T054615
         Piece Name:
E:\APP\FLASH_RECOVERY_AREA\MMDEV1\BACKUPSET\2010_03_12\
O1_MF_NCSNF_TAG20100312T054615_5SNBH7Z5_.BKP
   SPFILE Included: Modification time: 12-MAR-10
   SPFILE db_unique_name: MMDEV1
   Control File Included: Ckp SCN: 1905411        Ckp time: 12-MAR-10

BS Key   Size         Device Type Elapsed Time Completion Time
-------  ----------   ----------- ------------ ---------------
16       58.13M       DISK         00:00:09     12-MAR-10
         BP Key: 16   Status: AVAILABLE  Compressed: NO
         Tag: TAG20100312T054803
         Piece Name:
E:\APP\FLASH_RECOVERY_AREA\MMDEV1\BACKUPSET\2010_03_12\
O1_MF_ANNNN_TAG20100312T054803_5SNBHRFM_.BKP
   List of Archived Logs in backup set 16
   Thrd Seq    Low SCN    Low Time  Next SCN   Next Time
   ---- ------- ---------- --------- ---------- ---------
   1    35      1757126    08-MAR-10 1782135    09-MAR-10
   1    36      1782135    09-MAR-10 1802422    09-MAR-10
   1    37      1802422    09-MAR-10 1828159    10-MAR-10
   1    38      1828159    10-MAR-10 1853573    10-MAR-10
   1    39      1853573    10-MAR-10 1879239    11-MAR-10
   1    40      1879239    11-MAR-10 1902061    12-MAR-10
   1    41      1902061    12-MAR-10 1905455    12-MAR-10
```

To list the details about the archive logs, you can use the sequence number or SCN.

```
RMAN> list archivelog sequence=36;
List of Archived Log Copies for database with db_unique_name MMDEV1
=====================================================================
Key     Thrd Seq     S Low Time
------- ---- ------- - ---------
18      1    36      A 09-MAR-10
        Name:
E:\APP\FLASH_RECOVERY_AREA\MMDEV1\ARCHIVELOG\2010_03_09\
O1_MF_1_36_5SDDN6X8_.ARC
17      1    36      A 09-MAR-10
        Name:
        E:\APP\PRODUCT\11.1.0\DB_1\RDBMS\ARC00036_0710094395.001
```

This example shows two archive log files with the same sequence number. This means that a copy was included in the backup set and is also still in the archive log file on the database server. This is the case when the `DELETE ALL INPUT` option isn't used with the backup command. But the archive logs can also be cleared out another way: by being expired and deleted, as discussed in the next section.

In OEM, you can see the same backup set listing on the Backup Sets tab of Manage Current Backups, as shown in Figure 6-9. This page also offers the options to catalog additional files, so if a backup was taken and not recorded in the catalog, you can add those files, cross-check all of the archive logs and backups, delete obsolete files, and expire obsolete files.

Data dictionary views and recovery catalog tables also provide views into the backup sets, to help manage backups and know which backups are available for restoring. These are also good places to check to make sure backups are running properly.

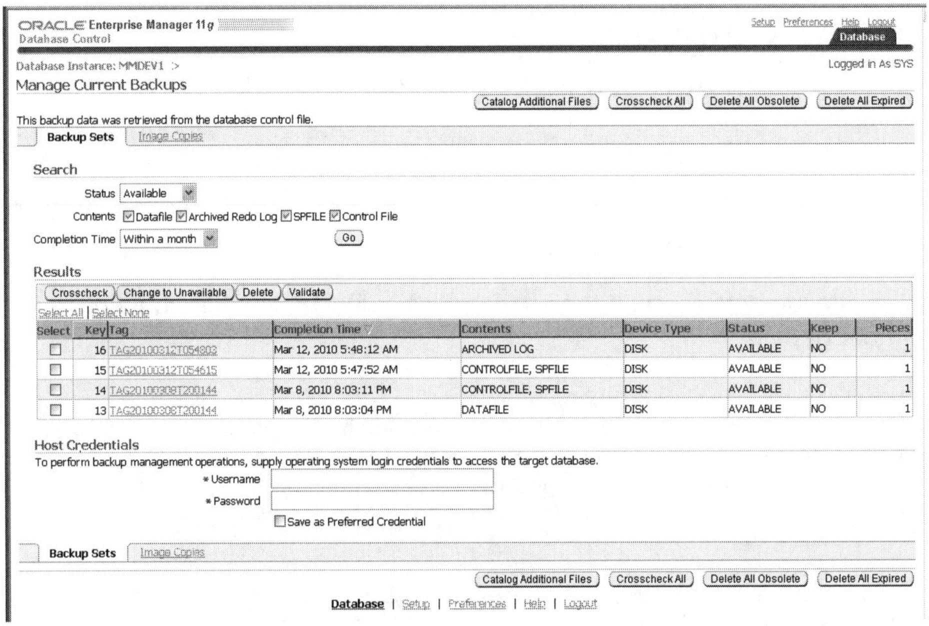

FIGURE 6-9. *Managing backups in OEM*

In the RMAN catalog, `RC_DATABASE` has the list of databases that are registered in the catalog. `RC_BACKUP_SET` has the completion time of the backup, type of backup, and some additional information. It might seem like duplicate information, but remember that the RMAN catalog can keep the information for multiple databases, so a report can be run for all of the databases in the catalog. The data dictionary view `v$backup_set` has the same details, but it is valid for only the database server, not all of the databases registered in the catalog.

The scripts are also stored in the RMAN catalog. The `RC_STORED_SCRIPT_LINE` table contains details about the scripts that are scheduled. Other tables that might be useful are `RC_BACKUP_SET_DETAILS`, `RC_BACKUP_FILES`, and `RC_RMAN_BACKUP_JOB_DETAILS`. The corresponding data dictionary views are `v$backup_datafile`, `v$backup_set_details`, and `v$rman_backup_job_details`.

You can build reports from these tables outside OEM or RMAN to provide details about the backups that are running against one of the database servers or multiple databases (from the RMAN catalog).

Purging Obsolete Files

Keeping the catalog a manageable size is part of backup maintenance. In SQL Server, you can handle this when you schedule a database backup by setting an expire time on the backup, by number of days or on a specific date. In Oracle, the parameters `REDUNDANCY` and `RECOVERY WINDOW` set the number of backups and number of days for retention policies. Table 6-2 shows the options for expiring and deleting backup files in SQL Server and Oracle.

You can run reports to get the status of the backup pieces, including which ones have been marked obsolete by the retention policy, deleted, or expired. First, run a cross-check to check the files that have been deleted or marked obsolete. Then run the RMAN `DELETE OBSOLETE` command to remove the files.

```
RMAN> CROSSCHECK BACKUP;
RMAN> CROSSCHECK ARCHIVELOG ALL;
RMAN> DELETE EXPIRED BACKUP;
--If not deleting archive logs as they are backed up,
--delete from file system via DELETE
RMAN> DELETE ARCHIVELOG ALL BACKED UP 2 TIMES;
```

Option	SQL Server	Oracle
Expire	Part of backup job or script parameters EXPIREDATE or RETAINDAYS (number of days or on a date)	RMAN parameters REDUNDANCY and RECOVERY WINDOW (number of days or number of backups)
Delete (from msdb/catalog)	sp_delete_backuphistory	DELETE EXPIRED
Delete expired backup files	Maintenance Cleanup task	DELETE OBSOLETE BACKUP ARCHIVELOGS DELETE ALL INPUT

TABLE 6-2.   *Delete and Expire Backup Options in SQL Server and Oracle*

It is possible to override the defaults for retention policies as well as force the backups to be deleted by using the RMAN DELETE FORCE command.

Backing Up and Restoring Objects

With SQL Server, it is typical to restore a database to get a copy of just the objects that are needed. With Oracle, restoring the database is normally to restore the full system, but there are utilities available to pull out just the objects by schema, or even at the table level. This allows you to secure backups for these objects or copy them to another system, perhaps to refresh a test environment with just the needed schema or tables.

Copying Objects at the Table and Schema Level

Using a SQL statement, you can create a table from an existing table for a quick backup of a table before data changes. A backup table can be defined (such as CREATE table TAB_BACKUP AS select * from TAB_PROD) with tablespaces, no logging (to avoid some of the logging in the redo logs), and with some of the other table options. The table will not include any of the indexes, constraints, or triggers that might be on the "real" table, but it will have the same datatypes and the same data. A WHERE clause can also be defined in the CREATE table AS statement to capture data that might be archived or deleted, as an extra security blanket.

SQL Server also has a couple of utilities to pull out table-level data as well as the table definitions. The bcp utility could be used copy table objects on the SQL Server side.

Oracle has the Data Pump utility, which handles both exports and imports, as well as older EXP and IMP utilities. For example, you might export a schema with just the simple EXP, and remap the schema to a new user to refresh a test schema. Chapter 5 covered some other tools, such as SQL Developer, that can pull the structure information for tables and also help copy objects to another environment or schema. However, the Data Pump utilities are easier to use and generally perform better, so we'll take a closer look at them here.

Using Data Pump

Since Oracle Database 10*g*, the new improved version of the export and import utilities is Data Pump. You can set up a Data Pump export job to allow you to recover just a table or another object, such as a view or stored procedure. The exports include the Data Definition Language (DDL), which creates the structures of the tables, procedures, trigger, indexes, views, and other objects. Exports can also be done without data, to provide just these structures, which you can then copy to another schema or save as a backup.

Data Pump does require some setup and permissions. Since the export file is being written out, it needs a directory for the file to write to. Directories are defined in the database, and permissions are given to read or write to the files for users that need to perform these tasks. If the exports and imports are being used only by the DBA for backups or refreshes, then these are privileged accounts.

A job is created with each Data Pump execution. A name can be specifically given to a job to be able to view its progress. The dba_ datapump_jobs view shows the jobs.

The Data Pump job can also export the full database by setting the parameter FULL=Y, and then be used to restore only a schema or table. Tablespaces and queries can also be exported. Even if you're exporting a full schema or tablespace, you can exclude a table or object by using the EXCLUDE parameter. This is useful for skipping over history tables or very large tables that might be used only for reading or reporting. To view the different parameters available for these utilities from the command line, execute `expdp help=Y`.

Here are a few examples of creating a directory and exporting and importing with Data Pump from the command line:

```
SQLPLUS> create directory DATAPUMP_DIR
   as '/oraexport/DB01/dpdump';
SQLPLUS> grant read, write on directory DATAPUMP_DIR to MMTEST;

## To run an datapump export from the command line
## This will export a couple of tables
> expdp mmprod/mmpasswd schemas=MMPROD tables=TAB1,TAB2
directory=DATAPUMP_DIR dumpfile=exp_tables.dmp log=Exp_tables.log

## This will export one schema
> expdp mmprod/mmpasswd schemas=MMPROD directory=DATAPUMP_DIR
dumpfile=exp_mmprod.dmp log=Exp_mmprod.log

## To run a datapump import to refresh the
## test schema from the dump
> impdp mmtest/mmpasswd remap_schema=MMPROD:MMTEST
directory=DATAPUMP_DIR file=exp_mmprod.dmp log=Imp_mmtest.log
```

Just as you can schedule RMAN backup jobs in OEM, you can also schedule Data Pump jobs. Figure 6-10 shows the selection of an export to a

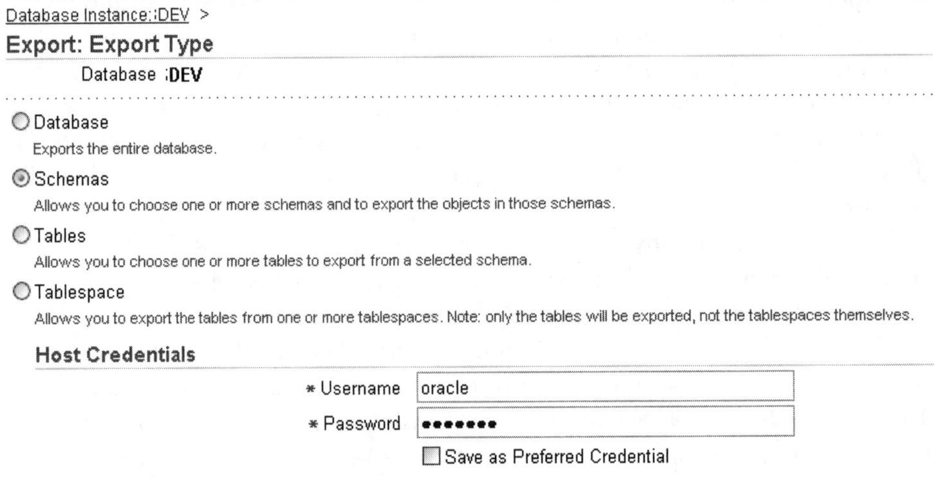

Database Instance::DEV >
Export: Export Type
   Database :DEV

○ Database
   Exports the entire database.
◉ Schemas
   Allows you to choose one or more schemas and to export the objects in those schemas.
○ Tables
   Allows you to choose one or more tables to export from a selected schema.
○ Tablespace
   Allows you to export the tables from one or more tablespaces. Note: only the tables will be exported, not the tablespaces themselves.

Host Credentials

* Username	oracle
* Password	●●●●●●●

☐ Save as Preferred Credential

FIGURE 6-10. *Choosing what to export in OEM*

file, which is found under the Data Movement tab. The options are to export the database, schemas, tables, or tablespace.

After selecting what to export, you can get an estimate of the disk space and set other parameters, as shown in Figure 6-11. Estimating the disk space would be useful in planning the directory space for the job, especially if you're keeping a couple of copies of the export files. You can choose whether to use the actual data blocks or the table statistics to gather this information. You select the directory here, or you can create one if you are using an account with the appropriate permissions (the actual file name for the export file is specified in the next step). You also can choose whether or not you want a log of the export. The advanced options allow for selections of data and structures, just data, or just structures. Objects can be either included or excluded—choosing the one that makes the shortest list is recommended.

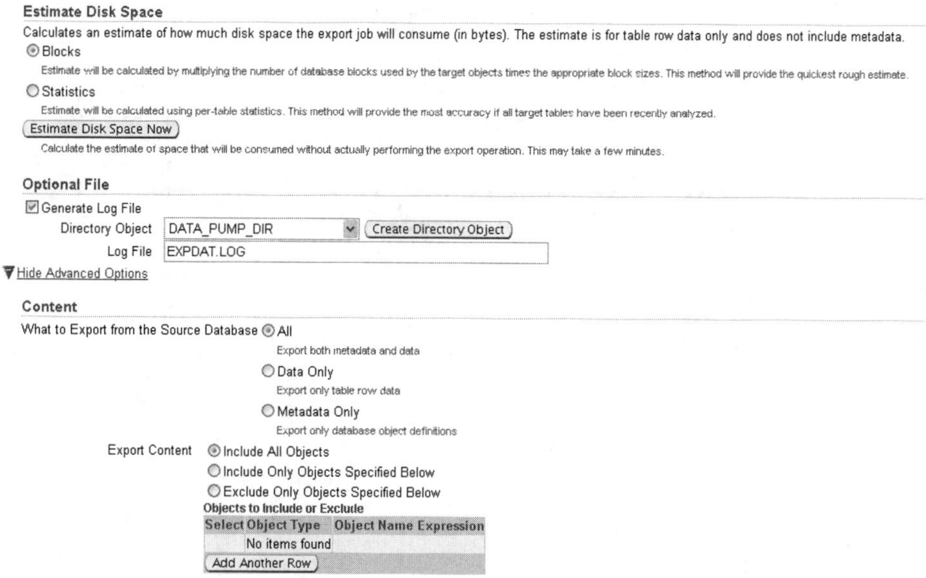

Estimate Disk Space

Calculates an estimate of how much disk space the export job will consume (in bytes). The estimate is for table row data only and does not include metadata.

◉ Blocks

Estimate will be calculated by multiplying the number of database blocks used by the target objects times the appropriate block sizes. This method will provide the quickest rough estimate.

○ Statistics

Estimate will be calculated using per-table statistics. This method will provide the most accuracy if all target tables have been recently analyzed.

(Estimate Disk Space Now)

Calculate the estimate of space that will be consumed without actually performing the export operation. This may take a few minutes.

Optional File

☑ Generate Log File

Directory Object | DATA_PUMP_DIR ▼ | (Create Directory Object)

Log File | EXPDAT.LOG

▼ Hide Advanced Options

Content

What to Export from the Source Database ◉ All

　　　　　　　　　　　Export both metadata and data

　　　　　　　　　　○ Data Only

　　　　　　　　　　　Export only table row data

　　　　　　　　　　○ Metadata Only

　　　　　　　　　　　Export only database object definitions

Export Content   ◉ Include All Objects

　　　　　　　　○ Include Only Objects Specified Below

　　　　　　　　○ Exclude Only Objects Specified Below

Objects to Include or Exclude

Select Object Type	Object Name Expression
No items found	

(Add Another Row)

FIGURE 6-11.   *Defining an export job in OEM*

Figure 6-12 shows the OEM options for scheduling a Data Pump job. After you have set up the Data Pump job, even if it is a one-time run of the job, it will be listed in the job activity for the export jobs and other scheduled jobs. You can monitor it by clicking its name (DAILY_EXP in the example in Figure 6-12).

Another option available in OEM is to set up a connection to a different database through a database link when importing, as shown in Figure 6-13. This would be run from the server to which you want to copy the objects, and the database link would be created to the source database.

NOTE
I am sure I don't need to warn you about being careful with mixing production and test environments with links. Sometimes it is necessary to be able to refresh the test environment. This chapter has given you some examples of how to recover the database if something goes wrong.

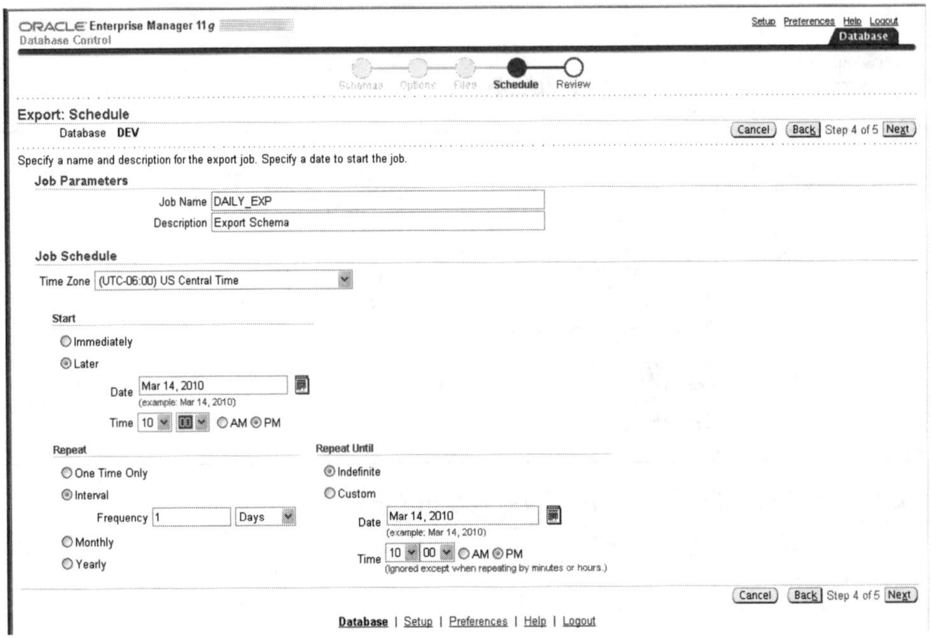

FIGURE 6-12. *Scheduling a Data Pump job in OEM*

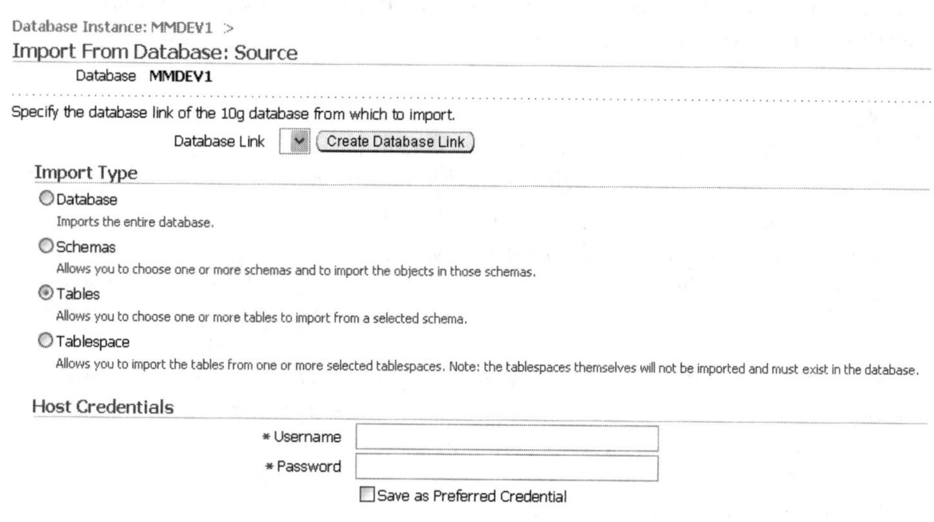

Database Instance: MMDEV1 >
Import From Database: Source
　　　Database **MMDEV1**

Specify the database link of the 10g database from which to import.
　　　　　　　Database Link 〔ⅴ〕〔 Create Database Link 〕

Import Type

○ Database
　Imports the entire database.
○ Schemas
　Allows you to choose one or more schemas and to import the objects in those schemas.
◉ Tables
　Allows you to choose one or more tables to import from a selected schema.
○ Tablespace
　Allows you to import the tables from one or more selected tablespaces. Note: the tablespaces themselves will not be imported and must exist in the database.

Host Credentials

　　　　　　　* Username 〔　　　　　　　　　　　　〕
　　　　　　　* Password 〔　　　　　　　　　　　　〕
　　　　　　　　　　　□ Save as Preferred Credential

FIGURE 6-13. *Importing objects with OEM*

Protecting Users from Users

Much of the thought put into backups and recovery is to protect the system from hardware issues or even disasters, but you also need to consider what damage people can do. Developers, users, and DBAs use the database environment for development, testing, running applications, making changes, and just doing their jobs. As a DBA, you probably confirm which environment you are logged in to before making a change. You probably run an extra backup just to give yourself that extra protection in case something goes wrong. But other users may not be so cautious. They may accidentally log in to the wrong environment and drop a table or change a stored procedure. Fortunately, Oracle offers some features to assist in protecting users from themselves.

Recycle Bin

How many times have you pulled something out of the Windows Recycle Bin after deleting it? The Oracle recycle bin works the same way with tables that have been dropped. For example, if you were refreshing a couple of tables, and realized you dropped the wrong tables, you can retrieve those objects from the recycle bin. The recycle bin has been available since Oracle Database 10*g* and is on by default. Users have their own recycle bins.

NOTE
The recycle bin does not provide protection from truncating the data from the table or other data manipulations. However, changes like deletes and updates can be handled with commits and rollbacks.

The `user_recyclebin` and `dba_recyclebin` views show information about the contents of the recycle bin. The `dba_recyclebin` view has an owner column, which lists who owns the object.

```
SQLPLUS> desc DBA_RECYCLEBIN;
 Name                                      Null?    Type
 ---------------------------------------- -------- ------------
 OWNER                                     NOT NULL VARCHAR2(30)
 OBJECT_NAME                               NOT NULL VARCHAR2(30)
 ORIGINAL_NAME                                      VARCHAR2(32)
 OPERATION                                          VARCHAR2(9)
 TYPE                                               VARCHAR2(25)
 TS_NAME                                            VARCHAR2(30)
 CREATETIME                                         VARCHAR2(19)
 DROPTIME                                           VARCHAR2(19)
 DROPSCN                                            NUMBER
 PARTITION_NAME                                     VARCHAR2(32)
 CAN_UNDROP                                         VARCHAR2(3)
 CAN_PURGE                                          VARCHAR2(3)
 RELATED                                   NOT NULL NUMBER
 BASE_OBJECT                               NOT NULL NUMBER
 PURGE_OBJECT                              NOT NULL NUMBER
 SPACE                                              NUMBER
```

Since the names of the objects in the database need to be unique by owner and object name, the name of the object in the recycle bin is system-generated and starts with `BIN$`. Here is an example of a quick query against `dba_recyclebin`:

```
SQLPLUS> select owner, object_name, original_name, droptime from dba_recyclebin;
OWNER    OBJECT_NAME                 ORIGINAL_NAME   DROPTIME
WK_TEST  BIN$7qfPJ4jvSjOSTM1Vng==$0  TAB_CUST_PK     2010-02-04:16
WK_TEST  BIN$oxgITJMlRtmNZOVYtw==$0  TAB_CUST        2010-02-04:16
WK_TEST  BIN$rdtRhxXVSANuLmU6+w==$0  TAB_INV_PK      2010-02-04:16
```
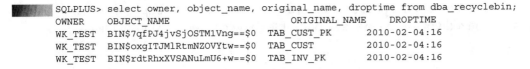

Or you can run a SHOW RECYCLEBIN:

```
SQLPLUS> show recyclebin;
```

As you can see from the description of the view and the sample query, the object name is definitely unique, and the only way to relate it back to the original object is through the original name and owner. The change number and the time that the object was dropped are also provided.

Since the object isn't really dropped and the data is there, you can actually run queries against the object by using the new system name.

```
SQLPLUS> select * from "BIN$LGYYp0ydRYyeNUiq66IHHw==$0";
```

Restoring Tables from the Recycle Bin

To "undrop" a table in the recycle bin, you flashback the table.

```
SQLPLUS> flashback table TAB_CUST to before drop;
Flashback complete.
```

When flashed back, the table will no longer be in the recycle bin. If multiple versions of a table exist in the recycle bin, the most recent one is returned. You can continue to issue `flashback table` until you get the correct object. Alternatively, you can use the system name (BIN$) to identify the table that should be flashed back.

```
SQLPLUS> flashback table "BIN$LGYYp0ydRYyeNUiq66IHHw==$0"
    to before drop;
Flashback complete.
```

NOTE
Any constraints on the tables are not maintained when restoring the table from the recycle bin.

Purging the Recycle Bin

As long as the dropped tables remain in the recycle bin, they are taking up space in the user tablespace. You won't want to allow the objects to stay there forever, unless you have completely unlimited disk space. Like backups, the recycle bin versions are great to have, but they need to be managed for size and which objects are being kept.

The objects in the recycle bin can be cleared out with the `purge` command. Users can clear their own recycle bins:

```
SQLPLUS> purge recyclebin;
```

Purging the DBA recycle bin clears out all of the user recycle bins.

```
SQLPLUS>  conn / as sysdba
SQLPLUS> purge dba_recyclebin;
```

If you are absolutely sure about the table you are dropping, include the `purge` command after the `DROP table` command, and the table will not appear in the recycle bin.

After a purge, when you query the system tables, no rows are returned (which can be used as validation that the objects have been cleared).

You can also turn off the recycle bin by running either of these commands:

```
ALTER SESSION SET RECYCLEBIN=OFF;
ALTER SYSTEM SET RECYCLEBIN=OFF;
```

Flashback

As you saw in the previous section, the `flashback` command lets you pull a table out of the recycle bin. But flashback also has a greater purpose in the recovery strategy. You can flashback a query, table, and even the database. But before you can use flashback in this way, you must configure a recovery area.

Configuring the Recovery Area

Just as with archiving, the flashback feature is either on or off, and to turn on flashback, archiving needs to be on, too. This can be set up as part of the database creation.

Additionally, you need an area to store the flashback information, which is a file destination that is allocated and configured in a parameter setting. This location is known as the flashback recovery area in Oracle Database 10*g* and 11*g* R1; in 11*g* R2, it is called the fast recovery area. Both names become FRA for short.

```
SQLPLUS> startup mount restrict
ORACLE instance started.
Total System Global Area   535662592 bytes
Fixed Size                   1334380 bytes
Variable Size              243270548 bytes
```

```
Database Buffers              285212672 bytes
Redo Buffers                    5844992 bytes
Database mounted.
SQLPLUS> alter database flashback on;
Database altered.
SQLPLUS> alter database open;
Database altered.
SQLPLUS> alter system set db_recovery_file_dest='/oraFRA/MMDEV1'
    scope=both;
System altered.
SQLPLUS> alter system set db_recovery_file_dest_size=100G
    scope=both;
System altered.
SQLPLUS> alter system set db_flashback_retention_target=1440
    scope both;
System altered.
```

The DB_RECOVERY_FILE_DEST_SIZE parameter allocates how much disk is available for the FRA. The size and the destination parameters are required. The DB_FLASHBACK_RETENTION_TARGET parameter is the limit in minutes of how far back to keep files available in the FRA to be able to flashback the database.

The FRA should be able to hold backups of the database, archive logs, and control files. The appropriate sizing depends on the database size and how many backups should be held there. The size can be adjusted with more disk space or by changing the location. The v$flashback_database_log view shows information about the FRA.

```
SQLPLUS> desc v$flashback_database_log;
 Name                                      Null?     Type
 ----------------------------------------- -------- -------------
 OLDEST_FLASHBACK_SCN                                NUMBER
 OLDEST_FLASHBACK_TIME                               DATE
 RETENTION_TARGET                                    NUMBER
 FLASHBACK_SIZE                                      NUMBER
 ESTIMATED_FLASHBACK_SIZE                            NUMBER
```

The estimated size should be based on the retention target and size of the current files in the FRA. The default retention value is one day.

Other views are available for monitoring the FRA, showing the files it currently contains and how they are being used. The v$flash_recovery_area_usage view shows how the FRA is used.

```
SQLPLUS> select file_type, percent_space_used as "%_used",
number_of_files
```

```
from v$flash_recovery_area_usage;
FILE_TYPE                % used NUMBER_OF_FILES
-------------------- ---------- ---------------
CONTROL FILE                  0               0
REDO LOG                      0               0
ARCHIVED LOG               6.45              19
BACKUP PIECE              27.41               4
IMAGE COPY                    0               0
FLASHBACK LOG              1.12               6
FOREIGN ARCHIVED LOG          0               0
```

The `v$recovery_file_dest` view provides similar information, as well as space limits that might be set for a file type.

Flashing Back Items

To flashback the database, you use RMAN to run the commands and can go back to a point in time, SCN, or restore point—starting to sound familiar?

```
RMAN> shutdown immediate
RMAN> startup mount
RMAN> flashback database to SCN 2126976;
Starting flashback at 18-MAR-10
allocated channel: ORA_DISK_1
channel ORA_DISK_1: SID=153 device type=DISK

starting media recovery
media recovery complete, elapsed time: 00:00:07

Finished flashback at 18-MAR-10
RMAN> alter database open;
-- this will cause an error because logs need to be reset
  --since the database went back to a point in time.
RMAN-00571: ===========================================================
RMAN-00569: =========== ERROR MESSAGE STACK FOLLOWS =============
RMAN-00571: ===========================================================
RMAN-03002: failure of alter db command at 03/18/2010 05:49:09
ORA-01589: must use RESETLOGS or NORESETLOGS option for
database open

RMAN> alter database open resetlogs;
database opened
```

Now that the database has been flashed back to the appropriate SCN, things can continue running against the database. This is similar to RMAN restore, but the files are probably more available because they are in the FRA.

The FRA is also useful for flashing back queries to see how the data was before the transaction happened. Transactions can be fairly complex, depending on constraints and what triggers and referential integrity are in place. For example, flashing back a query can be useful when you've updated the wrong table or modified data in an ad hoc query that doesn't have a simple rollback statement. You can even create another table or a view for the data if you want to just validate the change or compare the data to make sure it has the values expected.

Here is a simple example of how to create a table with the data that is flashed back:

```
SQLPLUS> desc mmalcher.emp
  Name                                         Type
  ------------------------------------------   ------------------------
  EMPNO                                        NUMBER(4)
  ENAME                                        VARCHAR2(10)
  JOB                                          VARCHAR2(9)
  MGR                                          NUMBER(4)
  HIREDATE                                     DATE
  SAL                                          NUMBER(7,2)
  COMM                                         NUMBER(7,2)
  DEPTNO                                       NUMBER(2)
SQLPLUS> insert into mmalcher.emp
values(9012,'MALCHER','DBA',2382,sysdate,1000,100);
1 row created.
SQLPLUS> commit;
Commit complete.
## To get the current database SCN
SQLPLUS> select dbms_flashback.get_system_change_number
  from dual;
GET_SYSTEM_CHANGE_NUMBER
-----------------------
2199747
SQLPLUS> delete from mmalcher.emp where ename='MALCHER';
1 row deleted.
SQLPLUS> commit;
Commit complete.
## Use the current database SCN before delete to get the
## values from the table as of that change
SQLPLUS> create table emp_compare as  select *
from mmalcher.emp as of scn 2199747;
```

```
Table created.
SQLPLUS> select * from emp where ename='MALCHER';
no rows selected.
SQLPLUS> select * from emp_compare where ename='MALCHER';
EMPNO ENAME    JOB    MGR HIREDATE        SAL       COMM    DEPTNO
----------- ------- --------------- --------- --------- -------
8901 MALCHER   DBA    2382 05-JAN-10     1000        40       10
```

As you can see, the transaction was committed, and yet you can create a table with the old values of the table. You can run queries against the new table and compare what data changed. You could also use a timestamp to go back as the information is available in the FRA, to bring back the query or changes to the data as needed.

This example gets the SCN before the delete, and you would only know what this value is before your change because you have queried for it. This could be useful in putting in rollback points into the code, and having the SCN values stored in a log table for the process.

Another way to confirm you're using the right SCN is to get the information about queries and SCNs by time and other details. You can query the `flashback_transaction_query` view for these details, which is especially useful when more than one table might be involved, as in the simple example:

```
SQLPLUS> desc flashback_transaction_query;
 Name                                      Type
 ----------------------------------------- -----------------------
 XID                                       RAW(8)
 START_SCN                                 NUMBER
 START_TIMESTAMP                           DATE
 COMMIT_SCN                                NUMBER
 COMMIT_TIMESTAMP                          DATE
 LOGON_USER                                VARCHAR2(30)
 UNDO_CHANGE#                              NUMBER
 OPERATION                                 VARCHAR2(32)
 TABLE_NAME                                VARCHAR2(256)
 TABLE_OWNER                               VARCHAR2(32)
 ROW_ID                                    VARCHAR2(19)
 UNDO_SQL                                  VARCHAR2(4000)
```

As you can see, being able to flashback a query or table lets you avoid that panic attack of "I think I updated something wrong" or "I might have dropped the production table or a key development table." Being able to restore what is needed is key to a DBA's peace of mind.

Summary

RMAN is the main tool for the Oracle backups, and it can be used through the command line or OEM. The RMAN catalog helps to manage the backups and backup pieces. RMAN can back up a tablespace, archive logs, datafiles, or even just control files, as well as the complete database. Incremental backups are an option after a full baseline backup. This tool also allows for parts of the backup to be restored, such as tablespaces, datafiles, or blocks of data. The backups do not need to be broken down into these pieces in order to just recover one file, but all of the backup set pieces that are needed to apply the archive log information must be available.

Oracle's Data Pump is another tool you can use if you need to pull a table back for comparison, or if the database isn't updated frequently, as a way to restore what is needed. The exports allow for imports into other environments for refreshing test or development databases, and jobs can be scheduled to use such a strategy.

The recycle bin offers a way to "undrop" tables, and with an FRA set up, you can also flashback a query, table, and even the database. You can't prevent all user errors, but you can be prepared to recover from them.

Backups are part of providing a secure and stable database environment. All of these options could be part of your backup and recovery strategies.

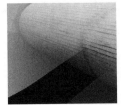

CHAPTER
7

Database
Maintenance

f there were no database users, data growth, or business modifications, the database could be installed and left alone. But as we all know, there are constant changes: application upgrades, new business requirements, different access needed by users, and just more data. So, installation isn't enough, and there is a constant need for monitoring databases and running maintenance jobs to maintain stable systems.

In the previous chapter, we looked at one big part of database maintenance: running backups and making sure you are able to recover from failures and errors. In this chapter, we will look at maintenance that can prevent some issues or serve as a warning to help you avoid problems about to happen.

Maintenance Tasks

As a SQL Server DBA, you've planned database monitoring and set up maintenance jobs. With various versions of SQL Server, some tasks may be more important than others; something that was a must for SQL Server 2000 might still need to be run in SQL Server 2008, but not as frequently because it's not as crucial. Oracle versions make a difference as well, especially if your database has older features, such as dictionary-managed tablespaces.

In large database environments, it is not possible to spend all of your time logging in to every database and validating logs and jobs. Automated tasks need to be developed to perform these tasks, and you will want to generate a report or summary to let you know that all systems are looking good. (I do tend to do a manual check occasionally—not that I don't trust the automated jobs, but a verification every now and then is reassuring.)

Generally, it's easier to develop maintenance jobs for a new database that you create, because you understand that database's setup. It may be more difficult to make sure that the maintenance jobs are running against existing systems, because jobs might be named differently or scheduled another way. However, you can use the database tools to verify that these tasks are running and if new ones need to be included.

In SQL Server, the Maintenance Plan Wizard helps you set up general maintenance tasks. These include checking for database integrity, cleaning up history, rebuilding and reorganizing indexes, shrinking the database, and updating statistics. In Oracle, you can schedule maintenance tasks in the Oracle Scheduler, and some system jobs are set up when the database is created.

Maintenance Area	SQL Server	Oracle
Database integrity	DBCC	DBVERIFY and ANALYZE VALIDATE structure
History cleanup	Manage backups and logs	Manage backups and logs
Indexes	Rebuild and reorganize	Rebuild indexes and reorganize tables
Statistics	Update statistics objects	Gather object and system statistics

TABLE 7-1. *General Maintenance Tasks in SQL Server and Oracle*

Table 7-1 lists some general database maintenance tasks. The specific tasks for SQL Server and Oracle may be different because of the nature of the different platforms and how they handle transactions and data blocks within the datafiles. And, of course, there are other maintenance tasks, depending on your environment.

In this chapter, we will review the general maintenance tasks and take a look at how to schedule these tasks and jobs in order to automate them.

Consistency Checks

Consistency checks validate database blocks and look for corruption in the datafiles. Here, we are not talking about the consistency of the data itself. Consistency checks look at the physical integrity of the data blocks and rows of objects. They can also validate the structures of objects, and that the tables and indexes still have the corresponding values.

In SQL Server, DBCC procedures perform database consistency checks. In Oracle, the DBVERIFY utility checks for data block corruption, as discussed in the previous chapter. Oracle also has an ANALYZE command that will perform structure checks.

The SQL Server command DBCC CHECKDB checks the logical and physical integrity of all objects in the database. The DBCC CHECKTABLE command checks only at the table level. The Oracle command for analyzing the tables is ANALYZE TABLE *table_name* VALIDATE STRUCTURE CASCADE. This will detect corruption between tables and indexes. In previous versions, the command was very expensive for large indexes, but its performance has been improved in Oracle Database 11g. The ANALYZE command does not put any locks on the tables, so that it can be run without any impact to users.

Oracle checks for block corruption as the database writers are handling the blocks of data. The DB_BLOCK_CHECKSUM parameter determines if blocks will be checked in memory. The TYPICAL setting for this parameter (the default) verifies checksums before writing to disk. With more data movement possibly happening in memory, detecting the corruption here before even writing to disk can be useful. To have Oracle check the blocks in memory (the buffer cache), set DB_BLOCK_CHECKSUM to FULL. This setting will perform checksums on all changes before and after writing to the log. This does add overhead to the system, but FULL is the only setting that will check for block corruption in the buffer cache. This parameter is dynamic, so it can be altered to check on its effects in your environment.

So, what about some of the other DBCC commands? The job of DBCC CHECKALLOC, which checks on space, is handled by the Segment Advisor in Oracle. This is another automatic job that runs against the database and can be configured to run against a table or tablespace. It will show details if an object or tablespace needs to be resized or reorganized. You can also run queries against the data dictionary tables for this information.

In a SQL Server environment, with the newer hardware and how transactions might be handled, DBCC procedures may need to be run less frequently. In Oracle, with the backups also able to validate and check for block corruption, ANALYZE TABLE might be scheduled to run as a monthly job, and against only the objects that have a lot of changes, instead of all of the objects. It could also be run on an ad hoc basis to perform the check (when there is not much activity on the database, of course).

Health Checks

By *health checks*, I'm referring to checks that run periodically against the databases. DBCC procedures/ANALYZE VALIDATE might be part of these checks. First, you will want to run health checks immediately after creating the database—if the database does not start off in a good state with all of the pieces that it is expecting, how is it going to be maintained? It's also a good idea to run health checks when taking over support for an existing system.

Health checks include validating the proper permissions for the administrator accounts, scheduling backups, scheduling maintenance jobs, checking the version of the database and patches, and checking options and parameters. This list might sound like tasks you perform after creating the database, but even permissions and parameters change over time, and checking that jobs are running as needed is important. Table 7-2 lists some common health checks in SQL Server and Oracle.

SQL Server	Oracle
Check password policies and `sa` and `sysadm` permissions.	Check password policies and `DBA` and `SYSDBA` permissions.
Check disk space for software, data, and logs.	Check disk space for software and datafiles.
Check version and patchsets.	Check version and patchsets.
Check backups are scheduled and running	Check backups are scheduled and running.
Check maintenance tasks (update statistics, shrink files, rebuild indexes).	Check maintenance tasks (update statistics, snapshots for performance, checks for any reorganization of tables or indexes).
Check for disk space/free space.	Check for monitoring of tablespaces and free space.
Check growth of transaction logs.	Check usage of undo and temporary tablespaces.
Check autostart for SQL Server and SQL Server Agent.	In Windows, check autostart of Oracle service and listener service. For Unix, check if scripts are in place to start up and shut down gracefully.
Check options and possible changes, FULL to SIMPLE, memory less than server memory.	Check parameters, and save copies of parameter files to track changes.
Check if using default ports or named instances.	Check listener permissions and ports.

TABLE 7-2. *Health Checks in SQL Server and Oracle*

Update Statistics

SQL queries tend to perform differently with more or less data, or when information about the object changes. An object that was originally 2MB may now be 2GB; more of the columns of a table might be populated after the initial load, which didn't have complete information. The information about the database objects and data is used by the database servers to figure out indexes and execution plans for queries.

In both SQL Server and Oracle, statistics are updated by default. In SQL Server, the AUTO_UPDATE_STATISTICS database option, when turned on, will update the statistics when they become stale. You can also run updates manually, using sp_updatestats or UPDATE STATISTICS.

In Oracle, the parameter STATISTICS_LEVEL set to TYPICAL or ALL enables automatic statistics gathering. In Oracle Database 10g, the GATHER_STATS_JOB job is scheduled to gather stale statistics and keep them updated. To make sure the job is enabled, you can query the dba_scheduler_jobs view. In Oracle Database 11g, the Optimizer Statistics Gathering task, rather than GATHER_STATS_JOB, is scheduled through Automated Maintenance Tasks, as shown in Figure 7-1.

If the STATISTICS_LEVEL parameter is set to BASIC or the automated jobs are disabled, you can use the DBMS_STATS package to gather the statistics. Even if automatic statistics gathering is configured to run, you can use DBMS_STATS to manually gather statistics for objects. There are options for this package to lock statistics on the table, export or import statistics, delete statistics, or run statistics gathering with different default settings.

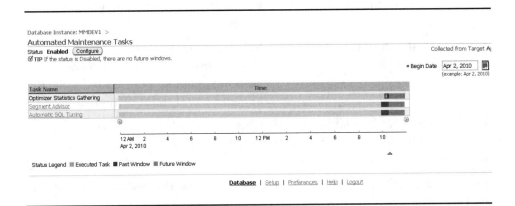

FIGURE 7-1. *Automated Maintenance Tasks in OEM*

The DBMS_STATS package can gather object-level statistics and system statistics.

System Statistics

The gathered statistics information is used by the cost-based optimizer to create query plans. Capturing statistics at different times for various activities is especially useful when the workload on the database is different, such as batch processing or reporting at night and processing transactions during the day.

```
sqlplus> exec dbms_stats.gather_system_stats('Start');
-- gather for an hour during peak activity
sqlplus> exec dbms_stats_gather_system_stats('Stop');
```

You can also capture system statistics on the fixed data dictionary tables, which should be done during regular workload and run once.

```
sqlplus> exec dbms_stats.gather_schema_stats('SYS', gather_fixed => TRUE);
sqlplus> exec dbms_stats.gather_fixed_objects_stats('ALL');
```

Gathering system statistics is an occasional type of maintenance. You might do this when performance issues arise, or when changes, such as upgrades or the amount of workload, happen on the database server. This will give the optimizer information for developing query plans.

Another reason for gathering the system statistics is that they can be exported from a production environment to import into a test environment, to be able to look at the queries and performance. This is also useful if the number of rows, size of the data and workloads are not the same from a production to test an environment.

```
## Create the statistics table
SQLPLUS> exec dbms_stats.create_stat_table
    ('MMPROD','STAT_TABLE_PROD');
## Export the statistics to the stats table
SQLPLUS> exec dbms_stats.export_schema_stats
    ('MMPROD','STAT_TABLE_PROD');
## export the table using datapump or exp utility
> exp file=Exp_prod_stats.dmp tables=stat_table_prod
## import the table into the test environment using imp
## utility or datapump
> imp file=Exp_prod_stats.dmp fromuser=MMPROD touser=MMDEV
## Import the statistics to the test environment
SQLPLUS> exec dbms_stats.import_schema_stats
    ('MMDEV','STATS_TABLE_PROD');
```

Now we have production statistics in the test environment even if the row counts are different between the two environments,

Object Statistics

For Oracle, statistics can be gathered at the schema level, table level, or index level. Having current statistics on the database objects is important for the optimizer to be able to choose an appropriate execution plan. As noted, Oracle Database 11g updates stale information as part of its automatic maintenance. However, you might need to gather, lock, or delete some of the statistics for an object. You may also need to get the information at another sample size. Like SQL Server, Oracle has procedures for handling statistics, as shown in Table 7-3.

With the automated jobs in place, first look at the values that are already being collected, and then consider gathering additional information or deleting statistics as necessary to deal with performance issues. Deleting statistics might also be useful if you're changing the type of information or sample size, to clear out what is currently there before gathering the new statistics. If you've adjusted the statistics gathering, you may want to lock the statistics on a table so that they don't change with each regular update.

sp_updatestats (SQL Server)	DBMS_STATS.GATHER_* (Oracle)
Name of table, index, or indexed view	Schema, table, or index

Sample size, either percent or rows
`Sample % or rows`
`FULLSCAN = 100%`
	Estimate percent is the sample size
	`estimate_percent => %`
	COMPUTE = 100%

`ALL` (default), `COLUMNS`, or `INDEX`	METHOD_OPT to include columns and indexed columns
`NORECOMPUTE` to disable statistics running after the update	LOCK_TABLE_STATS to lock the statistics on the table
	CASCADE set to TRUE to gather the indexes for the table

TABLE 7-3.   *Update Statistics Procedures in SQL Server and Oracle*

The following example shows how to use some of the commands for gathering statistics, locking statistics, and deleting statistics.

```
--Gather statistics for a table with a sample size of 75% and
--cascade through to indexes, run in parallel degree 8.
Sqlplus> exec dbms_stats.gather_table_stats('MYSCHEMA',
'MYTABLE', estimate_percent => 75, cascade => TRUE,
method_opt => 'for all columns size auto', degree => 8);
--Method_opt will determine which columns need histograms and
--will create them.

--Delete statistics for a column
sqlplus> exec dbms_stats.delete_table_stats('MYSCHEMA',
'MYTABLE');
--to include deleting the indexes with tables
sqlplus> exec dbms_stats.delete_table_stats('MYSCHEMA',
'MYTABLE',cascade_indexes => TRUE);

--Gathering schema statistics using gather auto to analyze
--the tables without statistics and objects that have
--stale statistics or changed more than 10%

sqlplus> exec dbms_stats.gather_schema_stats('MYSCHEMA',
options => 'GATHER AUTO', estimate_percent =>
dbms_stats.auto_sample_size)
```

You can gather statistics only for tables that do not have any statistics (GATHER EMPTY) or stale statistics (GATHER STALE). This example uses the GATHER AUTO option, which is a combination of the EMPTY and STALE options. There is also a filter to exclude tables when gathering schema-level statistics.

Jobs with additional statistics-gathering settings or to remove statistics can be set up to run along with the scheduled maintenance jobs created by Oracle. Figure 7-2 shows an example.

There are additional GATHER_TABLE_STATS options for running in parallel and for partitioned tables. GATHER_SCHEMA_STATS has the same options, but it doesn't require an object name and will perform the update on all of the objects in the schema.

Understanding the DBMS_STATS package will also help with previous versions of Oracle, as well as using the production statistics for test

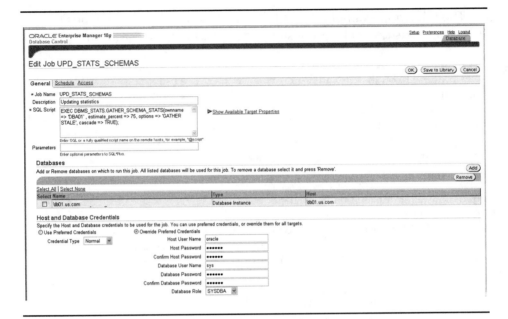

FIGURE 7-2. *Scheduling a DBMS_STATS script*

environments to mimic the sizing of tables. DBMS_STATS.EXPORT_TABLE_ STATS and DBMS_STATS.EXPORT_SCHEMA_STATS will pull the statistics from an environment, and IMPORT_TABLE_STATS and IMPORT_SCHEMA_ STATS will put them into an environment.

Several data dictionary tables show information about statistics collection:

- dba_tables includes a column that has last-analyzed information, which is the date that the statistics ran against the object.

- dba_tab_statistics has the information that was gathered, such as the number of rows, average space, chained row count, and sample size.

- dba_tab_stats_history shows when the statistics were last updated.

The following example shows a query against the `dba_tab_stats_` `history` table to retrieve the retention period of the statistics, which is how far back a restore of the statistics can go.

```
sqlplus> select dbms_stats.get_stats_history_retention
from dual;
GET_STATS_HISTORY_RETENTION
-----------------------------------------------------
                        31
sqlplus> select table_name, stats_update_time
from dba_tab_stats_history where owner='MYSCHEMA';
TABLE_NAME        STATS_UPDATE_TIME
---------------   -------------------------------------
TABLE1            02-APR-10 10.25.05.268000 PM -05:00
EMP               02-APR-10 10.25.05.377000 PM -05:00
EMP_COMPARE       02-APR-10 10.25.13.971000 PM -05:00
EMP               03-APR-10 01.57.36.941000 PM -05:00
sqlplus> exec dbms_stats.restore_table_stats('MYSCHEMA',
'EMP',' 02-APR-10 10.25.05.377000 PM -05:00');
```

Understanding which statistics are being gathered and their retention policy will help you to maintain the options to restore and manage the statistics for the schema and tables.

Object Maintenance

Along with gathering statistics information about the objects, some maintenance and checks need to be done on the objects themselves. There might be fragmentation, so that the object needs to be rebuilt. Invalid objects might need to be recompiled. Even grants and permissions can be considered part of object maintenance.

SQL Server has some of these tasks as part of the maintenance jobs. Oracle has advisors in place to advise if actions should be taken. Additionally, you can implement scripts to take care of object maintenance.

Index Rebuild

In examining the database objects, you may see some that appear fragmented and in need of a rebuild. Such rebuilds increase log activity, put additional resources on the system, and may put locks on the object. Therefore, you should be selective and plan which indexes to include in the tasks. You can generate reports to plan maintenance on indexes for another time, if necessary.

In SQL Server, clustered indexes are common, and these help to reorganize fragmented tables. Rebuilding clustered indexes in SQL Server will place some locks and possibly some blocking on the index. Rebuilding the clustered index also reorganizes a table. The performance of online rebuilds has improved with newer versions of SQL Server.

Oracle can use clustered indexes, but it seems to be more common to use nonclustered indexes. Oracle has an Automatic Segment Space Management (ASSM) feature, which has improved with each version and helps to reduce fragmentation during regular processing. As with SQL Server, online rebuilds in newer versions of Oracle are more efficient.

With SQL Server, you can use DBCC commands to evaluate if an index should be rebuilt. DBCC SHOWCONTIG shows fragmentation for tables, and a table with a clustered index probably has the same fragmentations. Also, the system table dm_db_index_physical_stats can return average fragmentation for all of the indexes in the database. With Oracle, the ANALYZE TABLE table_name VALIDATE STRUCTURE command makes sure the index is in sync with the table. When CASCADE is used with this command, information will be inserted into an index_stats table, which you can use to evaluate if indexes need to be rebuilt.

```
Sqlplus> analyze table emp validate structure cascade;
Table analyzed.
sqlplus> select height, blocks, lf_rows, del_lf_rows,
btree_space, used_space
from index_stats where name='IDX_EMP1';
HEIGHT      BLOCKS     LF_ROWS     del_lf_rows   BTREE_SPACE USED_SPACE
---------- ---------- ----------  ----------- ---------- ----------
1           8          14          3             8000        209
```

The index_stats table shows the height of the index. As a general rule, an index with a height great than 4 might be considered for a rebuild. Also look at the deleted leaf blocks (del_fl_rows) value. This amount should be under 20 percent of the total leaf rows.

As noted earlier, Oracle supplies advisors to help assess maintenance requirements. The Segment Advisor, part of the default maintenance jobs, reports on reclaimable space. This could be the result of fragmentation in the index or tables, or indicative of a bunch of deletions that have cleared out old data.

Figure 7-3 shows some of the Segment Advisor recommendations about chained rows, and it lists a couple of indexes that appear to have a BLOB datatype. Due to the nature of this datatype (it can vary on the space it consumes), chaining might be very typical here. In deciding on a course of

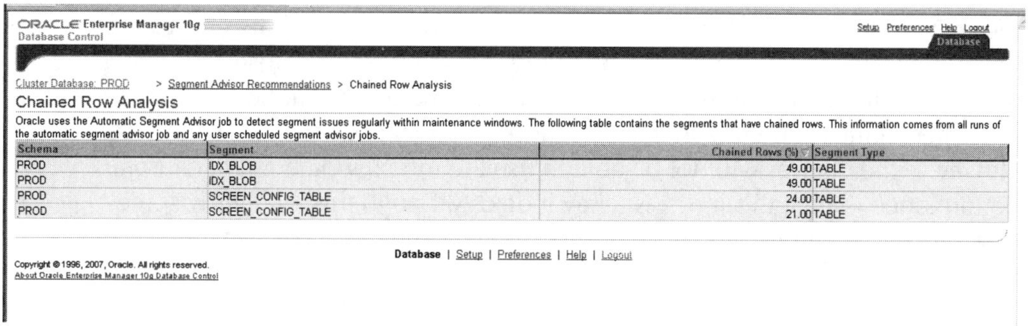

FIGURE 7-3. *Segment Advisor, chained row analysis*

action, you'll need to consider that rebuilds for these datatypes are more costly, and you might not be able to do them online.

You'll need to weigh the performance and benefits gained by a rebuild versus the actual cost of the maintenance in making your decision. If it appears to be regular behavior of the index and table with many deletions and insertions, and most of the space is able to be reused, that index might not be at the top of the list to rebuild. It is also not as common to rebuild b-tree indexes. Because of their structure, b-tree indexes tend to be self-managing. Even with a lot of deletions, the space is generally reused by new data being inserted, except if the primary key is on a sequence or date field. Other types of indexes, such as clustered or bitmap, or those that have a LOB datatype, might be considered for rebuilding. A coalesce of an index or an online rebuild might be worth it.

Another possibility is for an index to be in an unusable state. This could happen if a table was moved (rebuilding the indexes should always be done after a move) or when direct loads are made into a table. Using SQL*Loader, which is like using SQL Server's bcp utility, for a direct load and bypassing checking constraints could make a primary key index unusable. This can also occur with partitioned tables, where the index is a global index across all partitions, and one of the partitions was dropped to purge data, or partitions were merged, which would be like reorganizing the partitions.

An unusable index will need to be repaired or rebuilt.

```
sqlplus> select owner, index_name, table_name from dba_indexes
where status="UNUSABLE';
--simple fix for indexes listed
sqlplus> alter index index123 rebuild online;
```

When an index becomes unusable, any queries against the table, unless the parameter `SKIP_UNUSABLE_INDEX` are set to `TRUE`. In that case, Oracle will not report an error on the indexes, and will allow selects, inserts, updates, and deletes to occur against the table. (This parameter does not disable the error messaging for unique indexes because of possible constraint violations.) However, the queries will not be able to use the index, which might cause a performance issue if this index is a key index. Although this will allow some operations to continue, it's better to rebuild the index and not have it in an unusable state.

Table Reorganization

Like indexes, tables can become fragmented, due to chained rows, changes by updates, and deletions that leave space available that is not being reused. In some cases, these tables can benefit from reorganization. For example, a table might need to be reorganized after doing some data cleanup, or if monitoring shows free space can be reclaimed.

In SQL Server, the `DBCC SHOWCONTIG` *table_name* command gives clues as to whether a table needs to be reorganized. Also, rebuilding a clustered index on the table will reorganize the table, which is a typical way to handle table reorganization in SQL Server.

Oracle's ASSM feature manages the space within a segment. Allowing Oracle to manage the space in segments for tables reduces the fragmentation of the table. The Segment Advisor again comes into play with tables, checking for chained rows and space that can be freed up. Figure 7-4 shows an example of the Segment Advisor recommendations in OEM.

As with indexes, you'll need to carefully consider the value of table reorganization against its costs, especially with very large tables. In Figure 7-4, the Segment Advisor is showing that 53.64MB can be reclaimed, which is 12.16 percent of the space. But regaining 50MB of space is probably not worth reorganizing the table. Now, if this were 12 percent of 100GB, a reorganization might be worthwhile.

If you decide to go ahead with a table reorganization, you can use OEM to configure and schedule it. Under the Schema tab in the Database Objects area, select Reorganize Objects, as shown in Figure 7-5. Here, the reorganization of tables, indexes, schemas, and tablespaces can be set up in a job.

The options that are available in the following steps include doing the rebuild online or offline, as shown in Figure 7-6. If the downtime is available,

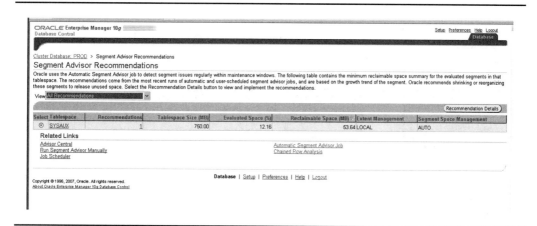

FIGURE 7-4. *Segment Advisor recommendations*

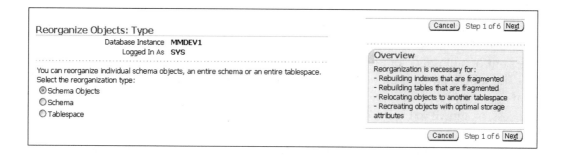

FIGURE 7-5. *Reorganize Objects: Type*

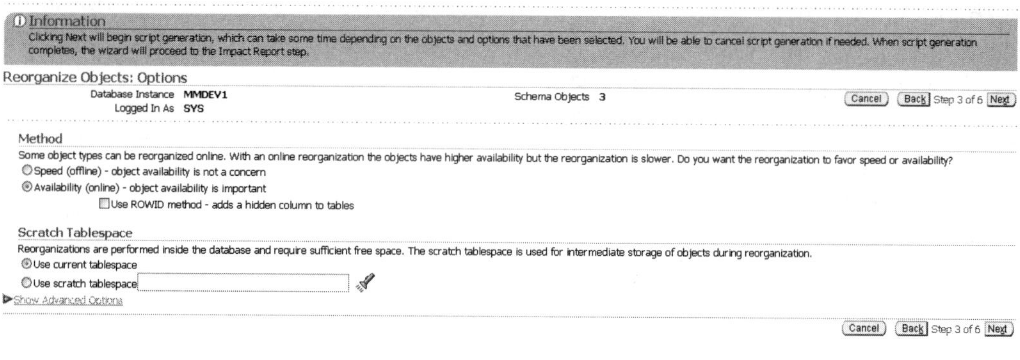

FIGURE 7-6. *Reorganize Objects: Options*

Reorganize Objects: Review

Database **PROD**	Schema Objects **4**
Logged In As **SYS**	Cancel Back Step 6 o

Job Name **REORGANIZE_PROD_22**
Job Schedule **Run Immediately**

Script

The script summary is a list of the database commands that will be used to reorganize the selected objects. The full script is a PL/SQL script that includes functions, procedures, and other commands needed during the reorganization. The full script will be created when you submit the job and will be executed by the job to perform the reorganization.

View ◯ Script Summary ◉ Full Script

```
set echo off
set feedback off
set serveroutput on
set pagesize 0

spool /u01/app/oracle/product/10.2.0/db_1/dbs/reorg22.log

-- Script Header Section
-- =============================================

-- functions and procedures

CREATE OR REPLACE PROCEDURE mgmt$reorg_sendMsg (msg IN VARCHAR2) IS
    msg1 VARCHAR2(1020);
    len INTEGER := length(msg);
    i INTEGER := 1;
```

FIGURE 7-7. *Reorganize Objects: Review*

the table reorganization will run faster if the object does not need to be available. Figure 7-6 also shows the option to perform the reorganization in the current tablespace or another tablespace.

The job can then be scheduled to run immediately or at another time. The final step has a summary of the commands that will be executed for this process, as shown in Figure 7-7. You can review the script to better understand the process.

Many tables can be reorganized by using the MOVE command to move the table from one tablespace to another tablespace, or within the same tablespace. There is also a DBMS_REDEFINITION package that will rebuild tables for those with datatypes (LOB, RAW, and LONG RAW) that cannot be handled by MOVE.

With some of the options to reorganize the table, space needs to be available to temporarily house the rebuilt table.

```
## Reorganize the table in the same tablespace
sqlplus> alter table emp_info move;
-- can specify a tablespace to move to another
-- tablespace or keep it in the same one
```

```
-- dbms_redefinition package example
sqlplus> create table myschema.mytable_redef as
select * from myschema.mytable where 1=2;
sqlplus>exec dbms_redefinition.start_redef_table
('MYSCHEMA','MYTABLE','MYTABLE_REDEF');
sqlplus> exec dbms_redefinition.sync_interim_table
('MYSCHEMA','MYTABLE','MYTABLE_REDEF');
sqlplus> exec dbms_redefinition.finish_redef_table
('MYSCHEMA','MYTABLE','MYTABLE_REDEF');
```

Indexes will need to be re-created after the table reorganization, and the old table will need to be dropped.

Invalid Objects

Objects such as procedures, functions, and views can become invalid if a dependent object is altered. Normally, the object will recompile the next time the procedure is executed or the view is accessed, as long as there are no errors in the code. However, making sure that the objects are valid should be included in a maintenance plan. Alerts will pop up in OEM about invalid objects in a schema, as shown in Figure 7-8.

With these alerts and a simple query against the dba_objects table, it is easy to find the objects that are invalid.

```
sqlplus> select owner, object_name, object_type from dba_objects where
status='INVALID';
OWNER               OBJECT_TYPE               OBJECT_NAME
------------------  ------------------------  ----------------------------
PROD_1              FUNCTION                  GET_ID_LIST
PROD_2              PACKAGE                   UPDATE_VAL1
PROD_1              VIEW                      ID_VW
```

Severity	Target Name	Target Type	Category	Name	Message	Alert Triggered
⚠	:db.us.drwholdings.com_db1	Database Instance	User Audit	Audited User	User SYS logged on from sup-chirefdb01.us.drwholdings.com.	Apr 3, 2010 10:56:28 PM
⚠	db.us.drwholdings.com	Cluster Database	Invalid Objects by Schema	Owner's Invalid Object Count	4 object(s) are invalid in the ACT_RO schema.	Apr 1, 2010 6:46:57 AM
⚠	:db.us.drwholdings.com	Cluster Database	Invalid Objects by Schema	Owner's Invalid Object Count	77 object(s) are invalid in the LEFT schema.	Apr 1, 2010 6:46:57 AM

FIGURE 7-8. *Invalid object alerts in OEM*

You can recompile invalid objects in a few ways:

- **Recompile all database objects that are invalid**   The utlrp.sql script, in the ORACLE_HOME/rdbms/admin directory, will recompile all of the objects in the whole database. You might consider running this script after applying a patch or doing overall database maintenance. You probably would not use this method to recompile one or two procedures that might be invalid, and you would not run it during a regular window of availability in the environment.

- **Recompile individual objects**   To recompile individual objects, you can alter the object or use DBMS_DDL.ALTER_COMPILE. For day-to-day maintenance, running a script to recompile individual objects will be less disruptive to the database than recompiling all of them. After the recompile, run a check to verify that the object was compiled successfully.

- **Recompile objects at the schema level**   You can compile objects at the schema level by using the DBMS_UTILITY package. If object changes were applied to one schema, you can run a script to recompile the objects just for that schema.

Here are examples of these options:

```
Recompile all database objects that are invalid
sqlplus> $ORACLE_HOME/rdbms/admin/utlrp;
Recompile objects at the schema level
sqlplus> exec DBMS_UTILITY.compile_schema(schema => 'MYSCHEMA');
Recompile individual objects
sqlplus> alter function prod_1.get_id_list compile;
sqlplus> exec DBMS_DDL.alter_compile('PACKAGE','PROD_2','UPDATE_VAL1');
```

Using a query to find the invalid objects, you can create a script to recompile the object.

```
Sqlplus> select 'alter '|| object_type|| ' ' || owner || '.' ||
object_name || ' compile;' from dba_objects where status='INVALID';
```

Grants

SQL Server has roles available to grant read-only or write permissions against a database for the users of that database. If these roles are used, individual grants on objects do not need to be maintained. However, you can also grant individual permissions against an object. Whether using roles or users for these permissions, knowing that these grants are present, or at least making sure the access for the application is still available, is best practice after doing maintenance.

Oracle does not have fixed roles for read-only or write permissions on a schema; the roles need to be created with permissions granted. This does not allow for granting permissions across the whole database, which provides for separation of the schemas and isolation of permissions.

The dba_tab_privs and dba_col_privs views show the current grants that have been added to either a role or a user. One way to maintain grants is to have a copy of the grants that have been granted in a table and compare that information against the current dba_tab_privs view. (The name dba_tab_privs might be a little confusing, because it does contain permissions on other objects besides tables, such as views, procedures, packages, and functions.)

You can also maintain grants by auditing, which will let you know which grants have been changed. This approach not only ensures that access is maintained during an object change, but it also provides audit logs of the roles and users who have permissions and any changes. This could provide a needed compliance report.

To set up auditing on the grants, turn on audits for granting the permissions, and set the parameter AUDIT_SYS_OPERATIONS = TRUE. This parameter audits the actions of anyone connecting with SYSDBA or SYSOPER permissions. With auditing enabled, the view dba_audit_statement is available to see the grants issued or permissions revoked. This provides good information about new grants, but not necessarily about objects that were dropped and re-created without the grants. You also need a table to capture which grants should be there, and not just what changed. The auditing will require purging the audit tables, and the copy of the table will need rows removed as grants are verified.

Here are a few quick examples of what can be done to maintain grants:

```
sqlplus> audit system grant;
Audit succeeded.
sqlplus> audit grant any object privilege by access;
Audit succeeded.
```

```
sqlplus> audit grant any privilege by access;
Audit succeeded.
sqlplus> audit grant any role by access;
Audit succeeded.
-- Create table to manage the grants
sqlplus> grant insert, update, delete, select on emp to mmtest;
sqlplus> create table grants_expected as select * from dba_tab_privs ;
Table created.
sqlplus> revoke delete on emp from mmtest;
Revoke succeeded.
## check the table that has the saved grants and compare
## the grant is still listed in the table with the stored
## grants even though the privilege is no longer available
sqlplus> select grantee, owner, table_name, privilege
from grants_expected where (grantee,privilege,table_name, owner)
not in (select grantee,privilege, table_name, owner
        from dba_tab_privs);
```

GRANTEE	OWNER	TABLE_NAME	PRIVILEGE
MMTEST	MMALCHER	EMP	DELETE

Synonyms

Users other than the schema owner may need access to a particular table or view, which requires them to fully qualify the object with *schema_name* .*object_name*. Alternatively, a synonym can be created for that object.

A good practice is to create the synonym as the user accessing the object, instead of as PUBLIC, which makes that name available to all users. The specific permissions for the table still need to be granted to the users. Once a public synonym is created, the same name cannot be used, even if it is pointing to an object in a different schema.

In SQL Server, a default schema can be assigned so that the user is, in a sense, accessing those schema objects by default; otherwise, the user needs to fully qualify the object with *dbo.table_name*.

In Oracle, when tables are altered, the synonyms created on the object are not changed and remain in place. However, if an object is dropped, the synonym will become invalid, and when the object is re-created, the synonym might need to be recompiled. The object will appear with INVALID as the status in the dba_objects table.

The data dictionary view dba_synonyms shows synonyms. The synonym name needs to be unique to the schema. If there are tables with the same name in different schemas, they can receive different synonym names, but at this point, it might be easier to fully qualify the table.

As you've seen so far, object maintenance in Oracle has several pieces. After database changes are rolled out, it's important to verify there are no invalid objects, and that grants and synonyms are still available. If you rebuild indexes or reorganize tables, you will need to validate that the indexes are still usable. Using alerts in OEM might be one way of verifying these objects. You can also create jobs to run against the database, and use the Oracle Scheduler to periodically run the scripts.

Job Scheduling

With SQL Server, the msdb database holds the information about jobs and schedules, and the SQL Server Agent service must be running for the jobs to be executed. It logs the information about the jobs and maintains a history of successful runs and failed jobs with errors. The jobs also can be extracted from SQL Server and created on another server.

In Oracle, the Oracle Scheduler handles job scheduling. PL/SQL and Java procedures can be scheduled, as well as scripts outside the database, such as shell scripts and executables. The Oracle Scheduler has an interface in OEM. Using the DBMS_SCHEDULER package, you can schedule jobs and get job information from the command line. The jobs are logged, and since Oracle Database 10g R2, they can have multiple steps. The Oracle Scheduler allows for using export and import to move the jobs from one database to another. It also can take advantage of the high-availability options since it is in the Oracle database. If the server failed, jobs can be recovered, as with other database processes.

Table 7-4 shows a summary of job scheduling in SQL Server and Oracle.

Creating a Job in Oracle Scheduler

The Oracle Scheduler is available from the Server tab in OEM (Oracle Database 11g). Selecting Jobs will show the current jobs scheduled against the database, and jobs can be viewed, edited, executed, and created from here.

Figure 7-9 shows an example of creating a job to rebuild an index. A job is defined with a name and description. You can choose not to log the running of the job, and to drop the job after completion. (Even if you are creating a job to run just once, it might be a better idea to disable it, in case you find that you need it again.)

SQL Server	Oracle
msdb	DBMS_SCHEDULER (DBMS_JOB)
SQL Server Agent	Job slave processes (parameter MAX_JOB_SLAVE_PROCESSES)
History and logs	History and logs in dba_scheduler_* views
Multistep jobs	Multistep jobs
Jobs inside and outside the database	Jobs inside and outside the database
Used for maintenance tasks	Used for maintenance tasks
Manage in SQL Server Management Studio	Manage in OEM or with DBMS_SCHEDULER
Permissions: SQLAgentUserRole in msdb	Permissions: "Create job" and "Select any dictionary"

TABLE 7-4. *Scheduling in SQL Server and Oracle*

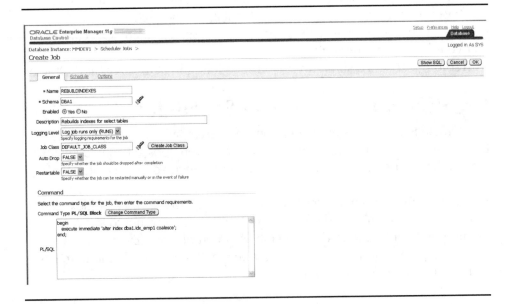

FIGURE 7-9. *Creating a job in OEM*

For the command type, you have the following options:

- Program name

- PL/SQL (enter the code in the text box)

- Stored procedure

- Executable

- Chain (to create steps and chain the jobs together)

Set up the schedule for the job on the Schedule tab. The Options tab lets you raise events (to handle success, failure, and other job statuses), set limits on runtime and failures, set priorities, and specify other options.

Creating a chain will set up different steps for the job. The programs should be created first. In OEM, make sure to enable the jobs that you want to run. After creating the steps, you can set up rules for what to do between the steps. The steps also do not need to go in order, and if one job fails, it can skip to another step. You can create rules for different status values. For example, you may set up rules that say if the job is successful, continue; if the job fails, run the last step, which might be to send an e-mail or update a table with information.

NOTE
By default, all of the programs and chains in a job are not enabled. If a job fails, first check that all its pieces are enabled.

Figure 7-10 shows an example of creating a chain for a job to reorganize a table, rebuild the indexes, and then recompile the stored procedures for that schema. The programs used for the job have the ALTER TABLE emp MOVE and ALTER INDEX emp_idx1 REBUILD ONLINE commands. The chain needs to start with a true value; otherwise, the chain will sit in the stalled state. That is why the first rule's condition is 1=1, and its action is to start the first step. The last step should be completed with an END.

To view the SQL for the job, click the Show SQL button in the upper-right corner of the job-creation page. The SQL statement shows how the job is created using DBMS_SCHEDULER and different steps along the way.

```
BEGIN
sys.dbms_scheduler.set_attribute( name => '"MMALCHER"."TAB_REORG"',
attribute => 'job_action', value => '"MMALCHER"."REORGEMP"');
END;
```

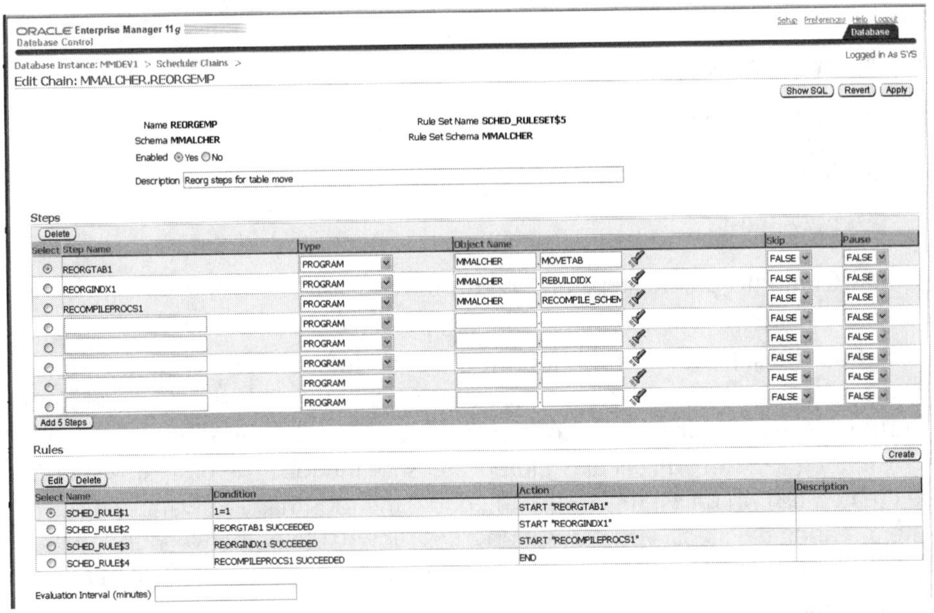

FIGURE 7-10. *Creating a chain for a job*

In the SQL statement that is created for the job, the value for `job_action` is actually the name of the chain. The chain is defined by the programs and the rules. For this example, programs were used, but another chain can be called, or an event can be used to trigger the next step.

The history of the job for the chained job will have the start of the chain and result from each step before completing. You can purge the history, either by removing all of the logs or setting the history to be kept for a specific number of days.

Using DBMS_SCHEDULER

You can also create jobs with the DBMS_SCHEDULER package. It takes parameters for job name, description, and action. You can set up a one-time job or a repeat interval, which can be by time, days, weeks, and so on. The start date could be the current time for immediate execution or a future date. Here is an example:

```
BEGIN
sys.dbms_scheduler.create_job(
job_name => '"DBA1"."REBUILDINDEXES"',
```

```
job_type => 'PLSQL_BLOCK',
job_action => 'begin
   execute immediate ''alter index dba1.idx_emp1 coalesce'';
end;',
repeat_interval => 'FREQ=WEEKLY;BYDAY=SAT;BYHOUR=1;BYMINUTE=0;
BYSECOND=0', start_date => systimestamp at time zone 'US/Central',
job_class => '"DEFAULT_JOB_CLASS"',
comments => 'Rebuilds indexes for select tables',
auto_drop => FALSE,
enabled => TRUE);
END;
```

For external jobs, such as running a script in Linux or an executable in Windows, you can set up attributes and credentials to be used by the job definition. In this example, the job action is the simple operating system command ls, to list the files in the directory:

```
sqlplus> Exec dbms_scheduler.create_credential (
credential_name => 'MM_WINDOWS',
username => 'mm1',
password => 'passwd',
windows_domain => 'domain1');
-- Linux credential is really the same but doesn't
-- require the domain.
-- attributes can be set with job arguments
begin
dbms_scheduler.create_job(
job_name => 'test_OS_job',
job_type => 'EXECUTABLE',
number_of_arguments => 1,
job_action => '/bin/ls',
auto_drop => FALSE,
enabled => FALSE);
dbms_scheduler.set_job_argument_value('test_OS_job',1,
    '/home/oracle');
dbms_scheduler.set_attribute('test_OS_job','credential_name',
    'MM_LINUX');
dbms_scheduler.enable('test_OS_job');
end;
/
```

Several procedures are part of the DBMS_SCHEDULER package. The chain can be built with CREATE_CHAIN, DEFINE_CHAIN_RULE, and DEFINE_CHAIN_STEP.

Using DBMS_JOB

Prior to Oracle Database 10g, DBMS_JOB was the package to schedule jobs. This package is still available to submit, change, run, and disable jobs.

Individual jobs that were created with the DBMS_JOB package can be converted to DBMS_SCHEDULER jobs. The basic definition of the job can be translated, and defining schedules and job classes can be done later.

For DBMS_JOB, the parameter WHAT becomes JOB_ACTION, NEXT_DATE becomes START_DATE, and INTERVAL becomes REPEAT_INTERVAL. The job can be created in DBMS_SCHEDULER and then removed from DBMS_JOB. Jobs can be running from both packages, but the parameters JOB_QUEUE_PROCESSES and MAX_JOB_SLAVE_PROCESSES will have to be set. If JOB_QUEUE_PROCESSES is set to 0, DBMS_JOB is disabled.

You can see the chain steps in the dba_scheduler_chain_steps view. The attributes and arguments are placed in a dba_scheduler_* view to define the job. As shown in the example, to set these attributes, the job name is used to link the arguments and attributes to the job in the scheduler. Selecting from dba_scheduler_running_jobs will show the current jobs that are running, and dba_scheduler_job_log will show the status of the job.

You can also use the DBMS_SCHEDULER package to change the status of a job, complete a job, start a job, and change the attributes of the job.

Setting Up System and User Jobs

When you create the database, you have the option to set up system maintenance jobs. These jobs include gathering statistics, running the Segment Advisor and other advisors, and performing some cleanup.

Maintenance windows are predefined and can be used by the system jobs or user jobs. You can also create maintenance windows to run maintenance jobs in other windows. The following three automated maintenance tasks are configured to run in all maintenance windows. The system jobs can be enabled and disabled using `DBMS_AUTO_TASK_ADMIN`.

```
sqlplus> exec dbms_auto_task_admin.disable(client_name=>'sql tuning
advisor',operation=> NULL,window_name=>NULL);
PL/SQL procedure successfully completed.
sqlplus> select client_name,status from dba_autotask_client;
CLIENT_NAME                                              STATUS
-------------------------------------------------------- --------
auto optimizer stats collection                          ENABLED
auto space advisor                                       ENABLED
sql tuning advisor                                       DISABLED
```

The system privilege "Manage Scheduler" allows users to manage the attributes, such as the job classes and maintenance windows; this should be treated like a DBA type role. Users can create jobs and schedule jobs without this privilege, but they do need the "Create job" system privilege and "Select any dictionary" privilege.

When the system jobs complete, they are tracked in the history view. Statistics are collected about the job, which are included in columns of the `dba_autotask_client` view.

Job information, logs, and history can be viewed from the user perspective in the `user_scheduler_*` views. These allow the users to get details about the jobs and create jobs as needed. But it is still left to an administrator to set up the configurations and settings that the Oracle Scheduler uses.

File Maintenance

Datafiles, log files, error logs, history logs, trace files—oh my! File maintenance is very important to the health of the database and maintaining a stable environment. Developing tasks and scripts will be useful for managing the many different files. We discussed backups and managing the backup files in Chapter 6. Here, we will look ways to maintain the datafiles, alert logs, and trace files.

Shrinking and Resizing Files

In SQL Server, you might shrink files as part of getting a production database to fit into a development environment. Especially if you are not running in FULL mode, large transaction files can be shrunk down to size. Also, if production backups have an issue, or a large transaction filled up more space than normally needed, you could shrink the log. In Oracle, the logs are sized and remain that same size, so shrinking the file is not the issue. However, depending on how many times the transactions are looping through the redo logs, there might be a reason to adjust the size of the logs.

Datafiles are slightly different, because they are normally growing. But you might need to clean up data or start an archive process that frees up the space. In SQL Server, you have the same options as with the transaction logs to shrink datafiles. There is some movement of the segments to bring down the high water mark so that the file can be shrunk down as much as possible. In Oracle, you can also shrink datafiles.

Logs

If there is not enough time to archive the logs, this issue will show up in the alert log as "checkpoint not complete." To address this issue, you might add more redo log groups at the same size or re-create the redo logs at a different size. If you resize the redo logs, you can create new groups with the bigger size. Then, as the older redo logs become inactive, they can be dropped. All of the redo log groups should have the same size set for the redo logs.

If the redo logs are too big, there might be issues with not having the logs switch for a long period of time. The `v$log_history` view will provide some insight into how frequently the log is changing. Here is an example of a query using the Oracle Database 11*g* pivot tables to get the breakdown of the number of log switches by hour for the previous five days:

```
sqlplus> select hour_of_day,
sum(decode(day123, to_char(sysdate-5,'MM/DD/YYYY'),
log_switches,0)) as  "5_days_ago",
sum(decode(day123, to_char(sysdate-4,'MM/DD/YYYY'),
log_switches,0)) as "4_days_ago",
sum(decode(day123, to_char(sysdate-3,'MM/DD/YYYY'),
log_switches,0)) as "3_days_ago",
sum(decode(day123, to_char(sysdate-2,'MM/DD/YYYY'),
log_switches,0)) as "2_days_ago",
sum(decode(day123, to_char(sysdate-1,'MM/DD/YYYY'),
log_switches,0)) as "1_day_ago",
sum(decode(day123, to_char(sysdate,'MM/DD/YYYY'),
log_switches,0)) as "Today"
from  (SELECT to_char(first_time,'MM/DD/YYYY') as
day123,to_char(first_time,'HH24') as hour_of_day,count(1)
as log_switches from gv$log_historyGROUP BY to_char(first_time,'MM/DD/YYYY'),
to_char(first_time,'HH24'))
group by hour_of_day
order by 1;
```

HO	5_days_ago	4_days_ago	3_days_ago	2_days_ago	1_day_ago	Today
00	6	71	6	4	4	6
01	4	81	4	4	6	6
02	4	81	4	4	4	4
03	8	63	8	8	8	8
04	4	76	4	4	4	4
05	4	62	4	4	4	0
06	4	76	4	4	4	0
07	4	83	6	4	4	0
08	4	48	4	4	6	0
09	4	4	4	4	4	0
10	39	4	4	4	4	0
11	77	4	4	4	4	0
12	77	4	4	8	4	0
13	79	8	4	4	4	0
14	10	4	4	4	4	0
15	51	4	4	4	4	0
16	80	4	4	4	4	0
17	83	4	4	4	4	0
18	70	4	4	4	4	0
19	66	4	6	4	6	0
20	81	8	6	8	10	0
21	75	6	6	4	4	0
22	80	6	4	10	12	0
23	78	4	6	6	4	0

24 rows selected.

These results show that five days ago at 10 A.M., there was a significant increase in log activity. This was due to a change made to the application that caused more transactions against the database. With an understanding of what changed, the decision was made to resize the redo logs to handle the additional load. Resizing was chosen in this example because 12 log groups are already set up, and the redo logs are not yet that big.

In summary, using an appropriate number of log groups and size for the redo logs will help you to keep up with the activity of the server, avoiding the "checkpoint not complete" alert in the alert log.

Datafiles

Oracle datafiles will have a high water mark, and the files can be resized to only this point to reclaim the space. If you attempt to shrink a file below the high water mark, the procedure will fail. Here is an example of a query to get this information:

```
###assumes that block size is 8k

sqlplus>select
  a.tablespace_name,
  a.file_name,
  a.bytes file_size_in_bytes,
```

```
   (c.block_id+(c.blocks-1)) * 8192 HWM_BYTES,
   a.bytes - ((c.block_id+(c.blocks-1)) * 8192) SAVING
from dba_data_files a,
   (select file_id,max(block_id) maximum
    from dba_extents
    group by file_id) b,
dba_extents c
where a.file_id = b.file_id
and c.file_id = b.file_id
and c.block_id = b.maximum
order by 6;
```

TABLESPACE	FILE_NAME	FILE_SIZE_IN_BYTES	HWM_BYTES	SAVING
USERS	/u01/oradata/MMDEV1/USERS01.DBF	10485760	9961472	524288
UNDOTBS1	/u01/oradata/MMDEV1/UNDOTBS01.DBF	41943040	37814272	4128768
SYSTEM	/u01/oradata/MMDEV1/SYSTEM01.DBF	754974720	746651648	8323072
SYSAUX	/u01/oradata/MMDEV1/SYSAUX01.DBF	92715520	659619840	33095680

To resize a datafile (to be either smaller or larger than its current size), use the `ALTER DATABASE DATAFILE` command, as follows:

```
sqlplus> alter database datafile '/u01/oradata/MMDEV1/users01.dbf' resize 100M;
```

CAUTION
When resizing a datafile, be careful not to make it too small. Otherwise, you might just run out of space much sooner than you expected.

You can adjust the datafile in OEM. From the Server tab, under the Storage category, choose Tablespaces. Select a tablespace, and from there you will be able to edit datafiles, as shown in Figure 7-11. The datafiles are part of a tablespace, so resizing the datafiles will affect how much space is available in the tablespace for the database objects.

Tablespace Monitoring

In SQL Server, the datafiles might be created with a fixed size or set to autogrow. With an autogrow setting, you need to monitor how much disk is available on the drive. With a fixed size setting, it's important to monitor database growth to check whether it is approaching the maximum size.

Oracle tablespaces are created with one or more datafiles. As the database grows, the tablespaces and datafiles need to be maintained to allow for the growth. Planning the size of the system tablespaces is recommended.

FIGURE 7-11. *Resizing a datafile in OEM*

Not having enough space in `SYSTEM` and `SYSAUX` could hang up the database. Allowing too much growth in the temporary and undo tablespaces could result in poorly performing queries and transactions, and fill up the file systems, causing issues with the database.

Oracle datafiles are set to a fixed size or to autoextend. You can monitor space at the tablespace level in OEM. From the Server tab, under the Storage category, choose Tablespaces to see a list of tablespaces, as shown in Figure 7-12.

Selecting the tablespace name drills down into the datafiles that make up the tablespace (see Figure 7-11). Along with setting the file size, as discussed in the previous section, you can set alerts and thresholds to monitor the tablespace usage. The free space available threshold can be a specific amount or a percentage. The actual size of free space is useful for very large tablespaces. For example, 20 percent free of a 10GB datafile and 20 percent free of a 2TB datafile may have very different levels of urgency. The percent of allocated space amount does not take into account autoextend for the datafiles.

The autoextend setting for datafiles allows the files to grow as needed. Using autoextend is useful when you do not know how much data is being loaded. However, as the database becomes more stable or consistent, setting a size limit is usually better. With unlimited growth on datafiles, the space on the file systems must be monitored, because filling up the file

Database Instance: MMDEV1 >
Tablespaces

Object Type Tablespace

Search
Enter an object name to filter the data that is displayed in your results set.
Object Name [   ]
(Go)
By default, the search returns all uppercase matches beginning with the string you entered. To run an exact or case-sensitive match, double quote the search string. You can use the wildcard symbol (%) in a double quoted string.

Selection Mode Single

(Edit) (View) (Delete) Actions Add Datafile ____ (Go)

Select	Name	Allocated Size(MB)	Space Used(MB)	Allocated Space Used(%)		Allocated Free Space(MB)	Status	Datafiles	Type	Extent Management	Segment
⦿	SYSAUX	660.6	620.4		93.9	40.2	✓	1	PERMANENT	LOCAL	AUTO
○	SYSTEM	720.0	711.4		98.8	8.6	✓	1	PERMANENT	LOCAL	MANUAL
○	TEMP	20.0	0.0		0.0	20.0	✓	1	TEMPORARY	LOCAL	MANUAL
○	UNDOTBS1	40.0	12.1		30.3	27.9	✓	1	UNDO	LOCAL	MANUAL
○	USERS	10.0	9.4		94.4	0.6	✓	1	PERMANENT	LOCAL	AUTO

Total Allocated Size (MB) 1,450.6   ✓ Online   ✗ Offline   ⊘ Read Only
Total Used (MB) 1,353.3
Total Allocated Free Space (MB) 97.3

Database | Setup | Preferences | Help | Logout

FIGURE 7-12.   *Tablespace listing in OEM*

system tends to cause some issues with the entire database, not with just the tablespace that has run out of space.

Also, a couple of tablespaces could possibly cause some issues if just left to autoextend. The undo and temporary tablespaces should be sized as needed. Joins, views, and sorts could take up a lot of the temporary tablespace. Just as you would look at actions that were using up more space in the `tempdb` database on SQL Server, you should investigate the statements running against the database before adding more space to the temporary tablespace.

When monitoring the tablespaces, it might appear that the temporary tablespace is completely used, but the space does get reused, just as with `tempdb`. The undo tablespace also could appear full, but the new transactions reuse the space if the old transactions are completed. Resizing the temporary and undo tablespaces might just open up the database for other issues, without solving the problem of transactions that are using up the space. One indicator of problems is when the temporary or undo tablespace is using two or three times the space used by all of the other tablespaces. When transactions are needing that much space, examining the queries is a good first step. We will take a closer look at this in the next chapter.

Maintaining the SYSAUX and SYSTEM tablespaces is somewhat easier than managing the user tablespaces. Placing user objects in either of these tablespaces is not recommended, and a quick check for user objects that are not owned by the system users could be run as a scheduled script or maintenance task. The SYSAUX tablespace has some automatic cleanup when the retention periods are set for the performance snapshots and other logs. The SYSTEM tablespace grows as new objects and more datafiles are added in the database. The initial size of the SYSTEM tablespace is normally about 500MB to 1GB. With applications that have a significant number of objects, it is not unusual for the SYSTEM tablespace to grow to 3GB or 4GB. Filling up the SYSTEM tablespace would not be good, so you should monitor its growth. You might consider letting SYSTEM grow to a size such as 8GB, which would give you enough time to resize it if needed.

The following is a sample query that will look at the total space in a tablespace and how many bytes are still free. It does not consider autoextend, and it looks only at the permanent tablespaces (excluding the temporary and undo tablespaces).

```
sqlplus>select sysdate,a.tablespace_name, sum(a.bytes), b.bytes
   from dba_data_files a, (select tablespace_name, sum(bytes) bytes
                        from dba_free_space
                        group  by tablespace_name ) b,
                     (select tablespace_name
             from dba_tablespaces
                     where contents='PERMANENT') c
   where a.tablespace_name = b.tablespace_name
   and c.tablespace_name=a.tablespace_name
   group by sysdate, a.tablespace_name,b.bytes;
```

SYSDATE	TABLESPACE_NAME	TOTAL SUM(A.BYTES)	FREE BYTES
---------	-------------------------------	------------	----------
07-APR-10	SYSTEM	754974720	9043968
07-APR-10	SYSAUX	692715520	40042496
07-APR-10	USERS	10485760	589824

Planning and monitoring the growth of your tablespaces could allow for larger allocations to tablespaces, reducing the need to resize tablespaces.

Error Logs, Alert Logs, and Trace Files

SQL Server error logs cycle through with restart of the server. There is also a retention policy to keep logs.

Oracle alert logs contain information about the status of the database and error messages. The alert log errors are on the first page of OEM. When the instance is restarted, the alert log is not cycled to the next log; writing continues to the current log.

You might consider saving the current log (using operating system commands) to allow Oracle to write to a new log. You could then run a purge script against the file system to delete any trace files and logs that are older than a certain date.

The directories as set by the parameters `background_dump_dest`, `user_dump_dest`, and `background_core_dump` contain trace files and log files. In Oracle 11g there is also the diagnostic_dest which can be single directory for the trace and log files. If there is enough space allocated to the server to have unlimited files here, not much maintenance needs to be done. Otherwise, these directories should be purged by days.

Using operating system commands, you can find the files in the dump destinations, and the `mtime` sets how many days the files should be retained.

```
find "/u01/oracle/product/11.2.0/db_1/admin/orcl/udump"
-name "*.trc" -type f -mtime +15 -exec rm -f {} \;
find "/u01/oracle/product/11.2.0/db_1/admin/orcl/bdump"
-name "*.trc" -type f -mtime +15 -exec rm -f {} \;
find "/u01/oracle/product/11.2.0/db_1/admin/orcl/cdump"
-name "*.trc" -type f -mtime +15 -exec rm -f {} \;
```

You should clean up the older alert logs as well. The command to do so might include the date or `*.log`, depending how the alert log is named when rotating logs.

Summary

Having a stable and consistent database environment is a primary goal for any DBA. Having good maintenance plans in place to monitor and fix pieces of the database before they become issues will help you to achieve this goal. Developing health checks that start after first creating the database and continue as the database changes allows you to assess the environment and keep things running smoothly.

Along with backups, your maintenance plans should include validating data block consistency and object structures for fragmentation and updated statistics. Even though the Oracle database has become more automated in handling statistics and fragmentation, applications and transactions running against the database might require additional statistics gathering or other handling.

Maintenance checks can be scheduled in the Oracle Scheduler. You can create and manage jobs to run health checks and perform maintenance as necessary.

And what would database maintenance be without monitoring space and managing all of the files associated with the database? In Oracle, this means watching database growth and managing the tablespaces. Running jobs to purge older log and trace files and monitoring the information in the alert logs are parts of maintaining the files for the database.

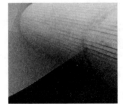

CHAPTER
8

Performance
and Tuning

 e would all like the fastest possible access to the data in the database. Planning the system should account for how the system is going to be used and the areas of growth. This helps determine the initial database instance setup for best performance. However, just as we talked about in the previous chapter on maintenance and monitoring, things change. Monitoring for performance issues and doing the regular maintenance against the database will keep the database tuned and running faster.

In this chapter, we will look at the ways to do some proactive performance tuning, as well as how to troubleshoot performance issues that arise. You'll see that there are some differences in the areas to check and tools available in SQL Server and Oracle environments.

Better-Performing Systems

Planning the initial database design, monitoring, and maintenance are the proactive steps to achieving better-performing systems. This applies to any database environment. As a DBA, you know that database performance is a priority, and you make sure the system is running well. The differences between SQL Server and Oracle systems tend to lie in the areas of the database that might be more prone to problems and the configurations available to tune the database for better performance.

Along with the proactive monitoring and tuning for performance, DBAs need to deal with performance issues that arise. We are all familiar with that call or e-mail message complaining that the database is slow. These types of fire drills are always fun, and whatever the cause, troubleshooting the problem starts with the same question: What do you mean by slow?

- Is it currently slow, or was it running slowly earlier and is now back to "normal"?

- What is running slowly—the application, a query, or something else?

- How fast does it normally run?

- Slow compared to what—yesterday, last night, last month?

- Is this a new report or a new query that is running slowly?

- Did something change?

- Does this normally run at a different time?

- Is this the case for one user or all users?

- Have the data volumes changed?

- Are you performing a normal activity that you do every day at this time?

This list can go on and on, and it's similar for any database platform. However, where you start looking first for the issue may vary.

In SQL Server, you can use the Session Monitor and Profiler to see what might be running now. The first items to check are blocking sessions, then currently running SQL statements, and then maybe that the objects have the correct indexes and statistics.

Oracle has a view into the sessions and a way to see the current statements that are running against the database. Looking at the queries running and validating that statistics are current on the tables might be first steps. With the cost-based optimizer, current statistics are important for the queries to choose the right plan. In OEM alerts, waits are shown with the alert, and OEM provides a list of top queries running and also shows if any process is being blocked. In Oracle, blocking normally is checked after figuring out what is running and validating statistics. This is in the opposite sequence that you would follow with SQL Server.

For performance tuning, there are differences in what is available in the SQL Server and Oracle environments. Let's start with the type of indexes and how they affect database performance.

Indexes

Indexes exist to help speed up queries. Having the proper columns indexed can reduce the logical I/Os for queries. However, creating an index to make one query run faster may not be a good solution. Begin by examining the SQL statements that are currently being run against the database. If the query can be adjusted, that would be a logical first step. This is the same for both SQL Server and Oracle platforms.

There are costs associated with data changes when the indexes are involved. The maintenance requirements should be considered. The performance gains of adding the index should be more than the cost of maintaining the index. Also, too many indexes can add to performance issues instead of resolving them. Indexes should be used selectively and their usage monitored.

Index Monitoring

By enabling index monitoring, you can see which indexes are being used in Oracle. The owner of the index can alter the index to enable monitoring, and leave monitoring on for a set period. The `v$object_usage` table will show whether or not the index is used.

```
SQLPLUS> alter index IDX1_EMP_DEPT monitoring usage;
Index altered.
SQLPLUS> select empno from emp where deptno=10;
...rows returned...
SQLPLUS> select index_name,used, monitoring
from v$object_usage;
INDEX_NAME                        USED          MONITORING
----------------------------- ------------- --------------
IDX1_EMP_DEPT                     YES           YES
```

The `v$object_usage` table has two other columns that show the time the monitoring was started and stopped. To end the monitoring of the index, use this statement:

```
alter index index_name nomonitoring usage
```

Index monitoring will not track how many times the index is used, but it does offer a way to find out if there are unused indexes on a table, assuming you leave monitoring on long enough. Watch out for indexes added only for month-end or year-end processing, which can appear unused if you don't turn on monitoring during that time period.

Index Types

Indexes are definitely a useful tool for improving access to the data in the database. Several types of indexes are available on both database platforms. Table 8-1 shows the types of indexes available in SQL Server and Oracle.

Understanding which type of index is being used and how to improve that index will help in performance tuning. Knowing how the various index types affect data changes and improve SELECT statements will help you to decide if the benefits of the index outweigh the costs for putting it in place.

SQL Server Index Types	Oracle Index Types
Unique clustered	B-tree
Nonunique clustered	Function-based
Unique Nonclustered	Reverse key
Nonunique nonclustered	Index-organized tables (IOT)
Indexed views	Bitmap
Full text	Bitmap join
Spatial	Compressed
Filtered	Descending
XML	Partitioned
	Domain
	Invisible
	Intermedia (for LOBs and text)

TABLE 8-1.   *Index Types in SQL Server and Oracle*

Primary Key Indexes

Creating indexes on primary keys is a good place to start. In SQL Server, it is typical to create a clustered index for the primary key. The clustered index organizes the table for efficient access. Clustered indexes even help with the reorganization of tables when they are rebuilt. But just because this is an effective practice in SQL Server doesn't mean that it translates to Oracle databases.

In Oracle, the primary key index is created for a table when a constraint is added, and you can either use an existing index or create a new one. The concept of a clustered index for Oracle corresponds to that of the index-organized table (IOT). Organizing a table like this would make it fast when using the primary key for the joins or using just the primary key as the part of the WHERE clause. If the table is normally searched by other columns than how the table is organized, creating an IOT might not be the solution.

Here's how to check if a table is an IOT:

```
SQLPLUS> select owner, table_name, IOT_TYPE from dba_tables
where IOT_TYPE='IOT';
OWNER                              TABLE_NAME         IOT_TYPE
------------------------------     -----------------  ---------
ACB01                              MSTR_TBL           IOT
ACB02                              WORK_TBL           IOT
```

```
## If not IOT the column IOT_TYPE is blank
SQLPLUS> select owner, table_name, IOT_TYPE from dba_tables;
OWNER                           TABLE_NAME          IOT_TYPE
------------------------------  ------------------  ---------

. . .
ACB01                           MSTR_TBL            IOT
ACB01                           PRODUCTS
ACB01                           SALES
ACB01                           WORK_TBL            IOT
```

An `IOT_TYPE` of `NULL` means that the table is not an IOT.

In Oracle, it is typical to use b-tree indexes for the primary keys. The primary key indexes for Oracle are unique and help enforce data integrity, but they do not need to be clustered. So if using an IOT is faster for access to a table, why would you use a b-tree index instead?

As an example, consider a table in which the primary key is an ID for the object or symbol that makes the row unique, but you typically access the table by the date (perhaps the effective date or load date). You could place an additional index on the IOT table, but access might not be as fast as it would be if there were a b-tree index to access the table by date. And then both indexes must be maintained, which might slow down the updates and inserts.

Function-Based Indexes

Oracle's function-based index type can dramatically reduce query time. In SQL Server, if you need to use a string function or another function to compare the column in the `WHERE` clause, the index will not be used. However, in Oracle you can create function-based indexes with the exact function to use, so you can use an index instead of a full-table scan. Function-based indexes can be useful for large tables even with simple functions like `UPPER` to do string comparisons.

```
## Example of using a function-based index
SQLPLUS> select employee_name from tbl1
where to_char(hiredate,'MON')='MAY';
Plan
-------------------------------------------------
SELECT STATEMENT
  TABLE ACCESS FULL TBL1

SQLPLUS> create index IDX_TBL1_FUNC
on TBL1(to_char(hiredate,'MON'));
Index created.
```

```
SQLPLUS> select employee_name from tbl1
where to_char(hiredate,'MON')='MAY';
Plan
------------------------------------------------
SELECT STATEMENT
 TABLE ACCESS BY INDEX ROWID TBL1
  INDEX RANGE SCAN IDX_TBL1_FUNC
```

The function-based index can be a composite index with other columns included in the index. The function that is used needs to match what is being used in the WHERE clause. For example, if the WHERE clause has SUBSTR(col1,1,12), the function-based index cannot be SUBSTR(col1,1,15). User-defined functions can also be used, but if the function changes, the index might become unusable.

NOTE
Composite indexes will use multiple columns of the table, with the most selective going first. In general, limiting the number of columns used for the index will make the index more usable. In Oracle, the optimizer may even skip the first column in a composite index. The skip scan of the index is probably more efficient than a full-table scan. This allows you to avoid creating more indexes to support possible searches based on the secondary columns of the indexes.

If the index is not part of the query plan, statistics for the index (and the table) should be updated.

To use function-based indexes, you need to set the QUERY_REWRITE_ ENABLED=TRUE and QUERY_REWRITE_INTEGRITY=TRUSTED parameters. The user needs to have permissions to execute any of the user-based functions and also must be granted the "query rewrite" privilege to be able to create the index.

As an alternative to having the function-based index, in Oracle Database 11*g*, you can use a virtual column on the table. The virtual column can be a calculation or function, which is stored in the table definition. For example, you might use this type of column to keep the month that is derived from another date column or a symbol that is created from concatenating some of the fields or parts of the fields together. The advantage of the virtual column is that statistics can be gathered for this column. This virtual column can then be indexed.

Indexes for Views

Views use the indexes on their associated tables to build the information in the view, but there might be a need for an index for selecting from the view. SQL Server has indexed views—you create a view, and then create an index on the view. Oracle has materialized views, which are similar to views but are a snapshot of the data. They can be a join of one or more tables, and can be refreshed automatically or on demand. Indexes can be created on materialized views. For both the SQL Server indexed view and the Oracle materialized view, the query results are stored, so they require storage space, unlike a regular view.

The indexed view and materialized view both provide a useful tool to access expensive joins. SQL Server indexed views are limited in that they cannot reference another view or subqueries. Oracle materialized views can have functions and aggregations, along with subqueries and other views, including self-joins.

Materialized views are great for summarizing information and aggregating functions to allow this information to be queried faster. Oracle provides several ways to work with and manage materialized views. They are key to managing performance in large environments and data warehouses.

The materialized view log is associated with the master table for the view to be able to perform fast refreshes. As changes are made to the data in the master table, they are stored in the materialized view log, and then the log information is used for the refresh of the materialized view. There can be only one materialized view log on a table.

Here are a couple of examples of how to create materialized views and refresh them:

```
## Fast refresh requires a log
SQLPLUS> create materialized view log on scott.emp;
Materialized view log created.
SQLPLUS> create materialized view emp_sal
build immediate
refresh fast on commit
as select empno, sal*1.10
from scott.emp;
Materialized view created.
```

```
## Complete refresh does not need a log
SQLPLUS>create materialized view dept_sal
build immediate
refresh complete
as select deptno,sum(sal)
from scott.emp
group by deptno;
Materialized view created.

## Build deferred will build view later to refresh
SLQPLUS> exec dbms_mview.refresh('dept_sal','C');
```

Using a materialized view requires setting the same parameters as for function-based indexes: QUERY_REWRITE_ENABLED=TRUE and QUERY_REWRITE_INTEGRITY=TRUSTED.

Whether you should use a materialized view in your environment depends on the performance gains it can provide and the complexity of the view. A fast or complete refresh time also factors into this decision.

Bitmap Indexes

Bitmap indexes are stored differently than b-tree indexes. Instead of storing the row ID, a bitmap for each key is used. Because of this, these indexes are typically smaller in size and are useful for columns that have a low cardinality (such as a region or marital status column). Bitmap indexes are also good for read-only tables. They might be more expensive than other types of indexes for tables in which the data changes.

Bitmap join indexes store the join of two tables. This type of index is useful in a data warehousing environment and with a star data model schema, because it will index the smaller table information on the larger fact table. The row IDs are stored for the corresponding row ID of the joined table. This is really an extension of the materialized view, and allows for compression of the index, which is more efficient for storage.

```
SQLPLUS> create bitmap index idx_sales_prod
on sales(product.name)
from sales, product
where sales.prod_id=product.prod_id;
SQLPLUS> select sales.amount, product.name
from sales,product
where sales.prod_id=product.prod_id
and product.name='Thingy';
```

```
## Sample output from explain plan
|   0 | SELECT STATEMENT                |
|   1 |  NESTED LOOPS                   |
|   2 |   NESTED LOOPS                  |
|   3 |    TABLE ACCESS BY INDEX ROWID | SALES
|   4 |     BITMAP CONVERSION TO ROWIDS|
|*  5 |      BITMAP INDEX SINGLE VALUE | IDX_SALES_PROD

## Can also create composite bitmap join indexes
SQLPLUS> create bitmap index idx_sales_prod_2
on sales(product.name,states.name)
from sales, product, states
where sales.prod_id=product.prod_id
and sales.state_id=states.state_id;

## Pulls in the data from the state table for sales.
SQLPLUS> select sales.amount, stats.name, product.name
from sales, product, states
where sales.prod_id=product.prod_id
and sales.state_id=states.state_id;
Execution Plan
---------------------------------------------------------
| Id  | Operation                      | Name
|   0 | SELECT STATEMENT               |
|   1 |  NESTED LOOPS                  |
|   2 |   NESTED LOOPS                 |
|   3 |    NESTED LOOPS                |
|   4 |     TABLE ACCESS BY INDEX ROWID | SALES
|   5 |      BITMAP CONVERSION TO ROWIDS|
|   6 |       BITMAP INDEX FULL SCAN    |
Predicate Information (identified by operation id):
   8 - access("SALES"."STATE_ID"="STATES"."STATE_ID")
   9 - access("SALES"."PROD_ID"="PRODUCT"."PROD_ID")
```

The fact table has the index based on the ID being joined and could have another column in the index as well. In this example, the information is on the joins of the IDs for the other tables. The columns from the other tables are included in the index so that the query doesn't need to go back to the other tables to get the information; it can use the bitmap join index.

Reverse Key Indexes

Reverse key indexes are a nice little trick to spread out index blocks for a sequenced column. With a sequence, there can be thousands of records that all start with the same number. Reversing the numbers will allow for the index to have different beginning values and use different blocks in the index b-tree structure. This is especially useful for RAC environments. When you are doing inserts, the reverse index will minimize the concurrency on the index blocks.

```
## To create a reverse key index
SQLPLUS> create index on idx_prod_id on product(prod_id) reverse;
## To alter an index to remove the reverse key
SQLPLUS> alter index idx_prod_id rebuild noreverse;
## To alter an index to a reverse key
SQLPLUS> alter index idx_prod_id rebuild reverse;
```

Partitioned Indexes

Partitioning is a useful way to tune a large database environment. Oracle offers options for partitioning table, such as LIST, HASH, RANGE, and COMPOSITE. The partition key is how the table is partitioned. You can create partitioned indexes for these tables. The index can be a local partitioned index based on the partition key and set up for each partition. Local indexes are easier to manage because they are handled with each partition, as partitions might be added, dropped, or merged.

```
## Example: EMP table partitioned by deptno
## Create local partitioned index
SQLPLUS> create index idx_emp_local on emp (empno) local;
```

Global partitioned indexes are indexes that can have a different partition key than the table. Maintenance against the partitioned table could mark the global partitioned index unusable.

```
## Same emp table partitioning, create global partitioned index
SQLPLUS> create index idx_emp_global on emp(empno);
## Partition maintenance with global index
SQLPLUS> alter table drop partition P1 update global indexes;
```

Understanding how local and global indexes could become unusable and how they benefit by accessing the data on each partition is helpful when looking at the performance of large tables. (It never seems to be the small tables that cause the performance issues.)

Invisible Indexes

Invisible indexes are hidden from the optimizer, but not from being maintained, so as rows are changed, so is the index. I am sure you are thinking that seems backwards. The optimizer is looking for good indexes to use to create the best query plan, so why make an index invisible?

One reason to use an invisible index is to test the performance of the queries without the index. Suppose you have found that the index on a large table is not being used. Creation of indexes on large tables can take a lot of time, so you want to be sure you don't need the index before you drop it. You can alter the index to be invisible. Then if you find the index is needed, you can alter it to be visible again, rather than needing to re-create it.

```
SQLPLUS> alter index idx_prod_date invisible;
Index altered.
SQLPLUS> select index_name, visibility
from dba_indexes where index_name='IDX_PROD_DATE';
INDEX_NAME                                VISIBILITY
----------------------------------------  ----------------
IDX_PROD_DATE                             INVISIBLE
SQLPLUS> alter index idx_prod_date visible;
Index altered.
```

You can also use an invisible index to see if an index would be beneficial. Create an index and make it invisible. At the session level, alter the session:

```
alter session set OPTIMIZER_USE_INVISIBLE_INDEXES=TRUE
```

This will allow the session to see the index, and you can even gather statistics for the index in this session. At this point, the index should not affect any statements other than the ones in the current session. The query plan can be run against the query to validate that the index will be used and confirm if there are performance benefits from using the index. The index then can be made visible, as in the preceding example. If it does start to drag down the performance of the insert and update statements, the index can be made invisible again, and then dropped.

NOTE
Rebuilding an index will make the index visible.

So, it turns out that invisible indexes do make sense. They allow you to monitor index usage as well as test if an index would be useful.

Locking

Holding locks on a database object will also cause another concurrent session to wait. Waits to acquire a lock or perform a transaction could even cause blocking, depending on the locks required to perform a select or transaction.

Both SQL Server and Oracle have exclusive modes for modifying data and shared lock modes for sharing resources among multiple users. The locks are held for the duration of the transaction, and the first statement to acquire the lock will release it after the first transaction is committed or rolled back. The exclusive lock is obtained at the row level for all of the rows of the insert, update, or delete operation.

SQL Server offers different levels of isolation to help minimize some of the locking that happens with shared and exclusive locks. In Chapter 2, we discussed how Oracle doesn't need to provide dirty reads just to avoid a nonblocking read of the data. Oracle automatically uses the lowest level of lock to provide data concurrency and consistency.

Oracle also allows the users to lock data manually. A user can issue a SELECT FOR UPDATE statement. This is when the lock needs to be more restrictive, but then can be converted to row locking as the rows are updated. This can cause problems when long-running SELECT statements put locks on the table longer than necessary. A worst-case scenario would be a user issuing a SELECT FOR UPDATE statement and then going for lunch without issuing the UPDATE statement or a commit, causing several other sessions to be blocked (and sending a red flag to the DBA to kill that process).

A *deadlock* is when two or more users are waiting to access data locked by each other. When the deadlock occurs, Oracle chooses a victim and rolls back the transaction, and allows the other process to continue. Oracle does not escalate locks that could possibly cause more deadlocks. Code that overrides Oracle handling of the transactions and locking tends to cause some of its own issues with deadlocks and blocking.

Tables 8-2 and 8-3 summarize the lock types available in SQL Server and Oracle.

Reads through regular `SELECT` statements are least likely to interfere with other SQL statements. `INSERT`, `UPDATE`, and `DELETE` statements need an exclusive lock only on the row of data that is changing. The queries used as part of the transaction statement can have shared locks on the data being read.

Because of how Oracle handles locking, blocking is not always the first area that I check for performance, unless I know that the application is trying to explicitly handle the locking outside Oracle. Access outside of the application, such as using query tools for ad hoc queries, could open a transaction, and since the flow of the query is waiting on the user, the Oracle database will also wait on the user and hold onto the locks. So, if an `UPDATE`, `INSERT`, or `DELETE` statement is open in such a tool, there is no autocommit that will release the locks. If the user does not issue a commit or rollback, this would leave an uncommitted transaction open, which could block others.

Lock Type	Description
Shared	Reads but can't modify
Update	Combination of shared and exclusive locks
Exclusive	Writes; only one transaction can hold the lock at a time
Intent	Notifies another transaction that a lock will be needed; prevents other transactions from acquiring the lock
Schema	Locks to modify object structures
Bulk update	Bulk operations using `TABLOCK`

TABLE 8-2. *SQL Server Lock Types*

Lock Type	Description
Row	No limit. Readers do not wait for writers, and writers do not wait for readers. If attempting to update the same row at the same time, writers will wait for writers.
Table	DML statements—INSERT, UPDATE, DELETE, and SELECT FOR UPDATE. Table locks prevent DDL and structure changes while the transaction is occurring.
Row share table	Lock with intent to update data. This is the least restrictive lock and allows for other transactions to have the same row share lock.
Row exclusive table	Changes being made—INSERT, UPDATE, DELETE. This is slightly more restrictive than a row share lock. It allows other transactions on the same table.
Share table	Locks the table for updates. It allows reads of the table but no other writes.
Share row exclusive table	Only one transaction at a time can acquire a shared row lock on a table.
Exclusive table	Most restrictive lock. Only one transaction can have this lock on the table.
DDL	Dictionary lock for the structure of the objects, indexes, table, and view definitions.
Internal lock and latch	Lock on datafiles and internal structures.

TABLE 8-3. *Oracle Locking Types*

Current Activity Views

Oracle has various system views that provide current session and wait information. These are very helpful for performance tuning and troubleshooting.

Current Sessions

Obviously, when there are performance issues, it is necessary to take a look at the current sessions on the database. There is no sp_who, sp_who2, or sp_lock in Oracle, but there is the v$session view. This view shows which sessions are active. You can join this with another view to see which queries a session is running.

```
SQLPLUS> select username, schemaname,osuser, lockwait,status
from v$session
where status='ACTIVE' and username not in ('SYS','SYSTEM');
USERNAME          SCHEMANAME    OSUSER          LOCKWAIT STATUS
----------------- ------------- --------------- -------- -------
DBSNMP            DBSNMP        oracle          (null)   ACTIVE
MMALCHER          MMALCHER      mmalcher        (null)   ACTIVE
USER1             APP1          user1           (null)   ACTIVE
## Lockwait will be a non-null value when waiting on a resource
## such as a lock or a latch
## Another view to see this would be v$session_wait

## To see a SQL statement from one of the users currently active
SQLPLUS> select sa.sql_text
from v$sqlarea sa, v$sqltext st, v$session s
where sa.sql_id=st.sql_id
and s.sql_hash_value=st.hash_value and s.username='SCOTT';
SQL_TEXT
------------------------------------------------------------------
INSERT INTO log_messages (id,service,processed_date, log_date)
VALUES(:"SYS_B_0",:"SYS_B_1",TO_TIMESTAMP(:"SYS_B_2",:"SYS_B_3"),
:"SYS_B_4",TO_DATE(:"SYS_B_5",:"SYS_B_6"))
INSERT INTO log_messages (id,service,processed_date,log_date)
VALUES(:"SYS_B_0",:"SYS_B_1",TO_TIMESTAMP(:"SYS_B_2",:"SYS_B_3"),
:"SYS_B_4",TO_DATE(:"SYS_B_5",:"SYS_B_6"))

## To see what locks are current on an object
SQLPLUS> select session_id, owner, type, mode_held,
mode_requested
 from dba_ddl_locks;
SESSION_ID  OWNER       TYPE                MODE_HELD MODE_REQUESTED
----------- ----------- ------------------- --------- --------------
871         YELL1       Table/Procedure/Type Null      None
627         SNAP        Table/Procedure/Type Null      None

284         SNAP        Table/Procedure/Type Null      None

286         ADB         Table/Procedure/Type Null      None
357         ADB         18                   Null      None
```

Activity Monitors

In OEM, under the Performance tab, you'll find additional monitoring links for looking at the top activity, instance activity, blocking sessions, and currently running SQL, as shown in Figure 8-1. There are statistics that are gathered as part of the Automatic Workload Repository to provide reports for analyzing the health of the database and looking for performance issues. The historical views are based on snapshots that have been gathered. (The Automatic Workload Repository is discussed a little later in the chapter.) Viewing these areas of activity can help you to troubleshoot performance issues by pointing to an area that might be responding slowly or be experiencing an overload, such as too many physical I/Os or hard parsing of SQL statements.

Figure 8-2 shows the Top Activity section. This has information about the resources that are being used, top SQL statements, and top sessions in the database. This can be the current information or information from another point in time. Viewing historical information is useful when a user drops by in the afternoon to say that he was having issues in the morning, although everything is fine now. From here, you can drill down to the SQL statements and look into SQL tuning. Drilling down on the session ID or SQL hash value can get back to the SQL being run. (Remember the `SQL_hash_value` from the `v$session` table from the example under the Current Sessions section?)

The Instance Activity section shows values since the database has been up and running or back until the last snapshot that is available. By default, these snapshots are kept seven days. Figure 8-3 has a chart of instance activity about cursors, transactions, physical and logical I/O, and other activity. It is useful to see the workload on the database server and look at what is currently running, as well as the snapshots.

Additional Monitoring Links

Top Sessions and Top SQL data from ASH can be found on the Top Activity page.

- Top Activity
- Top Consumers
- Duplicate SQL
- Blocking Sessions
- Hang Analysis

- Instance Locks
- Instance Activity
- Search Sessions
- Search SQL
- Snapshots

- AWR Baselines
- SQL Tuning Sets
- SQL Performance Analyzer
- SQL Monitoring

| Home | Performance | Availability | Server | Schema | Data Movement | Software and Support |

FIGURE 8-1. *OEM monitoring links*

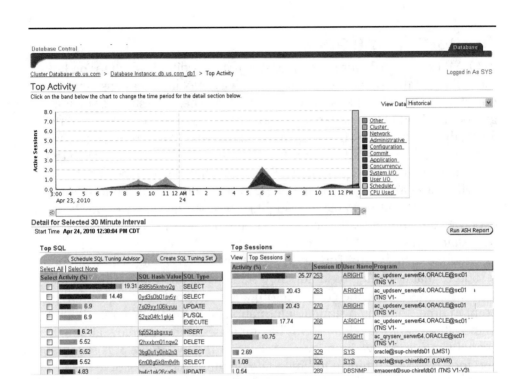

FIGURE 8-2. OEM Top Activity section

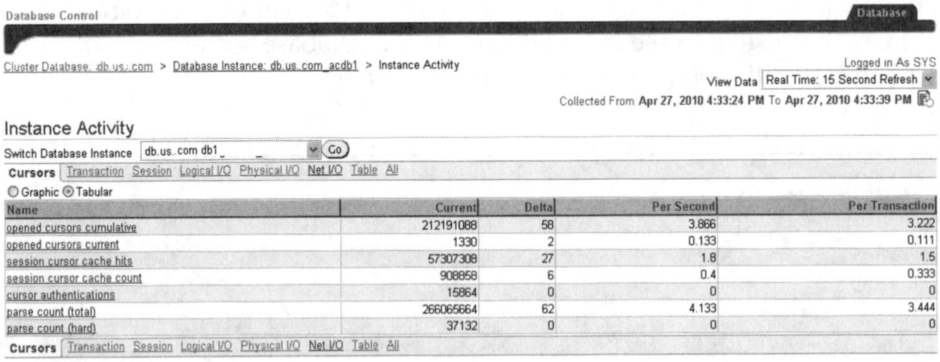

FIGURE 8-3. OEM Instance Activity section

Waits

Another area to check in Oracle for performance issues is wait events. This information will be available in the OEM views we just looked at, and also available to query in the v$ views such as v$session_wait. Here are a few examples of quick queries to check for current database wait events:

```
SQLPLUS> select sid, event, p1text, wait_time , p1, p2
from v$session_wait;
SID      EVENT                  P1TEXT      WAIT_TIME    P1           P2
-------  ---------------------  ----------  -----------  -----------  -----------
378      SQL*Net message from client    0             1952673792    1
385      SQL*Net message from client    0             1413697536    1
431      buffer busy waits  component    429           3             123
## p1 and p2 will provide additional information about
## the p1text so if it is an i/o wait, would have data file
## or could be about a latch type or object
SQLPLUS> select segment_name, segment_type
from dba_extents where file_id = 3
and 123 between (block_id and block_id + blocks -1);
SEGMENT_NAME                  SEGMENT_TYPE
----------------------------  ------------
IDX2_SALES_PROD               INDEX

SQLPLUS> select event, total_waits, time_waited
from v$system_event;
EVENT                         TOTAL_WAITS    TIME_WAITED
----------------------------  -----------    -----------
db file sequential read       3591611        2309586
SQL*Net message from client   3950929        1892
log file sync                 182955         1134406
```

Some waits give clues to performance issues; others are normal events that are to be expected. For example, a db file sequential read event is a block read by indexes. So the indexes are being used instead of full-table scans. On the other hand, db file scattered read waits could indicate the use of full-table scans. However, you should gather more information if you see that the waits are too high because of I/O issues.

The SQL*Net message from client event is the wait for the client to tell the database server to do something. It is just waiting for instructions, and really isn't contributing to issues—you can't blame the database for being slow because a session was waiting for an action while the user went to get coffee. There might be applications that open sessions and then just wait for responses before getting data from the database.

We'll look at some other ways to check waits in the "Automatic Workload Repository" section later in this chapter.

SQL Plans

As a DBA, you know that tuning SQL statements is a good place to start improving performance. If changes can be made to the code or available indexes, that is normally the quickest way to get results.

With SQL Server, you can get the execution plan from SQL Server Management Studio or by enabling `showplan_all`. This will provide information about the plan for which order to join the tables and the indexes to use.

Oracle plans are available through the OEM tools, and they can be traced through SQL*Plus as well. The plans can be saved in the plan table or just seen in the output from the trace.

Viewing Explain Plans

Let's first look at a quick way to use SQL*Plus to see the explain plan for a query.

```
## To see query results and the execution plan set autotrace

SQLPLUS> set autotrace on explain
SQLPLUS> select empno from emp where deptno=10;
EMPNO
----------
      7782
      7839
      7934
Execution Plan
----------------------------------------------------------
Plan hash value: 3956160932

-------------------------------------------------------------
| Id  | Operation          | Name | Rows |Cost (%CPU)| Time     |
-------------------------------------------------------------
|   0 | SELECT STATEMENT   |      |    5 |    3   (0)| 00:00:01 |
|*  1 |  TABLE ACCESS FULL | EMP  |    5 |    3   (0)| 00:00:01 |
-------------------------------------------------------------

Predicate Information (identified by operation id):
-------------------------------------------------------
   1 - filter("DEPTNO"=10)
## Traceonly will not execute the query but just
## show the plan
```

```
SQLPLUS> set autotrace traceonly explain
SQLPLUS> select empno from emp where deptno=10;
Execution Plan
-----------------------------------------------------------
Plan hash value: 3956160932

-----------------------------------------------------------
| Id  | Operation          | Name | Rows | Cost (%CPU)| Time
-----------------------------------------------------------
|   0 | SELECT STATEMENT   |      |   5  |    3   (0)| 00:00:01
|*  1 |  TABLE ACCESS FULL | EMP  |   5  |    3   (0)| 00:00:01
-----------------------------------------------------------
Predicate Information (identified by operation id):
-----------------------------------------------------------

   1 - filter("DEPTNO"=10)
## Only difference was that the rows were not returned
## Notice the plan hash is the same
## Add index to see new plan
SQLPLUS> create index idx_emp1 on emp(deptno);
Index created.
SQLPLUS> select empno from emp where deptno=10;
Execution Plan
-----------------------------------------------------------
Plan hash value: 306890541  ## NEW PLAN VALUE
-----------------------------------------------------------
| Id  | Operation          | Name | Rows | Cost (%CPU)| Time
-----------------------------------------------------------

|   0 | SELECT STATEMENT   |      |   5 |     2   (0)| 00:00:01
|   1 |  TABLE ACCESS BY
               INDEX ROWID| EMP  |   5 |     2   (0)| 00:00:01

|*  2 |   INDEX RANGE SCAN | IDX_EMP| 5 |     1   (0)| 00:00:01
-----------------------------------------------------------
Predicate Information (identified by operation id):
-----------------------------------------------------------
   2 - access("DEPTNO"=10)
```

The plan table, if it does not already exist, can be created from the SQL provided in ORACLE_HOME/rdbms/admin/utlxplan.sql.

```
## To put the execution plan into the plan table for viewing
SQLPLUS> explain plan set statement_id='my_example' for
select * from claim where claim_id=100;
Explained.
## To see the results
SQLPLUS> select * from table(dbms_xplan.display);
```

```
PLAN_TABLE_OUTPUT
-----------------------------------------------------------
Plan hash value: 3956160932
-----------------------------------------------------------
| Id  | Operation          | Name  | Rows |Cost (%CPU)| Time     |
-----------------------------------------------------------
|   0 | SELECT STATEMENT   |       |    5 |    3   (0)| 00:00:01 |
|*  1 |   TABLE ACCESS FULL|CLAIM  |    5 |    3   (0)| 00:00:01 |
-----------------------------------------------------------
```

You can also see the explain plan through the SQL Developer GUI. In Figure 8-4, the icons to get the explain plan are circled.

Tuning Using Explain Plans

In the explain plan, look for how the tables and indexes are accessed. Also see if the indexes being used are the ones expected and if there are other options that would be better.

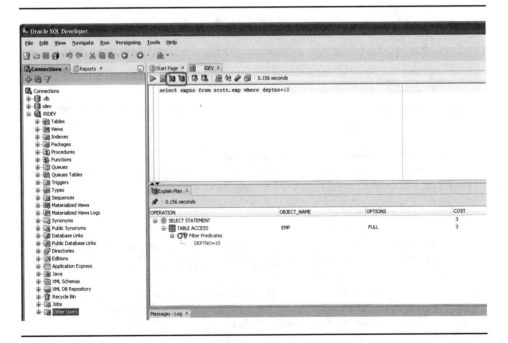

FIGURE 8-4.   *Viewing an explain plan in SQL Developer*

The explain plan will show the method used to access indexes:

■ A unique scan is normally seen with an unique index.

■ A range scan is used when multiple values could be returned for the nonunique index.

■ A full or fast full scan of the index may be performed when more data is being accessed or it is just more efficient to scan all the data instead of sorting for the range scan.

For tables, the quickest access method is by row ID. Seeing full-table scans might mean that you can use indexes to improve performance. How the tables are being joined also affects the query. The methods for joining tables include sort merge join, nested loops, and hash join.

The cost-based optimizer (CBO) pulls in the details about the system and objects to create execution plans. The CBO evaluates the details, and then it does transformation of the statements for complex queries. In performing these steps, it also calculates the cost to choose the access paths, join orders, and join methods. The cost of the query is included in the explain plan, which can help you with tuning and knowing which plan might be better.

The object statistics are needed for the CBO to be able to create the best execution plan. Incomplete or stale information could cause the optimizer to use a full-table scan or an inefficient method to access indexes. To make the CBO's job easier, you should ensure that the queries are coded the best they can be, the statistics are updated, and the required indexes are present.

NOTE
Earlier versions of Oracle used a rule-based optimizer (RBO). Then in the next couple of Oracle versions, you could choose between the RBO and CBO, and even let Oracle choose the best method. There were even times when deleting statistics from a table or using the RULE hint (no longer available with Oracle Database 11g) would improve performance. Now, with the automated statistics gathering and the use of the information that is available, as well as being able to do some transformations of the queries, the CBO has gotten smarter and can create efficient query plans.

You can use hints to suggest another path or direction for the CBO. Here are a couple examples:

```
## Hint to just append the rows to the end on an insert
SQLPLUS> insert /*+ APPEND */ into table1 select …
## Hint to use an index
SQLPLUS> select /*+ INDEX(a) */ col1, col2 from a where …
```

However, you should be careful about using hints. They might get you a performance boost for the current plan, but upgrades and other information might come along, and the CBO could have better information about a faster plan to use.

The CBO definitely needs valid statistics and information, and there are database parameters that can help to decide the best execution plans.

Statistics for Tables and Indexes

Because of the CBO, statistics is one of the first areas that I validate when looking at performance. Do the index and table have statistics? Are they current statistics? Do the row counts in the statistics match the current row count? The row counts could point to a load happening after or during the time statistics are being generated. The CBO uses the information available, and if the information is not current or valid, that will not lead to good execution plans.

```
SQLPLUS> select num_rows, last_analyzed
from dba_tab_statistics
where table_name='SALES';
  NUM_ROWS          LAST_ANALYZED
------------------ ----------------
    1490               15-MAR-10
SQLPLUS> select count(1) from sales;
  COUNT(1)
----------
    3919232
## Actual row count and number of rows in statistics different
## gathering statistics could be useful here.
```

You may consider making adjustments to the sample size and the frequency of the statistics collection. The statistics can also be adjusted to improve plans and methods of scans and access. Specific values can be set for an index such that it appears that there are more or less distinct values or a different number of rows.

```
SQLPLUS> exec dbms_stats.set_column_stats('SCHEMA1','TAB1',
'COL1', DISTCNT => 8, NO_INVALIDATE => FALSE);
PL/SQL procedure successfully completed.
## Once set the statistics can be locked
## Now lock statistics
SQLPLUS> exec dbms_stats.lock_table_stats('SCHEMA1','TAB1');
PL/SQL procedure successfully completed.
## Or if didn't help just unlock and gather the stats again
SQLPLUS> exec dbms_stats.unlock_table_stats('SCHEMA1','TAB1');
PL/SQL procedure successfully completed.
SQLPLUS> exec dbms_stats.gather_table_stats('SCHEMA1','TAB1',
CASCADE => TRUE);
PL/SQL procedure successfully completed.

## Or restore the statistics (schema, table and timestamp)
SQLPLUS> exec dbms_stats.restore_table_stats('SCHEMA1',
'TAB1','12-MAR-10 06.40.33.900462 PM -05:00');
PL/SQL procedure successfully completed.

## Number of rows might be useful if a table is loaded as a
## batch process and starts off with zero each time.
SQLPLUS> exec dbms_stats.set_table_stats('SCHEMA1','TAB2',
NUMROWS => 4000000, NO_INVALIDATE => FALSE);
```

Taking a look in the area of table and index statistics is well worth the time when it comes to tuning current statements. You do need to be careful to avoid overdoing adjustments or trying to outsmart the CBO. However, when other options are exhausted, a gentle nudge in one direction can help improve the execution of the queries.

Database Parameters

Not to say that these are the only parameters to look at when tuning queries, but Figure 8-5 has the list of database parameters that are classified in the optimizer area. For most parameters, the Help column includes a link to specific information about the parameter's default value and use.

ORACLE Enterprise Manager 11g
Database Control

Setup Preferences Help Logout
Database

Database Instance: MMDEV1 >

Logged in As SYS
(Show SQL) (Revert) (Apply)

Initialization Parameters

| Current | SPFile |

The parameter values listed here are currently used by the running instance(s). You can change static parameters in SPFile mode.

Name   Basic   Modified Dynamic Category
                    All ▼   All ▼   All ▼   Optimizer ▼   (Go)
Filter on a name or partial name

☐ Apply changes in current running instance(s) mode to SPFile. For static parameters, you must restart the database.

(Save to File)

Name	Help	Revisions	Value	Comments	Type	Basic	Modified	Dynamic	Category
star_transformation_enabled	Help		FALSE ▼		String	✓		✓	Optimizer
create_stored_outlines	Help				String			✓	Optimizer
optimizer_capture_sql_plan_baselines			FALSE ▼		Boolean			✓	Optimizer
optimizer_dynamic_sampling	Help		2		Integer			✓	Optimizer
optimizer_features_enable	Help		11.1.0.6 ▼		String			✓	Optimizer
optimizer_index_caching	Help		0		Integer			✓	Optimizer
optimizer_index_cost_adj	Help		100		Integer			✓	Optimizer
optimizer_mode	Help		ALL_ROWS ▼		String			✓	Optimizer
optimizer_secure_view_merging			TRUE ▼		Boolean			✓	Optimizer
optimizer_use_sql_plan_baselines			TRUE ▼		Boolean			✓	Optimizer
query_rewrite_enabled	Help		TRUE ▼		String			✓	Optimizer
query_rewrite_integrity	Help		enforced ▼		String			✓	Optimizer
skip_unusable_indexes	Help		TRUE ▼		Boolean			✓	Optimizer
sqltune_category	Help		DEFAULT		String			✓	Optimizer

(Save to File)

| Current | SPFile |

(Show SQL) (Revert) (Apply)

FIGURE 8-5. *Optimizer parameters*

Depending on the type of database that is running, several of these parameters may be useful for tuning, including the following:

■ The STAR_TRANSFORMATION_ENABLED parameter would probably be set to TRUE if the database has more of a data warehousing purpose, rather than is just used as a transactional database.

■ The OPTIMIZER_INDEX_COST_ADJ parameter can be adjusted to make the optimizer more willing to use indexes. The setting is a percentage to adjust the cost of using indexes in the query plans. For example, reducing the value of this parameter from 100 to 50 would cut the cost of using an index in half.

■ The OPTIMIZER_MODE parameter chooses the approach for the database instance. FIRST_ROWS will find a best plan to return the first set of rows faster. ALL_ROWS will develop the plan to return all of the values of the query in the session.

Adjusting the parameters can help change how the optimizer behaves, and can also give the database instance more resources, especially when increasing the memory parameters to allocate more memory to the system. Some of the default settings might be valid for simple database environments. The type of database environment and how it is being used in general should be considered when adjusting these parameters. Additional information from the snapshot reports and advisors that run in the database can help determine the appropriate settings and configurations for some of the parameters.

Automatic Workload Repository

The Automatic Workload Repository (AWR) contains significant information that can be helpful when it comes to tuning the database environment. The database takes regular snapshots to get information about the database settings and the workload in the environment, and stores them in the AWR metadata tables (WRM$_) and historical statistics tables (WRH$_).

In Oracle Database 11*g*, these reports and information are part of the Oracle Diagnostic Pack, which provides automated gathering of the information and ways to pull the information out of the workload and history tables for review and evaluation of performance issues. You can also create baseline templates to be able to compare information. Baselines are especially useful when you find that the database is not performing as it did before, and you need to understand what might have changed.

AWR Reports

AWR reports have information about the different waits. The reports list the top waits, providing a quick way to determine the areas that might be of interest or where to start looking for bottlenecks.

The AWR reports can be viewed in OEM, as shown in Figure 8-6. The reports are based on the snapshot times. If different intervals are needed, different reports can be generated.

In OEM, you can view the details in the list or see the reports in HTML format. The time period, activity on the server, and some information about

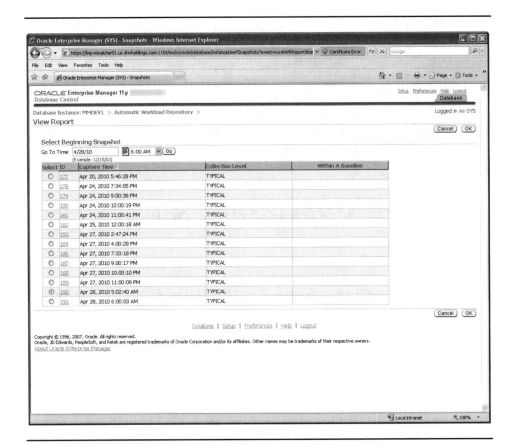

FIGURE 8-6. *AWR reports available for viewing in OEM*

the load on the server are summarized first. Figure 8-7 shows this information at the top of the report, as well as the wait information, which appears a bit further down in the report.

The first item listed in the wait information is DB CPU at the top. In the example in Figure 8-7, no waits are listed; it shows just the percent of the database time for CPU. I would suspect since there is no waiting for CPU, the time is just the regular activity against the database and what is needed for CPU.

As noted earlier in the chapter, the db file scattered read wait event points to full-table scans being done. If you see these waits, check the top SQL statements to validate query plans and consider placing indexes on the appropriate tables.

Host Name	Platform	CPUs	Cores	Sockets	Memory (GB)
LWP-MMALCHER01	Microsoft Windows IA (32-bit)	2	2	1	1.96

	Snap Id	Snap Time	Sessions	Cursors/Session
Begin Snap:	178	24-Apr-10 19:34:05	38	3.0
End Snap:	179	24-Apr-10 21:00:38	37	3.4
Elapsed:		86.55 (mins)		
DB Time:		1.18 (mins)		

Report Summary

Cache Sizes

	Begin	End		
Buffer Cache:	268M	268M	Std Block Size:	8K
Shared Pool Size:	220M	220M	Log Buffer:	5,708K

Load Profile

	Per Second	Per Transaction	Per Exec	Per Call
DB Time(s):	0.0	0.1	0.00	0.00
DB CPU(s):	0.0	0.0	0.00	0.00
Redo size:	2,184.1	7,399.0		
Logical reads:	84.2	285.4		

Instance Efficiency Percentages (Target 100%)

Buffer Nowait %:	100.00	Redo NoWait %:	100.00
Buffer Hit %:	98.05	In-memory Sort %:	100.00
Library Hit %:	97.61	Soft Parse %:	97.05
Execute to Parse %:	55.10	Latch Hit %:	100.00
Parse CPU to Parse Elapsd %:	0.01	% Non-Parse CPU:	59.54

Shared Pool Statistics

	Begin	End
Memory Usage %:	64.09	85.62
% SQL with executions>1:	54.73	72.81
% Memory for SQL w/exec>1:	47.06	72.42

Top 5 Timed Foreground Events

Event	Waits	Time(s)	Avg wait (ms)	% DB time	Wait Class
DB CPU		30		42.20	
db file sequential read	1,727	10	6	13.78	User I/O
control file sequential read	3,006	9	3	12.88	System I/O
library cache load lock	54	2	44	3.36	Concurrency
db file scattered read	189	1	7	1.92	User I/O

FIGURE 8-7.   *An AWR report in OEM*

Active Session History View

The Active Session History (ASH) view has information about waits and events based on the sessions that are occurring in the database. The following example generates a list of how many sessions had waits for an event.

```
SQLPLUS> select session_id||','||session_serial# SID, n.name,
wait_time, time_waited
from v$active_session_history a, v$event_name n
where n.event# = a.event#
SID          NAME                      WAIT_TIME   TIME_WAITED
----------   -----------------------   ----------- -----------
170,3        db file sequential read   0           28852
321,1        reliable message          0           977530
286,33215    db file parallel write    0           1108
240,25727    library cache lock         0          185
...
##plenty more events returned, so just a sampling
```

The TIME_WAITED column shows the actual time waited for the event, and will be updated when the event is completed. The WAIT_TIME column information matches up with the v$session_wait view. When the wait time is shown as zero, then the session is currently waiting; nonzero values indicate the session's last wait time.

The information about events and waits can be overwhelming. In tuning the database, you should focus on the top wait events, especially if the information gathered is during a period when performance was an issue. Getting information about which SQL statements were running and what Oracle was waiting on will help with this troubleshooting.

Also be aware that some waits are just routine in the system, such as the reliable message wait listed in the example of the ASH view. This is an idle wait event, meaning that it is just waiting for work—something to do—and not waiting on a resource.

Library Cache for SQL Statements

In the wait events listed in the sample AWR report and ASH view, you saw a couple events pointing to the library cache. The library cache is part of the shared pool and is the area in memory that handles SQL statements, PL/SQL packages, and procedures. This can be considered similar to the SQL Server procedure cache.

Oracle will first look in the library cache for code that is to be executed against the database, so there is no additional load into memory if the code is already there. The plans are also available there, so it is beneficial to be able to reuse SQL that is available in the library cache.

The following wait events appeared in the previous examples:

■ The library cache lock event is when two users want to compile the same piece of code.

■ The library cache load lock event is a wait for the lock to be able to load an object into the library cache.

The AWR reports show a library cache hit ratio to indicate how much of the code is found in the cache and available for reuse.

One reason for not finding code in the library cache is that the cache is too small to hold all of the statements; if there are a lot of ad hoc statements, it might be hard to hold all of the statements. Another reason could be due to the use of literal values instead of bind variables in the code.

```
SQLPLUS> select …
… where employee_name='George';
SQLPLUS> select …
… where employee_name=:empname;
```

The code with the variable will be getting the information passed in from a variable in the package instead of just using the string value that is passed in. Using bind variables is good practice and will help with management of the library cache.

There is also a parameter that can help make code seem similar enough that it can be reused: CURSOR_SHARING. This parameter can be set to one of the following:

■ EXACT   This makes the code match exactly. Using this value will result in either a large library cache/shared pool or a very low hit ratio of the library cache if literal values are used in the code and can't be matched up.

■ FORCE   This will force a substitute of a literal into a bind variable to reuse the code.

■ SIMILAR   This will allow Oracle to decide what to bind, so that code can be reused.

Other memory areas should also be examined for tuning and performance, but the library cache is important because it is related to the code running on the database. If you are able to design this code to use bind variables, or know how to take advantage of some other parameters to force it to behave in a more efficient manner, the database will perform better.

Summary

Tuning the performance of the database is a multiple-step process. First, you'll need to ask questions to figure out where the performance issue is and what the issue actually means. Several Oracle tools allow you to gather information and see history and current statistics, giving you more details regarding what is running and how the server is behaving.

The areas to check first in an Oracle database are different from those in a SQL Server database. Since locks and blocking are handled differently in Oracle, this area is further down on the list that it is in SQL Server. Indexes, statistics, and waits are the top areas to look at in an Oracle system to validate that the database has what it needs as input to create good execution plans and that it is not waiting on resources while the code is running.

Oracle provides several different index types. You may be able to make code that may be less than optimal more efficient and access data faster, such as through function-based indexes. Also, indexes that can skip the first column may allow for fewer indexes to be created and maintained, which might benefit data change performance. Since the Oracle CBO takes into account the different costs of the indexes available and statistical information, it is important to have good indexes and up-to-date statistics on the tables and indexes.

The system views that provide session and wait information are valuable in the tuning process, and the summary reports from the AWR provide a quick glance at the information. Using these tools, you can drill down into an issue to see if there are bottlenecks or code that needs to be tuned.

CHAPTER
9
PL/SQL

he extended programming language for SQL Server is Transact-SQL (T-SQL). For Oracle, the programming language is PL/SQL. These programming languages provide additional capabilities beyond those available with standard SQL. They are used to develop applications and a way of accessing data. However, using the database programming languages is not just for developers. Besides doing code reviews, there are plenty of times for DBAs to use these languages to write procedures for monitoring databases, performing maintenance, and moving or loading data.

The database programming languages have some similar characteristics, but each takes advantage of some features that are platform-specific. For both, you define the variables and code to be executed, as well as pass in values and return values. They both provide ways to handle errors and process standard SQL statements. You can create triggers, stored procedures, and functions. Oracle also has packages that group functions and procedures together.

In previous chapters, you have seen several examples of SQL statements to look at the data in an Oracle database or change it in some way, as well as examples to execute PL/SQL system-supplied packages and procedures, such as DBMS_STATS and DBMS_SCHEDULER. This chapter provides more details about using PL/SQL. If you're migrating from SQL Server to Oracle, you'll probably need to spend some time converting the T-SQL procedures to PL/SQL procedures.

Database Coding Practices

PL/SQL is a programming language with close integration to the Oracle database. Some of the standard coding practices used with T-SQL don't translate to PL/SQL, and might even seem backward. However, some of the concepts correspond, although the coding will not be exactly the same. For example, the concept of SQL Server INSTEAD OF triggers are found in Oracle's BEFORE triggers. Table 9-1 shows some examples of commonly used programming tools in SQL Server and Oracle. As we look at PL/SQL examples throughout this chapter, you will see how these are used in blocks of code.

Usage	SQL Server Tool	Oracle Tool
Data type association	User-defined types	`%TYPE` or `%ROWTYPE` allows for using a column or row to have the variable be the same type
Select	`SELECT 'test'` Can select without `from` clause	`SELECT 'test' FROM dual;` Dummy table to use with `FROM`
Row ID	Can generate an ID column on select using functions	Row ID is automatically created as a pseudo column
Unique identifier	Identity	Sequences
If this, then this ...	`CASE`	`DECODE` or `CASE`
Set operators	`EXISTS` and `NOT EXISTS`	`INTERSECT` and `MINUS`
Cursors	For looking at one row at a time; tend to be slower way to process	Implicit cursors used for data processing; explicit use of cursors to manipulate the data of a `SELECT` statement
Delimiters	Statements continue when previous statement is completed without specific delimiter	Use of `;` to delimit statements
Create	If exists, drop, then create	Create or replace
Alter	Alters stored procedure code if exists	Create or replace

TABLE 9-1. *Common Code Usage in SQL Server and Oracle*

The SQL Developer tool provides a way to develop, unit test, and handle version control. In SQL Developer, you can set up basic frameworks for the database objects.

```
## Statements generated by SQL Developer when creating new object
## Create procedure with two parameters passed in
CREATE PROCEDURE EXAMPLE_PROC1
(  PARAM1 IN VARCHAR2  , PARAM2 IN NUMBER
) AS
BEGIN
  NULL;
END EXAMPLE_PROC1
;

/
## Create trigger on insert
CREATE TRIGGER EXAMPLE_TRIGGER1
BEFORE INSERT ON EMP
REFERENCING OLD AS OLD NEW AS NEW
FOR EACH ROW
WHEN (DEPTNO=10)
BEGIN
  NULL;
END;
/
```

As noted in Table 9-1, a semicolon (;) is the delimiter that marks the end of the block. The forward slash (/) says to execute the code in SQL*Plus.

NOTE
*SQL Developer and some of the other tools have ways to execute statements with a run or run script statement, which will run the code without the forward slash. However, in SQL*Plus, the / is required to have the code run, like saying "Go."*

In SQL Server, you get an identity column, but Oracle doesn't have an identity type. Insert triggers are useful for generating IDs for primary keys. Using a sequence, you can retrieve the next value for a unique number to be used as an ID. You could also use a procedure for inserts to pull in the next value from the sequence without a trigger. This could be used on every insert, as long as the application does not rely on ad hoc queries for inserts.

```
## Trigger for sequences and populating identity column
create sequence order_id_seq start with 1 increment 1;
create or replace trigger trg_i_orders before insert
for each row
begin
select order_id_seq.nextval
into :new.order_id from dual;
end;
/
```

You cannot use a role to grant permissions to the objects in a procedure that the procedure owner is using in that code. Permissions for the objects that are being accessed and used in the code must be explicitly granted to the procedure owner.

Also worth mentioning is a difference in create and replace operations with the database programming languages. In SQL Server, the object is dropped first and then re-created, normally after first checking if the object exists. In Oracle, there is no need to check first, because the create or replace command will create the object if it is not there or replace the existing object with the new code. This works for stored procedures, packages, triggers, and views.

Packages and Package Bodies

Along with the usual objects of triggers, functions, and procedures, Oracle also has packages and package bodies. The package is the collection of the definitions of the procedures and functions that are found in the package body. Variables, constants, and cursors are also declared in the package definition, and can be used in the subprograms found in the package body. Figure 9-1 shows an example of using SQL Developer to create the framework for a package.

Using subprograms makes the code more modular, so it is easier to manage changes to programs and global variables. Since the whole package is loaded into memory, execution becomes faster; it's not necessary to recompile because of dependencies on other programs. Error handling can also be defined at the package level for all of the subprograms to use, which makes programming more consistent and avoids repeating the same steps in several different procedures.

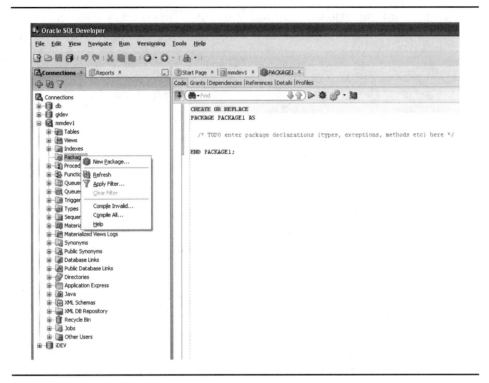

FIGURE 9-1. *Creating a new package in SQL Developer*

Here is an example of defining a package with package body, with error handling (discussed later in this chapter) and variable declarations:

```
create or replace package modify_product_info
as
TYPE ProductRec is record (prod_id number,longname varchar2(50));
cursor desc_prod return ProductRec;
procedure upd_prod_name(v_prod_id in varchar2);
procedure ins_new_prod
   (v_prod_id in varchar2,v_longname in varchar2);
function get_prod_id(v_prod_name in varchar2) RETURN ProductRec;
procedure raise_app_error(v_error_code in varchar2,
  v_text in varchar2, v_name1 in varchar2, v_value1 in varchar2);
END modify_product_info;
/
create or replace package body modify_product_info
as
cursor desc_prod return ProductRec is
  select prod_id, prod_name from orders;
```

```
procedure upd_prod_name(v_prod_id in number)
is
  var_count number;
  BEGIN
    . . .
    update products set prod_name = …

    . . .
    EXCEPTION
        WHEN OTHERS
        THEN
                Rollback;
                raise_app_error(v_error_code => 'UNANTICIPATED-ERROR',
            v_text => 'Details…',v_name1 => 'TABLE_NAME');
END upd_prod_name;

function get_prod_id(v_prod_name in varchar2)
RETURN ProductRec
is
 var_prod_id prod_id_type%TYPE;
 BEGIN
 . . .
 select prod_id into var_prod_id
 from orders
 where . . .
 . . .
 return var_prod_id;
EXCEPTION
  WHEN NO_DATA_FOUND
  raise_app_error(v_error_code => 'NO DATA…'
. . .
END get_prod_id;
. . .
## Define other procedures and functions
. . .
END modify_product_info;
```

This example shows the flow of the package and package body definition. As you can see, the functions and procedures are defined just with the input and output procedures in the package. The functions and stored procedures are then listed again in the body of the package with the details of the procedure and statements to be processed. If the package header has a procedure listed, the body must contain the definition. Of course, the code is filled in with processing, conditional statements, data processing, and so on.

Triggers

In both SQL Server and Oracle environments, triggers are available on logon, object changes, and data changes. Triggers can be fired for events such as startup or shutdown and when inserts, updates, and deletes are issued. The concept of the trigger is the same in both Oracle and SQL Server, but there are some differences in the types available and when they execute. Table 9-2 summarizes the types of triggers available on both platforms.

The triggers on the database system events, such as startup, shutdown, and server message events, can be used for auditing or changing session parameters.

```
##Audit logins via sqlplus into a table
create or replace trigger
after logon on database
begin
insert into logon_from_sqlplus (user_name,logon_time)
select username,sysdate from v$session where program='sqlplus.exe';
end;
/
##Trigger to prevent dropping of objects
create or replace trigger drop_not_allowed
before drop on database
begin
   RAISE_APPLICATION_ERROR(-20001,'Drop table not allowed');
end;
/
```

SQL Server Triggers	Oracle Triggers
DML triggers	DML triggers
After	Before and after
Instead of	Instead of
	Statement and row
DDL triggers	DDL triggers
Event triggers, system and user	Event triggers, system and user

TABLE 9-2. *SQL Server and Oracle Trigger Types*

```
##Alter the session to have a different parameter setting
create or replace trigger
after logon on database
begin
execute immediate 'alter session set optimizer_mode=FIRST_ROWS';
end;
/
```

The EXECUTE IMMEDIATE statement executes a SQL statement that can't be executed normally in a block of code, such as ALTER SESSION, ALTER TABLE, and other object changes. Dynamic SQL statements can also be built and then executed using the EXECUTE IMMEDIATE statement in the code of triggers, procedures, or functions.

```
. . .
sql_stmt        varchar2(300);
var_col         varchar2(30);
begin
. . .
select column_name into var_col from user_tab_cols
where table_name=v_table and column_name=v_column;
Sql_stmt := 'update '||v_table|| ' set price =  :1 where '
|| var_col || ' =:2';
execute immediate sql_stmt USING amout, column_value;
. . .
```

Triggers on tables that fire on update, insert, and delete offer some different options in Oracle than in SQL Server. In SQL Server, the triggers fire after the change, or they can do something instead of the action. Oracle triggers have the option of executing before or after, and they can be fired for each row that is changed or once for the whole statement. So, if a delete is run against the table, the statement-level trigger will fire once for the whole delete, which would be good for an audit record. The row-level trigger is useful for inserting the data that is being changed into another table, for example.

The BEFORE trigger is useful for validating the data and checking that the change should be performed. Being able to execute these actions before the change occurs could prevent rollbacks, and even disallow changes if an incorrect role or application is attempting to make them. The BEFORE trigger also allows for the adjustment of values or determination of values for another column, and could help maintain referential relationships. For use with row-level triggers, the variables :NEW and :OLD refer to the new and existing values for the columns, respectively. With BEFORE triggers, the old values cannot be updated, but the new values can change in the trigger body and be the "new" new values. BEFORE triggers are used on tables; they cannot be used on views.

AFTER and BEFORE triggers are used in combination with the statement and row triggers, which create the four types of triggers for actions on tables.

```
## Trigger examples
create or replace trigger trg_u_customers
after update on customers
for each row
begin
update orders set customer_name=:new.customer_name
where custumer_namer=:old.customer_name;
end;
/
## Trigger example to combine update, insert and deletes
create or replace trigger trg_iud_customers
after insert or update or delete on customers
for each row
declare
   v_order_date    date;
BEGIN
   v_order_date    :=    sysdate;
   if INSERTING THEN
      INSERT into orders
       values(order_seq.nextval, :new.customer_id,
       order_details,v_order_date);
      -- other possible inserts or code
    end if;
    if DELETING THEN
      INSERT into customer_hist_tbl
      values(:old.customer_id,:old.customer_name,
        :old_cust_details);

    end if;
    if UPDATING ('CUSTOMER_NAME') THEN
       update customer_hist_tbl set
       customer_name=:old.customer_name
       where customer_id=:new.customer_id;
    end if;
END;
/
```

Updates and Conditions

Before getting into the transaction part of the procedures and other useful information about PL/SQL, let's take a brief look at UPDATE statements, which tend to be very different in SQL Server and Oracle. The transition from doing SQL Server updates to handling them in Oracle is not easy. It may take several tries to not think in SQL Server syntax and get the correct statement for an Oracle update. Table 9-3 shows a couple of examples.

One difference is that in Oracle, you can group the columns being updated to set more than one column equal to the SELECT statement. Another is that instead of needing to list the table again for joins, Oracle can use the table being updated to join against in the query. To test the SQL Server UPDATE statement, you can just run the query after the FROM to

Update	SQL Server Example	Oracle Example
Update one column	`UPDATE titles    SET ytd_sales = t.ytd_sales + s.qty   FROM titles t, sales s     WHERE t.title_id = s.title_id`	`UPDATE titles t SET ytd_sales= (SELECT t.ytd_sales + s.qty FROM  sales s WHERE t.title_id=s.title_id)`
Update multiple columns	`UPDATE orders SET Customer_id=c.customer_id, item_id=p.item_id FROM   (SELECT c.customer_id, p.item_id FROM products p, customers c, orders o WHERE c.order_id=o.order_id and o.product_name=p.product_name) WHERE order_id=1234`	`UPDATE orders o  SET (customer_id, item_id)= (SELECT c.customer_id,p.item_id FROM products p, customers c WHERE c.order_id=o.order_id and o.product_nsme= p.product_name) WHERE o.order_id=1234`

TABLE 9-3. *UPDATE Statements in SQL Server and Oracle*

know which values you are getting. To test the update in Oracle, you can pull the update table into the query.

```
SQLPLUS> SELECT c.customer_id,p.item_id
FROM products p, customers c, orders o
WHERE c.order_id=o.order_id and o.product_nsme=p.product_name)

SQLPLUS> UPDATE orders o  SET (customer_id, item_id) =
(select c.customer_id,p.item_id FROM products p, customers c
WHERE c.order_id=o.order_id and o.product_nsme=p.product_name)
WHERE o.order_id=1234;
```

It does take some practice to get used to writing the updates differently. Other statements that select with joins translate fairly easily. Also, INSERT and DELETE statements are similar.

Since we are looking at some of the SQL statements here before putting them into the PL/SQL code, another function worth mentioning is DECODE. Like CASE (which Oracle also has), DECODE is useful for conditions.

```
SQLPLUS> select DECODE(deptno, 10, 'Technology',20,'HR', 30,
'Accounting','General') from departments;
## start with the value and if it matches then substitute the NEXT value
## the last value is the default which is optional
```

Ranges and not equal values are probably easier to define in a CASE statement, but DECODE is useful for other situations. For example, you might use it for date or number comparisons:

```
SQLPLUS> select DECODE(date1-date2)-abs(date1-date2), 0,
'Date 1 is greater than Date 2,
'Otherwise Date 2 is greater than Date 1')
from list_date_table;
```

These examples might be useful in developing your code and writing more effective PL/SQL.

Transactions

Transactions are a main reason for writing procedures, and planning transaction size, commits, and rollback points are part of good procedures. Transactions that are too big will cause issues like filling up log space or blocking in SQL Server, and possibly fill up the undo tablespace in Oracle. Transactions that are too small can have too many commits and checkpoints, which can slow down processing.

The starting point for a transaction is defining the blocks of code to be executed, where to roll back or commit, and then working in this framework to define transaction size. SQL Server has BEGIN TRAN, and then you can COMMIT or ROLLBACK TRAN after completion of the statement.

Beginning a Transaction

Oracle has a BEGIN statement to start the transaction, which works just like BEGIN TRAN in SQL Server. For marking a point to be able to commit or roll back to, you use SAVEPOINT *transaction_name*. This will start the transaction either in a block of code or a stored procedure, or even in a SQL*Plus session before executing a SQL statement.

```
SQLPLUS> begin
insert into emp values('Mandy',10);
end;
/
PL/SQL procedure successfully completed.
SQLPLUS> select * from emp;
EMP_NAME                EMP_DEPT
-------------------- ----------
Mandy                        10

SQLPLUS> begin
insert into emp values('Emily',20);
insert into emp values('Gabrielle',50);
savepoint savepoint_before_delete;
delete emp where emp_dept=10;
end;
/
PL/SQL procedure successfully completed.
SQLPLUS> select * from emp;
EMP_NAME                EMP_DEPT
-------------------- ----------
Emily                        20
Gabrielle                    50
SQLPLUS> rollback to savepoint_before_delete;
Rollback complete.
SQLPLUS> select * from emp;
```

```
EMP_NAME                    EMP_DEPT
-------------------- ----------
Mandy                           10
Emily                           20
Gabrielle                       50
SQLPLUS> rollback;
Rollback complete.
SQLPLUS> select * from emp;
no rows selected
```

This example uses an anonymous block of code, rather than a stored procedure. If you were to put this statement in a stored procedure, after executing the stored procedure, if you did not have the commits in the stored procedure, you could still roll back after the execution of the procedure.

```
SQLPLUS> create procedure INS_EMP
as
begin
insert into emp values('Mandy',10);
insert into emp values('Emily',20);
savepoint before_delete;
delete from emp where emp_dept=20;
end;
/
Procedure created.
SQLPLUS> select * from emp;
no rows selected
SQLPLUS> exec INS_EMP;
PL/SQL procedure successfully completed.
SQLPLUS> select * from emp;
EMP_NAME                    EMP_DEPT
-------------------- ----------
Mandy                           10
SQLPLUS> rollback to before_delete;
Rollback complete.
SQLPLUS> select * from emp;
EMP_NAME                    EMP_DEPT
-------------------- ----------
Mandy                           10
Emily                           20
SQLPLUS> commit;
Commit complete.
SQLPLUS> rollback;
```

```
Rollback complete.
## Rollback ineffective because commit already done.
SQLPLUS> select * from emp;
EMP_NAME                 EMP_DEPT
-------------------- ----------
Mandy                        10
Emily                        20

## Add commit to stored procedure
SQLPLUS> create or replace procedure INS_EMP
as
begin
insert into emp values('Mandy',10);
insert into emp values('Emily',20);
savepoint before_delete;
delete from emp where emp_dept=20;
commit;
end;
/
Procedure created
SQLPLUS> exec ins_emp;
PL/SQL procedure successfully completed.
SQLPLUS> select * from emp;
EMP_NAME                 EMP_DEPT
-------------------- ----------
Mandy                        10
## commit part of the stored procedure so rollback
## to a savepoint will error out
SQLPLUS> rollback to before_delete;
rollback to before_delete
*
ERROR at line 1:
ORA-01086: savepoint 'BEFORE_DELETE' never established
```

As you can see from the examples, in the same session without a commit, rollbacks are possible to the beginning of the statement or to the savepoints.

Defining Commits

With the transaction savepoints in place, you now need to confirm the changes and commit them. The transaction size is important, as noted earlier. You do not want commits every record; even every 500 can be too small. Locking is less of a concern with commit points in Oracle.

If looping through the data that is being processed can be validated, then a bulk of the updates can be committed or rolled back as a group in the transaction. The raising of errors in the procedure will also allow for rollbacks in the error handling, as discussed later in this chapter.

Commits should be put into the code as needed. It should not be expected that executing another procedure will automatically commit, or that a child procedure will commit automatically when completed. When changing tables and performing DDL statements with transactions in the same session, a commit does happen before and after the structure change. So, if you did some transactions, and then did an ALTER TABLE or CREATE INDEX, the changes would be committed.

```
## Example loop to commit every 10000
declare
loop_num number :=0;
cursor c_products is
select item_id from products;

begin
for i in c_products
    loop
        update products set prod_num = prod_num + 2000
        where item_id = i.item_id;
        loop_num := loop_num + 1;
        if mod(loop_num, 10000) = 0 THEN
            COMMIT;
        end if;
    end loop;
commit;
end;
```

This example can be modified to have a parameter passed in to adjust the commit value, or if it's part of a package, it can have a global variable defined for the number of rows to commit at a time.

Notice that the example loop first gathers the IDs to be updated in a cursor. Next, let's look at cursor processing in Oracle.

Cursor Processing

In SQL Server, because of the locking and processing of transactions, bulk transactions are normally the way to go. Looping through cursors is not normally the most efficient way to process transactions. However, in Oracle, implicit and explicit cursors are used to process transactions.

Implicit cursors are used automatically to process SELECT, UPDATE, INSERT, and DELETE statements. If you want to perform some other action with each row that is being processed, you will need to define an explicit cursor. Explicit cursors can be very useful in handling transactions that require additional work for the data or for handling the commit point size.

NOTE
SELECT INTO, which retrieves one row of data, also uses an implicit cursor. If there is more than one record returned with the SELECT INTO, an error is raised for handling of TOO_MANY_ROWS or NO_DATA_FOUND, as discussed in the "Error Handling" section later in this chapter.

The Oracle cursor works in a similar manner to a temporary table in SQL Server. The cursor pulls out the data set that is to be worked with and uses that in the rest of the code. It's true that SQL Server also has cursors, which can be declared and opened, and the next record can be fetched and then closed. But behind the scenes, SQL Server is handling this in a temporary table. With Oracle's version, we skip to the temporary table. And keep in mind that Oracle may already be using implicit cursors.

With a cursor, several attributes are useful in processing the rows: %NOTFOUND, %FOUND, %ROWCOUNT, and %ISOPEN. The %NOTFOUND attribute is good for error handling of the cursor to check if data is even returned in the SELECT operation. The cursor could be open for processing as long as new values are found or while the cursor stays open and hasn't been explicitly closed.

```
DECLARE
CURSOR c_emp_rec IS
    select emp_id, emp_name from emp
where emp_dept = var_in_dept_id;
BEGIN
    IF NOT c_emp_rec%ISOPEN
    THEN
        OPEN c_emp_rec;
    END IF;
--- Do stuff
 . . .
END;
```

BULK COLLECT or FOR loops can be used for cursor processing when you have an expected value of the set of results for the cursor or a manageable set of data.

```
DECLARE
TYPE dept_list IS VARRAY of varchar2(50);
v_dept_list         dept_list;
BEGIN
select dept_name
BULK COLLECT INTO v_dept_list
from departments;
FOR i IN 1 .. v_dept_list.COUNT
LOOP
        -- Do stuff with department names
END LOOP;
END;
```

Another cursor type is a REF CURSOR. This is a cursor variable that can be defined with different queries at runtime. Instead of just declaring a cursor as a SELECT statement, a datatype is defined as a REF CURSOR, and then can be associated with a variable. The SELECT statement can even be put together in a variable and then be used with the cursor.

```
SQLPLUS> create or replace procedure products_query (
var_prod_id         product.prod_id%TYPE,
var_prod_name       product.name%TYPE)
IS
prod_refcur         SYS_REFCURSOR;
v_prod_id           product.prod_id%TYPE;
v_prod_name         product.name%TYPE;
v_stmt_sql           varchar2(300);
BEGIN
v_stmt_sql := 'SELECT prod_id, name from product where ' ||
'prod_id = :productid and prod = :prodname';
OPEN prod_refcur FOR v_stmt_sql USING var_prod_id, var_prod_name;
LOOP
   FETCH prod_refcur INTO v_prod_id, v_prod_name;
   EXIT WHEN prod_refcur%NOTFOUND;
   DBMS_OUTPUT.PUT_LINE(v_prod_id || '     ' || v_prod_name);
END LOOP;
CLOSE prod_refcur;
END;
/
```

```
Procedure created.
## To see the output from DBMS_OUTPUT for example purposes
SQLPLUS> set serveroutput on
SQLPLUS> exec product_query(4,'Product 2');
4     Product 2
PL/SQL procedure successfully completed.
```

The cursor in the example can be set to another SELECT statement as long as the cursor was closed first. Using a variable to build the SELECT statement gives you a lot of flexibility in the queries that are in the cursor. For example, in application packages, instead of just outputting the information, values can be updated or used for comparison.

Processing with FORALL

With a PL/SQL FORALL loop, you can collect data and perform insert, update, or delete operations.

```
## Create sample table of months
SQLPLUS> create table forall_months (
  id           NUMBER,
  description VARCHAR2(50));
Table created.
## Insert some data for example
SQLPLUS> INSERT INTO forall_months VALUES (1, 'JAN');
1 row created.
SQLPLUS> INSERT INTO forall_months VALUES (2, 'FEB');
1 row created.
SQLPLUS> INSERT INTO forall_months VALUES (3, 'MAR');
1 row created.
 . . .
SQLPLUS> COMMIT;
Commit complete.

## Create procedure that uses FORALL loop to collect
## the data and update it.
SQLPLUS> create or replace procedure update_with_year
AS
  TYPE t_forall_months_tab IS TABLE OF forall_months%ROWTYPE;
  l_tab t_forall_months_tab;
BEGIN
  SELECT *
  BULK COLLECT INTO l_tab
  FROM   forall_months;
```

```
   FOR indx IN l_tab.first .. l_tab.last LOOP
     l_tab(indx).description := l_tab(indx).description||
' 2010 Information';
   END LOOP;

   FORALL indx IN l_tab.first .. l_tab.last
     UPDATE forall_months
     SET    description = l_tab(indx).description
     WHERE  id          = l_tab(indx).id;
   COMMIT;
END;
/
Procedure created.
## Execute procedure and look at the data.
SQLPLUS> exec update_with_year;
PL/SQL procedure successfully completed.

SQLPLUS> SELECT * FROM forall_months;
        ID DESCRIPTION
---------- --------------------------------
         1 JAN 2010 Information
         2 FEB 2010 Information
         3 MAR 2010 Information
         4 APR 2010 Information
         5 MAY 2010 Information
         6 JUN 2010 Information
         7 JUL 2010 Information
         8 AUG 2010 Information
         9 SEP 2010 Information
        10 OCT 2010 Information
        11 NOV 2010 Information
        12 DEC 2010 Information
12 rows selected.
```

Functions

A function in Oracle is the same thing as it is in SQL Server: a program to return some value. In general, the functions in Oracle are scalar-valued functions. They return a value to what called the function. In contrast, stored procedures do not return anything. Table 9-4 summarizes function types in SQL Server and Oracle.

Coding functions is similar to creating procedures. Functions can take input parameters and handle errors, but they always return a value. Here is

SQL Server Functions	Oracle Functions
System- and user-defined functions	System- and user-defined functions
Table-valued functions	Pipelined table functions
Scalar-valued functions	Functions

TABLE 9-4. *Function Types in SQL Server and Oracle*

an example of a simple function that takes in some parameters and returns a value:

```
SQLPLUS> create or replace function
get_customer_name(var_cust_id in number)
return varchar2
v_cust_name varchar2(40);
as
BEGIN
    SELECT cust_name into v_cust_name
    from customers where cust_id = var_cust_id;
    return v_cust_name;
END;
/
```

You can write code to modify and manipulate the values as needed or pull information from other tables.

Oracle provides multiple system-defined functions for working with values, dates, and characters. Instead of the SQL Server functions of CAST and CONVERT, Oracle has TO_ functions: TO_DATE, TO_CHAR, and TO_NUMBER. These allow for formatting and converting a datatype to another type. The following demonstrates some of the system-defined functions.

```
SQLPLUS> select amount from sales
where sales_date >= TO_DATE('05/01/2010','MM/DD/YYYY');
SQLPLUS> select TO_CHAR(sysdate,'YYYYMMDD:HH24:MI') from dual;
20100501:21:23   ## Now a character string
## Add 2 months to a date
SQLPLUS> SQL> select add_months(sysdate,2) from dual;
ADD_MONTH
---------
14-JUL-10
```

```
## Find the first occurrence of some characters
SQLPLUS> select INSTR('Michelle','ich') from dual;
INSTR('MICHELLE','ICH')
-----------------------
                      2
## Replace character with another
SQLPLUS> select replace('Gig Grown Gear','G','B') from dual;
REPLACE('GIGGR
--------------
Big Brown Bear
## Replace characters and remove spaces
SQLPLUS> select replace(replace('Gig Grown Gear','G','B'),' ','')
from dual;
REPLACE(REPL
------------
BigBrownBear
## Substitute a value for NULLs
SQLPLUS> select sales_state,NLV(amount,0) from sales;
  STATE_ID     AMOUNT
---------- ----------
        IL       3000
        WI       4000
        MN       6520
        IN          0
        IA        789
        MO          0
. . .
## Handling CASE
SQLPLUS> select UPPER('Michelle'), LOWER('MicHelle') from dual;
----------------------- --------------------
MICHELLE                    michelle
```

Functions can be used to do comparisons or change data. As discussed in Chapter 8, function-based indexes improve performance when using these types of functions to access tables. Even user-defined functions can be used in indexes.

The pipelined table functions are used to return a collection that can be queried in the same way as a table.

```
## first create the needed types
SQLPLUS>  create type emp_row_type as object (
empname varchar2(20),
empid  number,
deptid number,
status varchar2(10));
/
```

```
Type created.
create type emp_table_type as table of emp;
/
Type created.
SQLPLUS> create or replace function get_all_names (
p_empname in varchar2,
 p_empid in number,
 p_deptid in number,
 p_status varchar2)
 RETURN emp_table_type as
 v_tab emp_table_type := emp_table_type();
BEGIN
 for cur in (select ename,empno,deptno,job from emp2
 where hiredate < sysdate - 1)
 LOOP
 v_tab.extend;
 v_tab(v_tab.last) := emp_row_type
(cur.ename,cur.empno,cur.deptno,cur.job);
END LOOP;
return v_tab;
end;
/
Function created.
```

Oracle Database 11*g* has a result cache for functions. Return values can be cached to reduce the time needed to get the data out of the function. The following shows the basic structure for defining a function to use the result cache.

```
create or replace function get_product (p_in in NUMBER)
return varchar2
result_cache
as
  . . .
BEGIN
  . . . . function code
END;
/
```

The optional clause RELIES_ON will invalidate the cache if the dependent objects are modified. Oracle Database 11*g* Release 2 uses RELIES_ON by default, so it will automatically track dependencies and invalidate the cached results when necessary. This way, the cache will continue to return the correct result set.

Debugging Procedures and Unit Testing

Procedures are made up of the functions, transactions, and cursors we have been discussing in this chapter. They are also part of the packages. Understanding how to write stored procedures is important for a DBA. Understanding how to review procedures and find the good and the bad in them may be even more important.

When you're experiencing problems with procedures, check their permissions on objects. Also check for the dreaded missing semicolon somewhere. These are quick areas to check, and in a small stored procedure, they might be easy to spot.

Privileges needed for running in debug mode for PL/SQL are "Debug any procedure" and "Debug connect session." Figure 9-2 shows an example of compiling a procedure in debug mode in SQL Developer. Clicking an error message shown here will take you to the line in the code that is causing the issue.

FIGURE 9-2. *Debugging procedures in SQL Developer*

Breakpoints can also be set to walk through the procedures to validate code and variables. Another way to get output throughout the procedure to see what is happening is to use DBMS_OUTPUT.PUT_LINE to output a statement, value, or step in the procedure.

SQL Developer also has unit testing functionality. Test plans can be set up as an unit test repository that is created in the database. You can seed some data and pass in parameters from tables to do the testing. To set up a repository for unit testing or to connect to an existing repository, select the Unit Test option from the Tools menu, as shown in Figure 9-3. Create a new repository if one is not yet available. SYSDBA permissions are required to create a new repository, but users can be added with lesser permissions to run unit tests and create the test plans.

Figure 9-4 shows the first step in creating a unit test using the wizard. All of the packages, procedures, and functions are listed and available for testing. Other objects can be pulled in for using data or as part of the test in later steps.

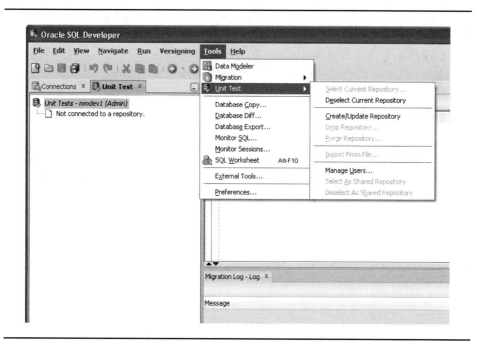

FIGURE 9-3. *Setting up a unit testing repository in SQL Developer*

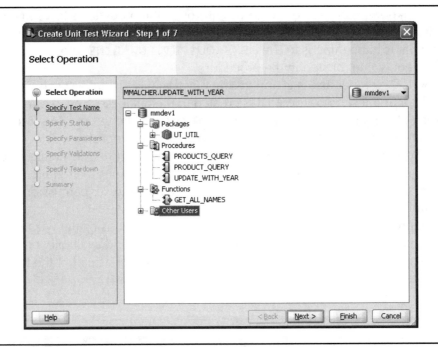

FIGURE 9-4. *Creating a unit test in SQL Developer*

Error Handling

With error handling, if something in a procedure fails, it goes to the routine for handling that exception. In SQL Server, the TRY CATCH block can be used for error handling. This is almost like wrapping the code in a transaction with a BEGIN TRY and then executing some code. If errors come up, it goes to the BEGIN CATCH.

```
BEGIN TRY
    . . . . . . . . (T-SQL Code
END TRY
BEGIN CATCH
....... (Error handling code)
END CATCH
```

With PL/SQL's exception handling, the errors that are raised can be user- or system-defined.

```
DECLARE
        .......... (variables defined)
BEGIN
        .......... (Blocks of code)
EXCEPTION
    WHEN exception_name THEN
            ............(Exception handling code)
END;
```

The error functions in SQL Server and Oracle provide information about the error or failure, as shown in Table 9-5. Oracle's SQLCODE function returns an error number. SQLERRM returns a message.

Exceptions do not cause DML statements to roll back unless this happens by default without an exception handler routine. The exception handler routine would need to handle commits and rollbacks depending on the failure. Within the exception handler, there might be a separate commit for inserting into an error log. Using savepoints is a good way to handle the rollbacks, so this logging of errors does not become part of the transaction. Autonomous transactions are another way to handle this. Autonomous transactions are changes made with a block of code that can be saved or reversed without affecting the outer or main transaction.

SQL Server Error Functions	Oracle Error Functions
ERROR_NUMBER()	SQLCODE
ERROR_SEVERITY()	SQLERRM
ERROR_STATE()	
ERROR_PROCEDURE()	
ERROR_LINE()	
ERROR_MESSAGE()	

TABLE 9-5. *Error Functions in SQL Server and Oracle*

Let's take a look at a couple of examples of exception handling.

```
EXCEPTION
WHEN NO_DATA_FOUND THEN
        v_msg := 'Record not found' || TO_CHAR(v_id);
        v_err := SQLCODE;
        v_prog := 'get product';
                insert into errlog
                values(v_err,v_msg, v_prog, sysdate);
```

Error Handling Packages

You can create a package to call your error procedures. Using a standard package makes it easier to have error handling at the end of each procedure and provides a centralized place to gather the failure information.

```
## Create a table to hold the error information
SQLPLUS> create table errlog (
errcode integer,
errmsg varchar2(4000),
prog_action varchar2(300),
created_on date,
created_by varchar2(30));
Table created.
## Create package with procedures for handling errors
SQLPLUS> create or replace package errlogs
IS
c_table     constant NUMBER :=1;
  PROCEDURE  handle (
    errcode   IN NUMBER := NULL,
    errmsg    IN VARCHAR2 := NULL,
    logerr    IN BOOLEAN := TRUE,
    reraise   IN BOOLEAN := FALSE);
PROCEDURE raise (errcode    IN    NUMBER := NULL,
     errmsg     IN    VARCHAR2 := NULL, prog_action IN VARCHAR2);
    PROCEDURE log (errcode IN NUMBER := NULL,
      errmsg IN  VARCHAR2 := NULL, prog_action IN VARCHAR2);
END;
/
CREATE OR REPLACE PACKAGE BODY errlogs
IS
    g_target   NUMBER      := c_table;
    PROCEDURE handle (
      errcode IN NUMBER := NULL, errmsg IN VARCHAR2 := NULL,
      prog_action IN VARCHAR2 := NULL, logerr IN BOOLEAN := TRUE,
      reraise IN BOOLEAN := FALSE )
```

```
IS
BEGIN
  IF logerr
  THEN
     log (errcode, errmsg, prog_action);
  END IF;
  IF reraise
  THEN
     errlogs.raise (errcode, errmsg, prog_action);
  END IF;
END;
PROCEDURE raise (
  errcode IN PLS_INTEGER := NULL, errmsg IN VARCHAR2 := NULL,
  prog_action IN VARCHAR2 := NULL   )  IS
  l_errcode   PLS_INTEGER := NVL (errcode, SQLCODE);
  l_errmsg    VARCHAR2(1000) := NVL (errmsg, SQLERRM);
  l_progact VARCHAR2(300) := NVL(prog_action,'Default Action');
BEGIN
  IF l_errcode BETWEEN -20999 AND -20000
  THEN
     raise_application_error (l_errcode, l_errmsg);
  ELSIF l_errcode != 0
  THEN
     EXECUTE IMMEDIATE
       'DECLARE myexc EXCEPTION; ' ||
       '   PRAGMA EXCEPTION_INIT (myexc, ' ||
            TO_CHAR (err_in) || ');' ||
       'BEGIN  RAISE myexc; END;';
  END IF;
END;
PROCEDURE log (
  errcode   IN   PLS_INTEGER := NULL,
  errmsg    IN   VARCHAR2 := NULL   )   IS
  PRAGMA AUTONOMOUS_TRANSACTION;
  l_sqlcode pls_integer := NVL (errcode, SQLCODE);
  l_sqlerrm VARCHAR2(1000) := NVL (errmsg, SQLERRM);
BEGIN
  INSERT INTO errlog
       (errcode, errmsg, prog_action, created_on, created_by)
       VALUES (l_sqlcode,l_sqlerrm,l_progact,SYSDATE,USER);
  COMMIT;
EXCEPTION
  WHEN OTHERS
  THEN  ROLLBACK;
END;
/
```

This package can be used in the exception handling of any procedure. The call to the package passes in the needed parameters, including information about what procedure was running, to put details in the error log.

```
SQLPLUS> create or replace procedure testing_errors
as
procedure_name varchar2(30) := 'testing_errors';
BEGIN
    . . .
EXCEPTION
    WHEN OTHERS
    errlogs.handle(SQLCODE,SQLERRM,procedure_name);
END;
/
```

Expanding on the error handling could then allow for different logs to be captured in a table or even a file. Rollback and commit information can be handled in the executing procedure, and then the error capture in the same error package for all procedures, to maintain consistency.

Standard Error Messages

PL/SQL can raise user error messages that can be passed along to the application for handling on the application side as well. Also, application errors can be raised to pass the information to the application.

The standard Oracle exceptions can be associated with a user-defined application error. You can also have other data or changes raise user-defined application errors.

Raised errors can be used in a trigger to disallow updates to a table:

```
raise_application_error(-20002,'Updates not allowed on this table');
```

If there is a check on a value, the procedure could raise an error stating that the value is not allowed or needs to be in a different range:

```
raise_application_error(-20001,'Salary not in correct range for department');
```

You can pass through additional information about the values of the columns or any of the variables in the procedure.

When standard Oracle messages come through, different information can be passed through to the application:

```
raise_application_error(-20004,'No Data Found, values not in table');
```

Here is a partial list of standard exceptions:

- NO_DATA_FOUND

- VALUE_ERROR

- OTHERS

- INVALID_CURSOR

- INVALID_NUMBER

- CASE_NOT_FOUND

- TOO_MANY_ROWS

- ROWTYPE_MISMATCH

Instead of having the exception handler looking at WHEN OTHERS, a different set of steps can be coded for each of these exceptions.

```
EXCEPTION
   WHEN exception1 THEN -- handler for exception1
     sequence_of_statements1
   WHEN exception2 THEN -- another handler for exception2
     sequence_of_statements2
   ...
   WHEN OTHERS THEN -- optional handler for all other errors
     sequence_of_statements3
END;


## Another example with the raise application
EXCEPTION
 WHEN TOO_MANY_ROWS THEN
    rollback to savepoint sales1;
    errlogs.handle(SQLCODE,SQLERRM,'Sales_records');
    raise_application_error(-20001,'Query return more rows
          than expected.');
 WHEN NO_DATA_FOUND THEN
    errlogs.handle(SQLCODE,SQLERRM,'customer_info');
    raise_application_error(-20002,
      'Data not available for this customer');
 WHEN OTHERS THEN
    errlogs.handle(SQLCODE,SQLERRM,'Oh No!');
    raise_application_error(-20003,'Unknow error details in log');
END;
```

Using DBMS Packages

System packages can be used in user packages as long as the user has permissions. SQL Server has several system procedures and extended procedures that are used in the same way as the Oracle packages.

We have already looked at DBMS_SCHEDULER and DBMS_STATS in previous chapters. The following are a few other packages you might consider using:

- DBMS_OUTPUT is useful for seeing what is running in a stored procedure. It sends output to the screen.

- DBMS_METADATA is useful for getting the definitions of the objects.

- DBMS_REDEFINITION offers a way to rebuild a table online.

- DBMS_SQL is used to create dynamic SQL in PL/SQL.

Here's an example of using the DBMS_METADATA package:

```
SQLPLUS> set long 200000 pages 0 lines 131
SQLPLUS> select dbms_metadata.get_ddl('TABLE','SALES') from dual;
  CREATE TABLE "MMDEV"."SALES"
   (    "SALES_ID" NUMBER NOT NULL ENABLE,
        "PROD_ID" NUMBER,
        "STATE_ID" NUMBER,
        "SALE_DATE" DATE,
        "CUSTOMER_ID" NUMBER,
        "REGION_ID" NUMBER,
        "AMOUNT" NUMBER,
         CONSTRAINT "SALES_PK" PRIMARY KEY ("SALES_ID")
  USING INDEX PCTFREE 10 INITRANS 2 MAXTRANS 255
  COMPUTE STATISTICS  STORAGE(INITIAL 65536 NEXT 1048576
  MINEXTENTS 1 MAXEXTENTS 2147483645  PCTINCREASE 0
  FREELISTS 1 FREELIST GROUPS 1 BUFFER_POOL DEFAULT)
  TABLESPACE "USERS"  ENABLE,
    CONSTRAINT "SALES_PRODUCT_FK1" FOREIGN KEY ("STATE_ID")
    REFERENCES "MMDEV"."STATES" ("STATE_ID") ENABLE     )
  PCTFREE 10 PCTUSED 40 INITRANS 1 MAXTRANS 255
  NOCOMPRESS LOGGING  STORAGE(INITIAL 65536 NEXT 1048576
  MINEXTENTS 1 MAXEXTENTS 2147483645 PCTINCREASE 0
  FREELISTS 1 FREELIST GROUPS 1 BUFFER_POOL DEFAULT)
  TABLESPACE "USERS"
```

There are many more useful packages, including several to help monitor databases and get details. Because of this access, permissions need to be granted carefully.

Summary

PL/SQL is an extremely useful database programming language, which you can use to develop robust applications as well as run maintenance tasks and monitor databases. This chapter presented examples of how to use PL/SQL to build packages, procedures, functions, and triggers. We looked at some of the ways to process data through cursors, the syntax for updates, and other differences between the database programming languages. As you can see, there is plenty of fun to have with PL/SQL!

The processing of statements is similar in both platforms, requiring transaction and points to commit or rollback. Oracle packages allow procedures and functions to be grouped together. Packages can be used for several of the transactions and processes that are written in PL/SQL. Error packages to be used with exception handling are useful to ensure consistent ways to log errors and raise application errors.

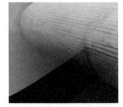

CHAPTER
10

High-Availability
Architecture

liminating single points of failure and decreasing planned or unplanned downtime make a database environment more highly available. Chapter 6 discussed failures and recovery options to help decrease some unplanned downtime. When planning high-availability solutions and failover capabilities, the failures also need to be considered. This includes not only unplanned outages, but planned ones as well.

Planning for unexpected failures is not an easy task, but with an understanding of database systems, you can have an idea of what might happen. So what are some of the unexpected failures? Hardware failures from servers, memory, storage, network, and other components of the server can be included in this area. Another area is data failures, which can come from changes and could be a result of another failure, such as storage.

Planned outages are a little more obvious. Patching, upgrading, and making configuration changes fall into this category. Some patches and upgrades can be applied with minimal (or no) downtime.

As a DBA, understanding the options that are available and the purposes that they serve to develop a high-availability system is critical. The options and components have pros and cons, whether you are working with an Oracle or a SQL Server system. You'll need to gather requirements, explore the available options, and then architect a solution for your particular database system. Usually, you'll use a combination of components and options to build a successful high-availability design and implementation.

In this chapter, you'll learn about the high-availability options available for an Oracle system. This will help you choose the most suitable solution for your database system.

Options for High Availability

Oracle and SQL Server have different components and features for ensuring a database system is highly available. Table 10-1 lists the main high-availability solutions on both platforms.

Oracle has a Maximum Availability Architecture (MAA), which includes a combination of the options with Data Guard and RAC environments.

Each of these solutions for high availability provides some failover capabilities. Combinations of these options provide even more protection. Depending on the environment and business needs, certain solutions will work better than others. Just as when you're planning the architecture for

SQL Server Options	Oracle Options
Clustering	Real Application Clusters (RAC)
Log shipping	Data Guard (primary and standby databases)
Replication	Streams/Advanced Replication
Database mirroring	Flashback

TABLE 10-1. *High-Availability Options in SQL Server and Oracle*

a SQL Server system, you need to decide which options are best suited for an Oracle environment that requires high availability.

Oracle RAC provides failover if a node has a failure and is no longer available. With RAC, you can apply rolling patches to eliminate downtime for patching. Additional nodes can be added to the cluster to provide more resources, since the nodes can use the CPUs and memory that are available on each server.

Take an Oracle RAC database and add a standby server with Data Guard, and now the system can be further protected by being in another location. Data Guard also provides a way to test an application rollout or database upgrade by using a snapshot of production database on the standby server.

ASM, when used in the RAC environment, is part of a high-availability solution. ASM manages the disks available to databases and instances on a server. It simplifies the management of Oracle database files and provides a clustered file system.

Replication and Oracle Streams might not be considered part of a high-availability solution for Oracle because RAC and Data Guard can provide the maximum availability without having to manage the replication processes. However, replication of data to other systems provides data availability.

Designing the high-availability database environment in Oracle may mean installing just a standby server with Data Guard or using the different options to combine RAC and an active standby server. Each of these components provides solutions for high availability. Including backups and flashback, as discussed in previous chapters, further reduces the risks for unplanned failures and planned maintenance.

In this chapter, we'll look at each of the high-availability options in detail.

Clustering with RAC

Clustering is ideal for two or more servers that have shared resources, such as disks. In case of a hardware failure on one server in the cluster, the other servers can pick up the workload until that server can be brought back up.

SQL Server clustering is dependent on operating system clustering. The file systems that SQL Server uses for the datafiles need to be on a clustered shared disk, and the software is installed on all of the nodes of the cluster. The SQL Server instance can be active on only one node (server) at a time, but there can be other SQL Server instances active on other nodes. Active/ passive clustering is when one SQL Server instance is installed on the cluster and running on one node, and the second node is just for failover. Active/ active clustering is when two or more nodes each has an active SQL Server instance, as illustrated in Figure 10-1. Either SQL Server instance can failover

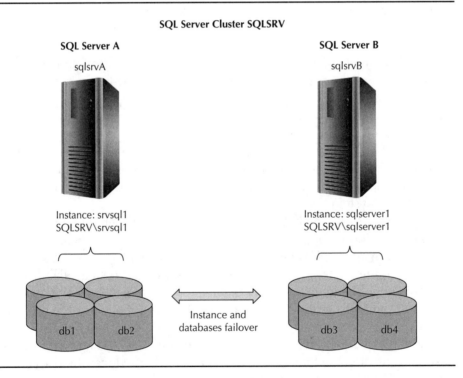

FIGURE 10-1. *SQL Server active/active clustering. The srvsql1 instance is primary and up on server A, and the sqlserver1 instance is primary and up on server B.*

to the other node, so you can have two instances running on one node. The client connection uses the cluster name with the instance name to connect to the server that currently has the instance active on it. The SQL Server instance is available on only one server at a time.

Oracle RAC servers share a disk and have the same Oracle database but with different instances running on each node, as shown in Figure 10-2. If one node fails, the connections failover to the other node. The instances do not failover, because the instances are just the processes on each server that access the same data. The Oracle database is available from any of the nodes in the cluster.

Comparing Figures 10-1 and 10-2, you can see that the whole instance and database must failover with the SQL Server cluster, but with Oracle, the

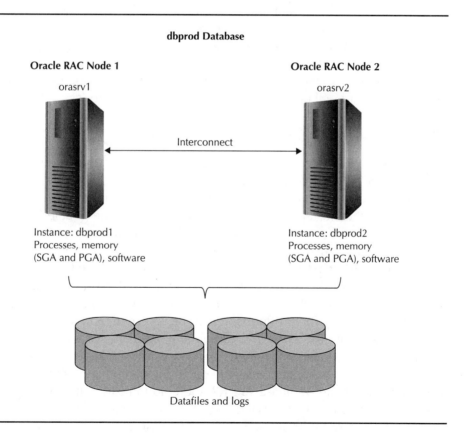

FIGURE 10-2. *Oracle RAC servers share the same database on all nodes.*

datafiles are what must be accessible from either node. The instances are the processes and memory on each of the nodes. It doesn't matter which of the nodes the user is connected to, because all of the tables and objects are available on all of the nodes for that database. There can also be multiple databases on a cluster.

The advantage of Oracle RAC is that the resources on both nodes are used by the database, and each node uses its own memory and CPU. Information is shared between nodes through the interconnect—the virtual private network. Parameters can be different on each node for the instance. This is because even though the application can connect to any of the nodes, certain applications or pieces, such as reporting, can be configured to connect to only one node, where the parameters for that instance can be configured specifically.

RAC provides high availability because of the failover of connections in the event of a hardware failure or server connection failure. The RAC environment also provides high availability for patching with rolling upgrades (Oracle Database 11*g*). And you can easily add a new server with memory and CPU to the cluster, make new connections to the new node, and the workload will be rebalanced between all of the nodes.

Configuring RAC

Configuring an RAC environment starts off similar to setting up a cluster of servers in a SQL Server environment. The servers need to have a private network between the machines and a set of disks that can be seen by all of the servers in the cluster. The disks will need space for the Oracle Cluster Registry (OCR) and voting disk, just as a SQL Server cluster needs a quorum disk for the cluster membership. After the network configuration and disk allocation, the Oracle Clusterware software can be installed. If the Clusterware software can see both nodes, then the database installation is available for an RAC database. The software will install on the available nodes in the cluster. The cluster name can be specified, and the node names will be visible, with each private and public IP address that is configured.

The Cluster Verification Utility (CVU) assists in the Clusterware setup and preinstallation tasks, including the operating system and network settings. With Oracle Database 11*g* R2, the Grid Infrastructure software has the installation for Clusterware and ASM. As mentioned in Chapter 3, Clusterware and ASM should be installed in a different Oracle home directory than the database, as shown in Figure 10-3.

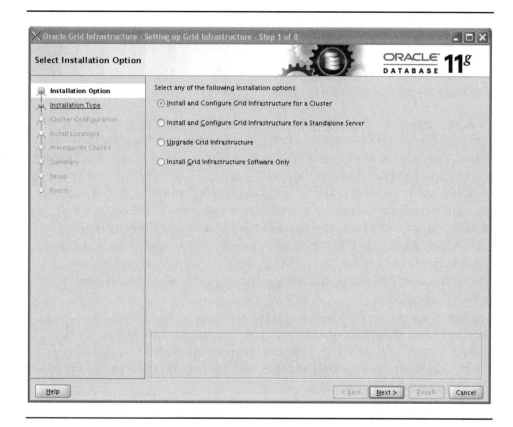

FIGURE 10-3. *Oracle installation of Grid Infrastructure components*

A few of the preinstallation steps require special consideration. The network configurations are key because you need a public IP and a private IP, for the interconnect and virtual IP (VIP). The network adapters need to be configured the same on all of the nodes of the clusters, so `eth0` should be set to public network on all of the nodes, and `eth1` set to the private network. For Linux environments, you can look at the /etc/hosts file to see the IP addresses and configurations.

```
cat /etc/hosts
#eth0 -- Public Network
orarac1.domain1.com                    orarac1
orarac2.domain1.com                    orarac2
```

```
#eth1 - Private / Interconnect Network
10.0.0.1          orarac1priv.domain1.com          orarac1priv
10.0.0.2          orarac2priv.domain1.com          orarac2priv
#VIPs - Virtual Network
192.168.10.104    orarac1vip.domain1.com           orarac1vip
192.168.10.105    orarac2vip.domain1.com           orarac2vip
```

CVU helps with these steps to make sure that everything is configured and that all of the IPs are available. If you attempt to continue the installation without addressing the failures or warnings from CVU, that is just asking for trouble and headaches down the line.

Once the network IPs, kernel parameters, and operating system settings are configured, and storage is available to the servers in the cluster, the installation walks through the setup of the Clusterware software. With Oracle Database 11g, you can choose to have the voting disk and OCR use ASM instead of just a shared file system. An advanced installation of Clusterware provides opportunities to configure the storage and additional networking options.

After Clusterware is installed and the databases are created, the databases and cluster services need to be monitored, and stopped and started as needed. Use the cluster and service commands to check the status, and start and stop the instances and listeners on each node. Here are some examples:

```
>crsctl check crs
Cluster Synchronization Services appears healthy
Cluster Ready Services appears healthy
Event Manager appears healthy
> ## Check nodes in the cluster
> crsctl check cluster
orasrv1        ONLINE
orasrv2        ONLINE
> ## Check the database instances
> srvctl status database -d oradb
Instance oradb1 is running on node orasrvdb01
Instance oradb2 is running on node orasrvdb02
> ## Start database or instance
> srvctl start service -d ORADB
> srvctl start instance -d ORADB -i ORADB1
> ## Stop database or instance
> srvctl stop database -d ORADB
> srvctl stop instance -d ORADB -i ORADB1
```

```
> ## Start and stop listener
> srvctl (stop/start) listener -n orasrvdb01
> ## See additional commands and details
> srvctl -h
> ## Or use the command and -h
> srvctl status asm -h
Usage: srvctl status asm -n <node_name>
    -n <node>            Node name
```

Using the Clusterware commands, you can put together a script to monitor the health of the cluster and validate that all of the pieces are up and available.

```
>export CRS_HOME=/u01/oracle/product/11.2.0/grid
> $CRS_HOME/bin/cluvfy comp clu
Verifying cluster integrity
Checking cluster integrity...
Cluster integrity check passed
Verification of cluster integrity was successful.
> $CRS_HOME/bin/ocrcheck
Status of Oracle Cluster Registry is as follows :
         Version                 :         2
         Total space (kbytes)    :    200560
         Used space (kbytes)     :      5136
         Available space (kbytes) :    195424
         ID                      : 852915171
         Device/File Name        : /dev/dbgroup/ocr1
                        Device/File integrity check succeeded
         Device/File Name        : /dev/dbgroup/ocr2
                        Device/File integrity check succeeded
         Cluster registry integrity check succeeded
##  Use to search for failures and output can go to log file
##  for creating a monitoring script
> $CRS_HOME/bin/ocrcheck | grep failed >> /u01/logs/ocrcheck.log
## nothing returned is a good thing
> $CRS_HOME/bin/crs_stat -t
Name            Type         Target    State    Host
-----------------------------------------------------------
ora....b1.inst application   ONLINE    ONLINE   svr-...db01
ora....b2.inst application   ONLINE    ONLINE   svr-...db02
ora.oradb.db   application   ONLINE    ONLINE   svr-...db01
ora....SM1.asm application   ONLINE    ONLINE   svr-...db01
ora....01.lsnr application   ONLINE    ONLINE   svr-...db01
ora....01.lsnr application   ONLINE    ONLINE   svr-...db01
ora....b01.gsd application   ONLINE    ONLINE   svr-...db01
```

```
ora....b01.ons application     ONLINE     ONLINE     svr-...db01
ora....b01.vip application     ONLINE     ONLINE     svr-...db01
ora....SM2.asm application     ONLINE     ONLINE     svr-...db02
ora....02.lsnr application     ONLINE     ONLINE     svr-...db02
ora....02.lsnr application     ONLINE     ONLINE     svr-...db02
ora....b02.gsd application     ONLINE     ONLINE     svr-...db02
ora....b02.ons application     ONLINE     ONLINE     svr-...db02
ora....b02.vip application     ONLINE     ONLINE     svr-...db02
## with crs_stat -t grep for OFFLINE for issues
> $CRS_HOME/bin/crsctl check crs
CSS appears healthy
CRS appears healthy
EVM appears healthy
## search for where it is not healthy
> $CRS_HOME/bin/crsctl check crs |grep -v healthy >> crsctlchk.log
```

Oracle RAC databases can also be managed with OEM. The home page of OEM lists the cluster database, and shutdown and startup options are available when you are logged in as SYSDBA. The instances on all of the nodes are listed with their status, showing any alerts at the instance level. If ASM instances are used, these will also be listed with each instance.

Testing RAC

Of course, you'll want to test the clustering before implementing it in a production environment. With SQL Server clustering, you test that the database failover from one node to another node is successful, validate that the disk is available, and check that the services start automatically with failover. You create a checklist and test plan to verify that the cluster is working properly.

With Oracle RAC, you can test the failover and confirm that the setup and configuration are working properly. Failover testing includes the client, network, and storage connections from both servers.

Simply rebooting the servers is first on the checklist. Make sure that the Clusterware software is still configured as needed and settings are persistent (the server did not revert to older settings). You can run CVU at any time to verify the cluster that includes the networking settings.

Another test is to pull the interconnect so that servers do not have their private network. Then validate that one of the nodes accepts the new connections, and that the failover of connections to the surviving node runs the queries as it should.

Next, test the connections from the application and from utilities like SQL*Plus. This is not just validating that the users can connect, but also checking what happens if a server goes down. Connect to the database through the different applications, and then actually shut down a server. The queries may take a little longer, as they transfer over. To verify, look at the sessions running on both nodes before the shutdown to confirm that there are connections to the node, and then look at the sessions on the node that is still running. If connections do not failover, double-check the tnsnames.ora file and connection strings to make sure that failover mode is in the string, as well as that the service name and virtual hostname are being used.

The testing of backups and restores in an RAC environment is basically the same as on a stand-alone server, and should be included as part of these tests.

Setting Up Client Failover

Having the capability to failover to another node if some part of a server or service failed on one node is a big reason to set up clustering of servers. Being able to handle the failover in the code that is running against the database to make the failover more transparent to clients is valuable from the user perspective. The Oracle RAC environment has different possibilities for failing over queries running against the database at the point of failure. Also, notifications from these events can be used by applications and PL/SQL to make failover seamless for the user.

These connections are through Fast Application Notification (FAN) and Fast Connection Failover (FCF). FAN notifies applications that instances are up or down. If an instance is not available, the application can rerun a transaction and handle this type of error. FCF makes the connection failover possible by being able to connect to whatever instance is available. A session, that has connected to an instance and is running a `SELECT` statement, will failover automatically and continue to run the `SELECT` statement on another instance. The error handling of transactions, such as update, insert and delete, will need to failover by using these configurations, and will have to pass the needed information about the transaction to the available instances. There is more to be handled by the application code to failover processes and transactions, but the information in the FAN can be by the application to make it RAC-aware.

Other failovers, such as SELECT statements, can be taken care of through the connection information, listeners, and tnsnames.ora files for a Transparent Application Failover (TAF) configuration. Here is an example of any entry in the tnsnames.ora file:

```
## Example tnsnames.ora entryPROD =
  (DESCRIPTION =
    (FAILOVER = ON)
    (LOAD_BALANCE = YES)
    (ADDRESS_LIST =
      (ADDRESS = (PROTOCOL = TCP)(HOST = srvora01-vip)
        (PORT = 1521))
      (ADDRESS = (PROTOCOL = TCP)(HOST = srvora02-vip)
        (PORT = 1521)))
    (CONNECT_DATA =
      (SERVICE_NAME = PROD)
      (SERVER = DEDICATED)
      (failover_mode =
        (type = select)
        (method = basic)
      )
    )
  )
```

And here is an example JDBC connection string:

```
jdbc:oracle:thin:(DESCRIPTION=(FAILOVER=ON)(ADDRESS_LIST=
(LOAD_BALANCE=ON)(ADDRESS=(PROTOCOL=TCP)(HOST=srvora01-vip)
(PORT=1521))(ADDRESS=(PROTOCOL=TCP)(HOST=srvora02-vip)
(PORT=1521)))(CONNECT_DATA=(SERVICE_NAME=PROD))
(FAILOVER_MODE=(TYPE=SESSION)(METHOD=BASIC)(RETRIES=180)
(DELAY =5)))
```

The TYPE setting for the TAF configuration allows for different types of failover:

■ SESSION creates a new session automatically but doesn't restart the SELECT statement in the new session.

■ SELECT fails over to an available instance and will continue to fetch the data and return the SELECT query.

■ NONE prevents the statement and connection from going over to the other node (no failover will happen).

With TAF, the RAC environment can eliminate single points of failure. Applications can use OCI packages to manage the transactions (otherwise, transactions are rolled back and regular PL/SQL would need to be restarted or rolled back because the session information is not persistent and variable settings are lost). This is also why FAN can provide the notifications about failover and restart the procedure with the needed information.

Setting Up RAC Listeners

Along with the client setup for failover, the listener needs to be set up on the server. This involves setting the parameter LOCAL_LISTENER on the database needs and configuring the local listener in the tnsnames.ora file on the server side.

The tnsnames.ora entry looks like this:

```
## tnsnames.ora entry for local listener
LISTENER_NODE1 =
    (ADDRESS_LIST =
        (ADDRESS = (PROTPCOL = TCP)(HOST = orasvr1-vip)(PORT = 1521))
    )
```

And here is how you set the LOCAL_LISTENER parameter:

```
## set the local_listener parameter
SQLPLUS> alter system set LOCAL_LISTENER='LISTENER_NODE1'
        scope=both  sid='oradb01';
## Same for other nodes
LISTENER_NODE2 =
    (ADDRESS_LIST =
        (ADDRESS = (PROTPCOL = TCP)(HOST = orasvr2-vip)(PORT = 1521))
    )
SQLPLUS> alter system set LOCAL_LISTENER='LISTENER_NODE2'
        scope=both  sid='oradb02';
```

The tnsnames.ora file on the client looks for the listener on the server and the configurations for the local listener. If the listener is running, the connections can be made, allowing for failover. If the listener is not running on a node, that node is considered unavailable to the client at that time.

Patching RAC

RAC environments also provide failover and increased uptime for planned maintenance as well as unplanned failures. With RAC environments, there are three ways to apply patches to all of the nodes of the cluster:

- Patching RAC like a single-instance database. All of the instances and listeners will be down. Patching starts with the local node and continues with all the other nodes.

- Patching RAC with minimum downtime. This method applies the patches to the local node, requests a subset of nodes to be patched first, and then applies the patches to other nodes. The downtime happens when the second subset is shut down for patching and the initial nodes are brought back online with the new patches.

- Patching RAC with the rolling method. The patches are applied to one a node at time, so that at least one node in the cluster is available while the patching is rolling through the environment. There is no downtime with this method. The node can be brought up again after being patched while the other nodes are still up and available. Then the next node is patched.

Not all patches are available as rolling patches. The patch will indicate if it can be applied with this method. The Oracle patching method is to use OPATCH to apply the patches to Oracle homes. Using OPATCH, you can verify if the patch is a rolling patch.

```
>export PATH=$ORACLE_HOME/OPatch:$PATH
>opatch query -all <patch_location> | grep rolling
## statement will return the line with true or false
Patch is a rolling patch: true
```

Deploying RAC

Adding another node to a cluster is an easy way to provide more resources to the RAC database. Using Oracle Grid Control or OEM, you can add a node with the same configuration and installation as the other nodes. Then the nodes are available for client connections.

An option pack is available for provisioning new Oracle servers. If you have several servers to manage or need to upgrade and patch a very large set of servers, these tools are useful for handling basic configuration and setup. They can use a golden copy or a template to verify the hardware installation, and then configure the operating system and database, which can be a stand-alone database server or Oracle Clusterware with an RAC database.

Configuring and Monitoring RAC Instances

In a SQL Server clustering environment, the same instance is configured with the server settings, and connections are being made only to that instance. The SQL Server instance can failover to another node, but those settings go with the instance as it fails over.

With an Oracle RAC environment, connections failover, and multiple instances are involved. There might even be multiple logs and trace files, depending on how the dump destination is configured for the instance. Each instance can have its own set of parameters that are different from those on the other instances in the database. For example, batch jobs, reporting, and backups can be set to go to one instance over another, but still have the ability to failover the connections if that node is not available. In the connection string, you might set FAILOVER=ON but LOAD_BALANCE=OFF to handle the connections to one instance.

The spfile and init.ora files can be shared by all of the instances in the RAC database, so the parameters will have a prefix of the instance SID if they are set for that instance. The view to see all of the parameters is gv$parameter, instead of v$parameter. Let's look at both of these views.

```
SQL> desc v$parameter
Name                              Null?     Type
--------------------------------  --------  ----------------
  NUM                                       NUMBER
  NAME                                      VARCHAR2(80)
  TYPE                                      NUMBER
  VALUE                                     VARCHAR2(512)
  DISPLAY_VALUE                             VARCHAR2(512)
  ISDEFAULT                                 VARCHAR2(9)
  ISSES_MODIFIABLE                          VARCHAR2(5)
  ISSYS_MODIFIABLE                          VARCHAR2(9)
  ISINSTANCE_MODIFIABLE                     VARCHAR2(5)
  ISMODIFIED                                VARCHAR2(10)
```

```
ISADJUSTED                              VARCHAR2(5)
ISDEPRECATED                            VARCHAR2(5)
DESCRIPTION                             VARCHAR2(255)
UPDATE_COMMENT                          VARCHAR2(255)
HASH                                    NUMBER

SQL> desc gv$parameter
Name                          Null?     Type
----------------------------- -------   ----------------
INST_ID                                 NUMBER
NUM                                     NUMBER
NAME                                    VARCHAR2(80)
TYPE                                    NUMBER
VALUE                                   VARCHAR2(512)
DISPLAY_VALUE                           VARCHAR2(512)
ISDEFAULT                               VARCHAR2(9)
ISSES_MODIFIABLE                        VARCHAR2(5)
ISSYS_MODIFIABLE                        VARCHAR2(9)
ISINSTANCE_MODIFIABLE                   VARCHAR2(5)
ISMODIFIED                              VARCHAR2(10)
ISADJUSTED                              VARCHAR2(5)
ISDEPRECATED                            VARCHAR2(5)
DESCRIPTION                             VARCHAR2(255)
UPDATE_COMMENT                          VARCHAR2(255)
HASH                                    NUMBER
```

Did you notice the difference? The global views have the `inst_id` to indicate for which instance the parameter is set, and join this with the `gv$instance` table to get the SID for the instance. Without the `gv$` views, the information would need to be gathered one node at a time, because `v$` views return the values for only that current instance. Here's an example:

```
SQLPLUS> select i.instance_name, p.name, p.value
  2   from gv$instance i , gv$parameter p
  3   where i.inst_id = p.inst_id
  4   and p.name in ('db_cache_size','processes','optimizer_mode');
INSTANCE_NAME    NAME                       VALUE
--------------   -----------------------    -------------------
db01             optimizer_mode             ALL_ROWS
db01             db_cache_size              8000M
db01             processes                  300
db02             optimizer_mode             ALL_ROWS
db02             db_cache_size              6500M
db02             processes                  300
```

The parameters that can be adjusted for an instance and are dynamic will need to be qualified with the SID. If you want to set it for all of the instances, you can use a wildcard.

```
SQLPLUS> alter system set db_cache_size = 8000M sid='db01';
System altered.
## Set all of the instances the same using a wildcard
SQLPLUS> alter system set db_cache_size = 8000M sid='*';
## If sid is not set for the current instance an error
## will be thrown
SQLPLUS> alter system set db_cache_size = 8000M;
alter system set db_cache_size = 8000M
*
ERROR at line 1:
ORA-32018: parameter cannot be modified in memory on
another instance
```

The v$ views mentioned in Chapter 8 are available as global views with the instance IDs to let you see what is happening on each of the instances collectively. The session information is in gv$session, and waits are in gv$session_waits.

Using the global views makes it easier to see all of the processes running across the nodes. But monitoring RAC performance is basically the same as checking performance on a single instance. You can verify what is running and check that the statistics are up to date. The same system information is available. Troubleshooting a query on an RAC database is the same as looking at the performance of any query on a single database—you check for the usual suspects.

The interconnect can play a role in the performance, as memory blocks are swapped between the nodes. Oracle Database 11*g* has improved the Cache Fusion protocols to be more workload-aware to help reduce the messaging for read operations and improve performance.

Primary and Standby Databases

SQL Server has an option to do log shipping to another database server. The logs are then applied to the database that is in recovery mode. The failover does not happen automatically, but the database is kept current by applying the recent transactions. If there is a failure on the primary server, the database on the secondary server can have the latest possible log applied, and then be taken out of recovery mode for regular use by connections.

Oracle offers the option of a standby database with Oracle Data Guard as another type of failover. The primary and secondary database servers do not share any of the database files or disk. They can even be servers located in completely different data centers, which offers a disaster recovery option. The redo logs from the primary server are transported over to the secondary server depending on the protection mode, and then they are applied to the database on the secondary server.

Oracle Data Guard has different protection modes based on the data loss and downtime tolerance:

- Maximum Protection provides for zero data loss, but the transactions must be applied synchronous to both the primary and secondary database servers. If there are issues applying the logs to the secondary server, the primary server will wait for the transaction to be completed on both servers to commit the change.

- Maximum Availability has zero data loss as the goal, but if there is a connectivity issue or the transaction cannot be applied to the secondary server, the primary server will not wait. The primary server still has a record of what has been applied for verification, and the standby database might fall slightly behind, but it is more critical to have the primary database available.

- Maximum Performance has the potential for minimal data loss. The transport of the logs is done asynchronously, and there is no checking back with the primary server about applying the logs and verifying the change has been completed.

Using Active Standby Databases

As noted, the physical standby database is a copy of the primary database and is kept in sync with the primary database. With Oracle Database 11g, the standby database can also be an active database, which remains open for reading while the database is still being synchronized with the primary. This is the Active Data Guard option.

Another option that allows for use of the secondary server is a logical standby database. With this type of standby database, the changes are applied by SQL statements that are converted from the redo logs. This allows for some of the structures of the data to vary from the primary database, and the changes can still be applied through the SQL statements.

A third standby database option is a snapshot database configuration. The standby database can be converted to a read-write snapshot. It continues to receive the redo information from the primary database, but does not apply the changes until converted back to being only a standby database. While in read-write mode, the snapshot standby database can be used to test various changes, such as new application rollout, patches, or data changes. Then the snapshot is set back to before the changes were made, and the redo log will be applied. Having a copy of the production database for testing like this is extremely valuable for successful rollouts of changes.

The standby database can also serve as a copy for disaster recovery purposes, because it can be at a different site than the primary database, as illustrated in Figure 10-4. With this setup, the disaster recovery plan is very simple: connect to the standby database and make it the primary database. The copies of the databases can also be used to offload work such as backups and read-only reporting. This takes advantage of the standby database, which would otherwise sit idle unless the primary database failed.

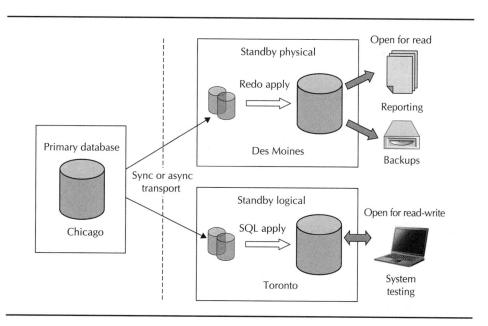

FIGURE 10-4. *Data Guard server design*

Setting Up a Standby Database

An existing database can be configured to have a standby database. The first step is to install the Oracle software on the standby server. The database already exists on the primary server. The primary database will need some configuration with standby logs and parameters. Connections to the secondary database can be set up, and then using RMAN, the initial copy of the database can be set up on the standby server.

On the primary database, the following needs to be done:

```
SQLPLUS> alter database force logging;
Database altered.
## Create the standby log files. They need to be the
## same size or larger than the primary database

SQLPLUS> alter database add standby logfile
'/u01/oracle/db01/stby01.log' size 50M;
Database altered.
SQLPLUS> alter database add standby logfile
'/u01/oracle/db01/stby02.log' size 50M;
Database altered.
  . . .
## Continue creating the log files. One more log group
## than on the primary is recommended

## Parameters
SQLPLUS> show parameter db_name
NAME                          TYPE          VALUE
------------------------- ----------- ---------
db_name                       string        DB01
## Name stays the same
SQLPLUS> show parameter db_unique_name
NAME                          TYPE          VALUE
------------------------- ----------- --------------
db_unique_name                string        DB01
## Standby and Primary will need unique names
## Names do not change even if roles switch

SQLPLUS> alter system set
LOG_ARCHIVE_CONFIG='DG_CONFIG=(db01,dbstby01)'
System altered.
SQLPLUS> alter system set log_archive_dest_2=
'service=dbstby01 async valid_for=(online_logfile,
primary_role) db_unique_name=dbstby01';
```

```
System altered.
## The standby database server should already have the
## software and the needed directories for the database
## Create a parameter file for the standby with just the DB_NAME
> cat initdbstby01.ora
DB_NAME=dbstby01
> export ORACLE_SID=dbstby01
SQLPLUS> startup nomount pfile=$ORACLE_HOME/dbs/initdbstby01.ora
ORACLE instance started.
. . .
SQLPLUS> exit
## To primary database run RMAN to copy database
RMAN> connect target
connected to target database: DB01 (DBID=1382128337)
RMAN> connect auxiliary sysdbstby01
connected to auxiliary database: DBSTBY01 (not mounted)
RMAN> run {
allocate channel disk1 type disk;
allocate auxiliary channel disk2 type disk;
duplicate target database for standby from active database
spfile parameter_value_convert 'db01','dbstby01'
set db_unique_name='dbstby01'
set db_file_name_convert='/db01/','/dbstby01/'
set control_files='/u01/oracle/oradata/dbstby01.ctl'
set fal_client='dbstby01'
set fal_server='db01'
set standby_file_management='AUTO'
set log_archive_config='dg_config=(db01,dbstby01)'
set log_archive_dest_1='service=db01 ASYNC valid_for=
(ONLINE_LOGFILE,PRIMARY_ROLE) db_unique_name=db01';
}
. . .
## Can test the standby by switching the log file on the primary
> export ORACLE_SID=DB01
SQLPLUS> alter system switch logfile;
System altered.
```

In summary, the basic steps are as follows:

1. Install the software on the standby server.

2. Configure the parameters on the primary server.

3. Make the connections by updating tnsnames.ora and listener.

4. Use RMAN to copy the database.

SQL Server has a manual process for the management of failover for log shipping. The Oracle Data Guard failover can be configured to occur automatically. You can use the Data Guard broker and management tools to set up the automatic failover and manage the standby servers. The Data Guard broker needs to be running on both the primary and standby server. A listener entry for the Data Guard broker on the primary and standby servers will help with failover and avoiding TNS errors.

```
## Parameter for starting the broker
SQLPLUS> alter system set DG_BROKER_START=TRUE scope=both;
System altered.
## Example listener entry
(SID_LIST =
  (SID_DESC =
    (GLOBAL_DBNAME = db01_dgmgrl)
    (ORACLE_HOME = /u01/oracle/11.2.0/db_1)
    (SID_NAME = db01)
  )
. . .
)
```

Using the Data Guard broker is similar to starting SQL*Plus from the command line. Enter dgmgrl to start the utility and then issue commands.

```
## Create a broker configuration
> dgmgrl
DGMGRL for Linux: Version 11.2.0.1.0 - 64bit Production
Copyright (c) 2000, 2009, Oracle. All rights reserved.
Welcome to DGMGRL, type "help" for information.
DGMGRL> create configuration 'DG_DB01'
AS PRIMARY DATABASE is 'db01'
CONNECT IDENTIFIER is 'db01';
Configuration "DG_DB01" created with primary database "db01"
DGMGRL> add database 'dbstby01'
AS CONNECT IDENTIFIER is 'dbstby01';
Database "dbstby01" added.
DGMGRL> enable configuration
Enabled.
DGMGRL> show configuration
```

```
Configuration
  Name:               DG_DB01
  Enabled:            YES
  Protection Mode:    MaxAvailability
  Databases:
      db01 - Primary database
      dbstby01 - Physical standby database
Fast-Start Failover: DISABLED
Current status for "DG_DB01': SUCCESS
```

Other utility commands can be used to do a switchover, which changes the roles of the servers between primary and standby, or failover, which will fail the primary over to the standby database.

The default configuration for `Fast-Start Failover` is disabled. When it is enabled, it can use triggering events to implement the failover to the standby server. Events include connection loss, instance crash, a shutdown abort on the primary, and different database health checks such as loss of a datafile. With these events, you can set thresholds to have more control over when the failover occurs. This lets you avoid situations where a small hiccup in the connection or a busy server that doesn't allow a quick check will cause the system to failover.

The Data Guard configurations can be modified to automate the failover for certain thresholds. If there is more than one standby database, the `FastStartFailoverTarget` property should be set so that the primary and standby database reference each other.

```
DGMGRL> edit database DB01 set property FastStartFailoverTarget =
   'dbstby01';
DGMGRL> edit database DBSTBY01 set property
   FastStartFailoverTarget = 'db01';
DGMGRL> edit configuration set property
   FastStartFailoverThreshold = '180';
```

NOTE
With automatic failover, the DBA can be assured of continuing service without having to log in. However, the DBA may need to be concerned about unnecessary failovers.

Maximum Availability Architecture includes a combination of these solutions, as shown in Figure 10-5. The Oracle RAC database can be a primary and a standby server. When the Maximum Protection option is chosen for the Data Guard configuration, having RAC set up on the standby database will reduce the risk for the logs to be applied. Figure 10-5 shows the architecture of the Oracle RAC database with the Data Guard standby database.

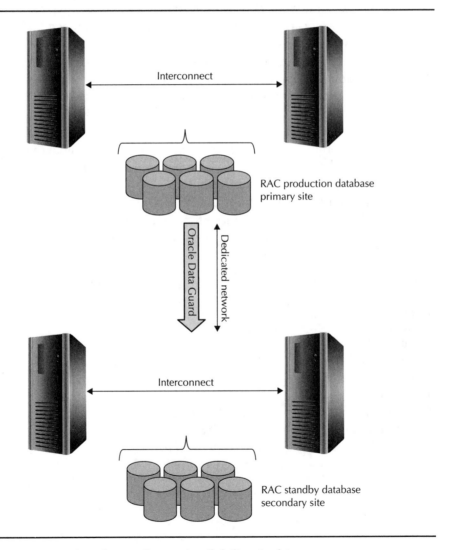

FIGURE 10-5. *Oracle Maximum Availability Architecture*

ASM in an RAC Environment

We have discussed how it is useful to have the ASM instance available for the disks of the database, but have not yet looked into the details about how to manage the instance. In the Oracle RAC environment, there needs to be an ASM instance for every node in the cluster, but one ASM instance can support multiple instances on that node.

Managing ASM Disk Groups

The ASM disk groups serve as containers for consolidating databases and file systems to be able to use the storage more efficiently and even share between databases. The ASM Configuration Assistant (ASMCA) helps you create and manage disk groups. As shown in Figure 10-6, new disks can be added to the disk group here, and attributes of the disk group can be edited. Other ASMCA options allow you to manage the volumes and file system in a clustered environment.

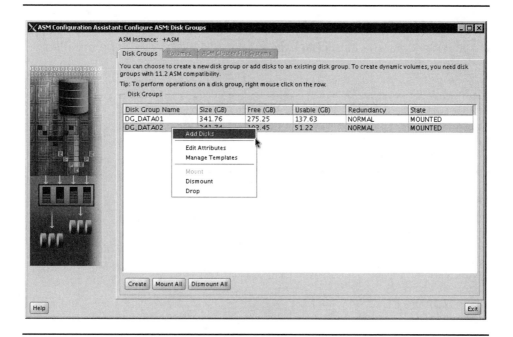

FIGURE 10-6.   *Using ASMCA*

ASM Configuration Parameters

The ASM instance is really a process and a bit of memory. Some parameters go into the spfile for configuration of this instance. These parameters provide the details about the type of instance and where the disks are located for creating the disk groups.

- INSTANCE_TYPE   Set to ASM (default is RDBMS)

- ASM_DISKGROUPS   Lists the disk groups that should be mounted

- ASM_DISKSTRING   A value that indicates where to discover the disks that are available to add to a disk group

- ASM_POWER_LIMIT   Maximum power for rebalancing operation, a value between 1 and 11 (higher number for faster rebalancing)

ASMLib is the support library for ASM. It is used for initialize the disk for usage with ASM. The Linux package for the ASMLib needs to be installed for usage.

```
>rpm -Uvh oracleasm-2.6.18-8.el5-2.0.4-1.el5.i686.rpm \
oracleasm-support-2.0.4-1.el5.i386.rpm \
oracleasmlib-2.0.3-1.el5.i386.rpm
## Configure ASMLib
>/etc/init.d/oracleasm configure
Configuring the Oracle ASM library driver.
. . .
## Create disks
>/etc/init.d/oracleasm createdisk ORADATA01 /dev/sda1
Marking disk "/dev/sda1" as an ASM disk:
## To see the disks that were created
>/etc/init.d/oracleasm listdisks
ORADATA01
ORADATA02
ORADATA03
ORADATA04
```

The information stored in the ASM instance is the metadata about the disks, disk groups, names, and directories. The Oracle database creates the data in the files when the disk groups are allocated to a database. The ASMCMD command-line utility can help you manage the files. It provides a quick way to find out information about what the ASM instance is managing and where the database files are located. You can take backups, make copies, and move files. ASMCMD commands are similar to file commands in a Linux environment. Here are some examples of using ASMCMD:

```
>asmcmd
ASMCMD> ls -l
State      Type     Rebal   Name
MOUNTED    NORMAL   N       DG_DATA01/
MOUNTED    NORMAL   N       DG_DATA02/
ASMCMD> cd DG_DATA01
ASMCMD> ls -l
Type Redund  Striped  Time           Sys   Name
                                     Y     ASM/
                                     Y     DADEV/
                                     Y     DSDEV/
                                     Y     SQLTEST/
ASMCMD> cd DADEV
ASMCMD> ls -l
Type        Redund  Striped  Time    Sys   Name
                                     Y     DATAFILE/
                                     Y     PARAMETERFILE/
                                     Y     TEMPFILE/
                                     N     spfileDADEV.ora =>
+DG_DATA01/DADEV/PARAMETERFILE/spfile.269.714035663

## Search for the spfile
ASMCMD> find / spfile*
+DG_DATA01/DADEV/PARAMETERFILE/spfile.269.714035663
+DG_DATA01/DADEV/spfileDADEV.ora
## Check SPACE
ASMCMD> du
Used_MB       Mirror_used_MB
  23798              47605
## Back up a disk group
ASMCMD> md_backup /bkup/dg1_backup -G 'DG_DATA01'
## The -G parameter is optional; if none chosen, it will
## back up all of the disk groups
## See all connected instances
ASMCMD> lsct
```

```
ASMCMD> lsct
DB_Name   Status      Compatible_version   Instance_Name Disk_Group
+ASM      CONNECTED        11.2.0.1.0           +ASM         DG_DATA01
DADEV     CONNECTED        11.2.0.1.0           DADEV        DG_DATA02
DBDEV     CONNECTED        11.2.0.1.0           DBDEV        DG_DATA02
SQLTEST   CONNECTED        11.2.0.1.0           SQLTEST      DG_DATA01
```

These simple commands demonstrate the following:

- Find out how much space is available on one of the disk groups

- Find out which instances are connected to which disk groups

- Find a file

- Execute a backup of one disk group

With ASM, even though everything is laid out in the directories of the disk groups, creating tablespaces is very simple. You just use a CREATE TABLE statement with a disk group and a size.

```
>export ORACLE_SID=DADEV
>sqlplus
SQLPLUS> create tablespace USER_DATA
    datafile '+DG_DATA01' size 2048M;
Tablespace created.
```

Then you have disk space available for users to start filling up with their tables, objects, and whatever data they need to store.

As you have come to expect, OEM also offers a way to manage the ASM disk groups and files. Figure 10-7 shows the OEM display of the disk groups of the ASM instance. In OEM, the ASM instance is available from any of the database instances that are using the ASM instance. You can mount the disk groups through this OEM view.

You can see information about the disks, including the status, the type of redundancy that the disk is configured for, and the space that is allocated and used. You can also do some health checks and rebalance the disks. Selecting one of the disk groups will drill down into a view of the files on the disks, as shown in Figure 10-8. If you find it difficult to work with the file names with all of those numbers, you can create an alias or rename files.

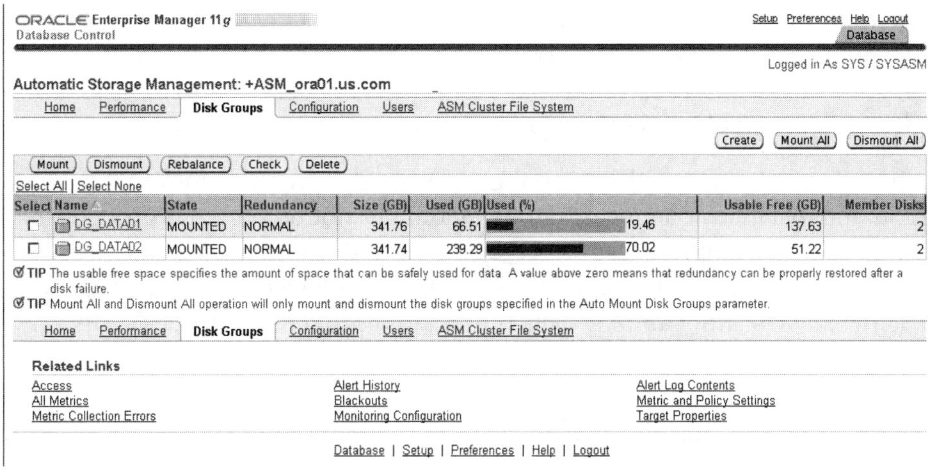

FIGURE 10-7. *OEM view of ASM disk groups*

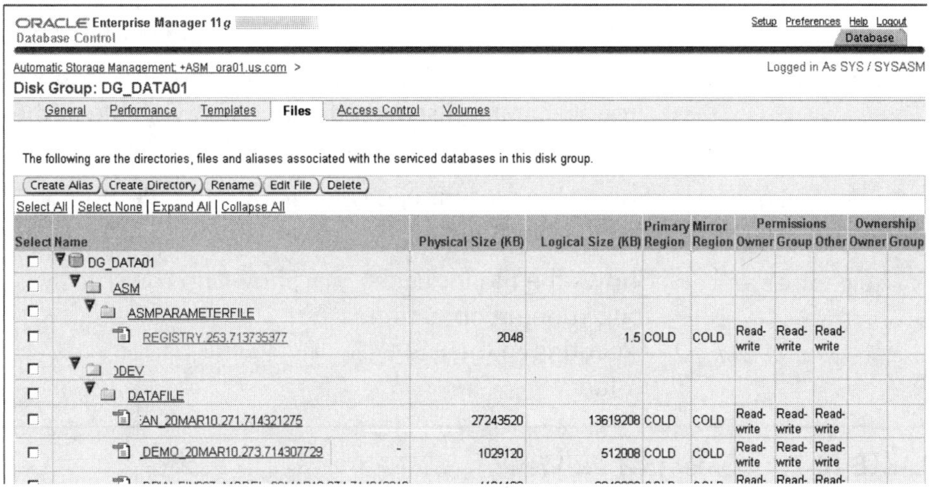

FIGURE 10-8. *OEM view of files in a disk group*

Deleting here might be useful for backups, but definitely not something you would want to do with database files. These are the options that are available with the ASMCMD utility.

Viewing ASM Information

When connected to the ASM instance, some v$ views give information about the instances connected, disks that might not be part of a disk group, and files. For example, the v$asm_disk view shows the disks that are being used by that database instance, and when viewed from the ASM instance, it will show all of the disks that are discovered. Table 10-2 lists some of the ASM v$ views.

View	Logged in to ASM Instance	Logged in to Database Instance
v$asm_client	Shows a row for each database instance using ASM	Shows a row for the ASM instance for the database
v$asm_disk	Shows all of the disks that are discovered	Shows only the disks in the disk groups being used by this instance
v$asm_diskgroup	Shows all of the disk groups that are discovered	Shows the disk groups that are available in the ASM
v$asm_file	Shows the files for each disk group mounted	Shows the files for the instance
v$asm_operation	Shows the file for each long-running operation executing in the ASM instance	Shows no rows

TABLE 10-2. *Some ASM v$ Views*

Here are some examples of using SQL*Plus to take a look at the views in ASM, making sure the environment is set up to log in:

```
>export ORACLE_SID= +ASM
>export ORACLE_HOME=/u01/oracle/11.2.0/grid
SQLPLUS> select name, state, total_mb from v$asm_disgroup;
NAME                               STATE        TOTAL_MB
---------------------------------- ------------ ----------
DG_DATA01                          MOUNTED        349962
DG_DATA02                          MOUNTED        349942
SQLPLUS> select name from v$asm_disk;
NAME
----------------------------------
ORADATA01
ORADATA02
ORADATA03
ORADATA04
SQLPLUS> select instance_name, db_name, status
from v$ASM_CLIENT;
SQL> select group_number, instance_name, db_name, status
from  v$ASM_CLIENT;
GROUP_NUMBER   INSTANCE_NAME    DB_NAME         STATUS
-------------- ---------------- --------------- ---------
1              DBDEV            DBDEV           CONNECTED
2              DB01             DB01            CONNECTED
1              +ASM             +ASM            CONNECTED
2              +ASM             +ASM            CONNECTED
4 rows selected.
>export ORACLE_SID=DB01
>export ORACLE_HOME=/u01/oracle/11.2.0/database
SQLPLUS> select group_number, instance_name, status
from v$asm_client;
GROUP_NUMBER INSTANCE_NAME      DB_NAME          STATUS
------------ ------------------ ---------------- ------------
1            +ASM               DB01             CONNECTED
```

Notice the difference between the view results on the ASM instance and the database instance. Also, if there are no disks available in v$asm_disk, this might indicate an issue with the parameter ASM_DISKSTRING or even permissions on the directories or devices.

Streams and Advanced Replication

Replication provides copies of data to different servers, and it can be used to move data. While it isn't a failover mechanism usually associated with high availability, it does help ensure that data is available and can provide a way to selectively pull out the important data.

SQL Server has replication to distribute transactions to a subscriber. You create the publisher, which can be various tables, and then you can make subscriptions to the publisher for replicating to another server. The SQL Server publisher, distributor, and subscriber fill the roles of capture, stage, and consume or apply. Some setup with a replication administration user and another database is required.

For replication, Oracle offers Oracle Streams and the Advanced Replication option. Which one you use depends on your replication requirements, including what needs to be replicated in your environment.

Oracle Streams

Oracle Streams, included as part of the Oracle database installation, captures data changes to distribute to another database. The phases of Streams are similar to the SQL Server publisher, distributor, and subscriber roles. A user needs to be created to manage the replication, and a tablespace is also required.

Setting Up Oracle Streams

The Streams administrator user needs the DBA permissions and admin privilege on the DBMS_STREAMS_AUTH package. Here is an example for granting the permissions to the user:

```
SQLPLUS> grant CONNECT, RESOURCE, DBA to streamadmin;
SQLPLUS> begin DBMS_STREAMS_AUTH.GRANT_ADMIN_
PRIVILEGE( grantee => 'streamadmin', grant_privileges => true);
END;
/
SQLPLUS> grant SELECT_CATALOG_ROLE to streamadmin;
SQLPLUS> grant SELECT ANY DICTIONARY to streamadmin;
```

The parameter configurations for Streams setup are GLOBAL_NAMES= TRUE, JOB_QUEUE_PROCESS higher than 2, and STREAMS_POOL_SIZE at least 200MB. A database link is used to connect to the target server, so the databases do not need to be identical.

Changes for data and objects are captured and replicated. Replication can be configured for the whole database, schemas, tables, or even tablespaces. You can set up Streams through OEM, as shown in Figure 10-9, or through the DBMS packages.

Through OEM, you can also choose to set up downstream capture and create an advanced queue. Downstream capture collects streams on a remote database other than the source. The archive logs can be shipped to where the downstream capture is configured, or the downstream can be a real-time data capture. The queue is a messaging system that queues up information to pass it along for other applications or databases to use to have persistent messages. This is used for distributed applications to communicate and coordinate processes in an asynchronous manner.

Having the flexibility to implement Streams for just a schema instead of the whole database allows you to choose which pieces are more highly available. The replication doesn't failover the application to a copy of schema, but provides a place to get the data, at least via a manual connection. The DBMS_ STREAMS_ADM package has procedures for adding schema and table rules, and setting up the queue table.

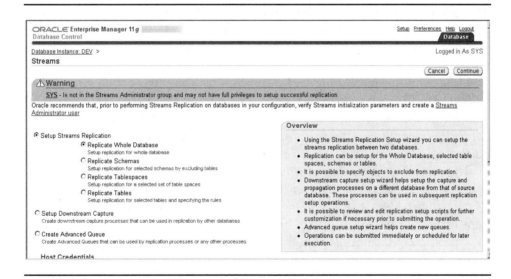

FIGURE 10-9.   *Setting up Oracle Streams in OEM*

Using Oracle Streams

Oracle Streams uses logical change records (LCRs) for each row of a table modified. Each LCR has the name of the table changed, old and new values for any changed columns, and values for the key columns. This information can be applied to the rows at the destination sites and resolve conflicts if they arise.

The changes are captured and staged based on the rules of what is to be replicated. For the capture side, log-based capture pulls the changes out of the redo logs. Capturing the information from the redo logs minimizes the overhead on the system and any of the table changes. The tables that are marked for replication need to log supplemental information in the redo logs, such as the primary key columns. The log-based capture has a reader service that reads the redo logs, and then prepares servers to scan the defined regions from the reader. The filter of the LCRs is based on the rules and definitions set up to replicate, so only the changes that are needed are captured. The builder server merges the records from the preparer and then passes the change to the staging area for processing. Capturing the changes from the redo logs can come from the log buffer, active redo, and the archive log files.

Another capture type is synchronous, which captures the changes as they are happening. This can be used for tables that might be updated often and are a smaller subset of tables. It captures the DML changes for each row and converts it to an LCR. The capture of this change is then passed along to the staging area.

Using rules for publishing and subscribing to the staging area offers flexibility in the routing of the streams. The staging area with the queues will even allow the information to be passed to a database that might not have a network connection to the main database, by passing through another database that has connections to both.

The consumption of the information is done by the apply engine. The apply engine detects conflicts and applies automatically captured DML and DDL changes. Here again, you have the flexibility of using declarative transformations or user-supplied functions to set up each LCR.

The source database is kept throughout the Oracle Streams processing. The administrator controls which changes are to be captured. The apply engine can be customized with PL/SQL procedures and functions, which can be registered with the Streams administrator. An example for this is to apply all of the changes except the deletions on a specific table.

Streams has an advisor that will help with performance and monitoring of the throughput and latency. The advisor looks at each of the areas in the process: capture, stage, and apply.

Advanced Replication

Along with Oracle Streams replication, Oracle offers an Advanced Replication option. This handles master replication with a single master or multiple masters.

Multimaster replication is known as *peer-to-peer*, and any of the servers can be updated. Advanced Replication processing to multiple masters can be asynchronous and synchronous.

For this type of replication, you need to set up a replication admin user. Tables in the databases should have primary keys. The DBMS_REPCAT package provides routines for administering and updating the replication catalog.

Advanced Replication offers the option of replicating to non-Oracle databases. This allows a way to provide data to several different systems. Also, with this type of replication, the Oracle database version and platform do not need to be the same for replication. Advanced Replication may be suitable for distributed or data warehouse databases, to have copies available for other systems or to maintain the workload on different servers.

Summary

The role of the DBA is to provide a reliable database environment. Businesses are requiring that systems be up and available 24/7.

The DBA needs to understand the options for the database system to provide high availability. This includes knowing the resource costs for each solution and what type of availability it provides.

Making a case for how a high-availability solution improves the management and reliability of the database, as well as provides for the needs of the business, is the responsibility of the DBA. Implementing, deploying, and administering the environment is the fun part for the DBA.

SQL Server has high-availability solutions that you might have considered and/or implemented. The options for SQL Server do not behave the same as those for Oracle. Even though both have clustering, there are significant differences. Looking at the differences is a good place to start to understand the Oracle solutions. However, you also should examine the specific features and possible configurations of Oracle RAC, Data Guard, and other high-availability options. Look into the Maximum Availability Architecture for Oracle, which combines solutions to handle different requirements and reduce the risks for failures.

APPENDIX

Mental Preparedness
for Multiple Platforms

y native language is English, but for some crazy reason, I wanted to learn German in high school. I learned about the language, discovered new words, and learned how to speak a couple of phrases. I started to learn about the syntax and gender of words. I was able to understand a very basic conversation, and I could read a simple article. My translations were straight word for word; I did not understand the slang.

At the university, I was exposed to more German. I studied the grammar and learned more about the culture, which helped me in understanding different meanings of phrases instead of just translating each word into English. Then I lived in Germany for several years, immersed in the language. I started to be able to speak the phrases and dialect. I even began to dream in German, and I realized I finally had made the German language a part of who I am.

Some of you might have experienced similar situations with learning a new language. We also experience this with computer languages and database platforms.

We have spent this book going through typical tasks and syntax of how to do things in Oracle, even though SQL Server is your native language. We used this as a baseline to understand the concepts of the database environment and tasks that need to be done. The translations were done into Oracle— some more direct than others. For example, the terms *database* and *instance* were matched up with each other. The database/instance comparison was to illustrate the Oracle environment—its objects and behaviors—and to truly convey what Oracle DBAs mean when they say "database."

Mental preparedness for multiple platforms is being able to distinguish between the different platforms. It is being able to speak the language of one platform one minute, and switch over to the language of another platform in the next minute. You start by learning enough of the differences to make the transition easier, but then begin to learn about the platform in more depth. It is still possible to translate between the different platforms, but in doing so, you might miss the real meaning or underlying concept. Take that extra step to try to "dream in Oracle." Try to stop comparing it with SQL Server, and start embracing some of the Oracle features for what they are.

This is definitely not an easy task. It might take a few years for you to be able to bounce between platforms without thinking about it. A good place to start is with some checklists for each platform to help smooth the transition.

Each of the platforms has a different starting point for troubleshooting a problem. Start a checklist for troubleshooting the problems based on each platform. It will increase the experience you have with the different database environments when looking at the issues from different perspectives. How do you go about looking at connection issues? What about performance? How about permissions and statistics? Consider where all of these types of issues fall as database administration activities—daily versus weekly, automatic versus manual, cause of an issue versus fix for an issue, and so on.

Resolving a performance issue in SQL Server might start with looking for locks and long-running queries, which could lead to needing to rebuild indexes. In the Oracle environment, the search might start with looking at session waits and checking if there are table scans because of stale statistics. These starting points are good to have for each environment to be able to jump into a different platform quickly. In not thinking about which platform, quite a few times I have gone down a path in SQL Server to research a performance issue by looking at statistics and indexes instead of looking at sp_who2 for blocking issues. In SQL Server, blocking issues might be higher on my list of things to check, but I might have skipped a quick check because I didn't think of the environment and may have even started to work on tuning the queries. On the other hand, even though that might not have been the solution, tuning queries is always worth it for better performance no matter what database environment. At some point, the troubleshooting may look the same or converge, depending on the issue, but understanding how the system behaves and what some of the main issues can be is a good place to start.

Of course, some of the DBA tasks in the environments are the same. For example, backups are important in any database system, but what is backed up and the options are different. That could even be said for different databases in the same platform. Not only are you translating to a different database platform, but you also must use different applications, which, as a DBA, you should be used to by now.

For maintenance jobs and tasks, be sure to look at the version of the database, the platform, and any new features that might make the task easier or even obsolete. Oracle did this with tablespaces. It was very typical to coalesce and reorganize the tablespaces and tables, but with locally managed tablespaces, this became less of a worry. SQL Server might have a higher priority to rebuild cluster indexes, where Oracle might be looking at statistics on the tables and indexes for the optimizer to have the correct information. What is new in the database, the tasks, and maintenance should be reviewed for each environment. A list of typical jobs and why they run will help keep your information current and useful for the system.

This all relates back to a DBA attitude toward learning. DBAs want to learn. And if you don't want to learn, why are you reading a book about a different platform? Be mentally prepared to learn with each new release of the database software, with each new application that is developed or installed, and with each new platform introduced to the environment. That is really what makes being a DBA fun—all of the new things to learn. We are constantly exploring and trying to find better ways to manage a stable and reliable system. We learn from what we have done in the past and try to discover what is new for the future.

Realize that you don't need to know everything, because honestly, that probably isn't possible. Just be aware of what's available and know how to get more information if that becomes necessary. Some pieces of the software may seem to be interesting and fun, but there might not be a business reason to implement them yet. Just knowing that these pieces exist and why they might be needed is the first step of the process. High availability is a good example. There are plenty of options with hardware, software, and ways to move transactions from one system to another. The willingness to learn about the solutions and be prepared to handle an implementation already makes you a great DBA. Understanding the options for different platforms and being willing to know what they have to offer make you even better. Be brave enough to try different things and throw out the old, familiar methods if they are no longer valid.

I bet you didn't even realize that learning new features can be like learning new database platforms. You're willing to give up some of the comforts and go explore what can be done. This is the exciting stuff. But don't just go for something because it is new and shiny. Use your experience and knowledge to see if it also makes sense. Be willing to think outside the box. Understanding more about databases in general helps with some out-of-the box thinking. Understanding the processing and tools available in multiple platforms provides additional resources to come up with different ways to gather information and integrate solutions. Just because you're gaining knowledge in one area, don't neglect what you already know.

Change is not always easy, but being in the technology business, we expect change and prepare for it. Learning new technologies and keeping up with the new features in the current technologies are part of our job. And this is why I enjoy being a DBA. The job continues to add new challenges and changes.

The roles of the job can change. I can explore the new technologies and work on the architecture of the database system. I can also work with developers to incorporate something that can solve a problem. The job also changes depending on how we monitor the systems and become more proactive in our administration of the databases. Being willing to learn and change are part of the DBA mental attitude and preparedness. Taking on multiple platforms is an excellent way to develop your skills.

Since databases touch so many environments, the learning does not stop with the new features and other database platforms but continues with operating systems, networking, and applications. The opportunities are just out there, waiting to be added to your experiences.

Again, you don't need to know everything about everything, but you do need to know what issues are important to the databases. Also, you need to talk to other teams to be able to maintain a well-performing environment, because it is definitely a team effort. Learning from other areas is good, but learning about the databases from other DBAs is also helpful. User group members and coworkers are great sources of information. Being prepared to support a different database and even a different operating system requires learning from others.

DBAs have the opportunity to be in the middle of things, and to work with different people and teams. Being prepared to offer ideas and knowledge about database solutions makes the job interesting and makes you more valuable. The teams will start to depend on your ability to evaluate why a database solution here makes sense, while using another solution for something else is a good idea. Being able to see the big picture, including how the application is getting the information, is a skill we are constantly improving. Being able to speak the database's language is valuable when drilling down into the environments.

In becoming a DBA, you might not have initially realized all of the learning that comes with the job. Those DBAs who challenge themselves and reach out to learn more are the ones who succeed in their careers. Learning from each other, being willing to explore new areas, and then being able to pull all of the information back to apply to the database environment are the tricks of the trade.

Being mentally prepared to handle multiple platforms means being willing to dive completely into one platform when dealing with it and being able to transition into another one as needed. Knowing that there are reasons for the database to run in a certain way and grasping the concepts behind how that database performs are key to being able to support the database environment.

Learning Oracle will broaden your perspective on databases. Keeping the skills you have already developed as a DBA and learning how to apply them in other environments will continue to challenge you as you develop more experience. The fun of the job is being able to be involved in several aspects of the systems we support as we develop reliable, secure, and robust database systems.

Be prepared to start dreaming in Oracle and database concepts, and be prepared to continue to learn new and exciting things about databases and their environments.

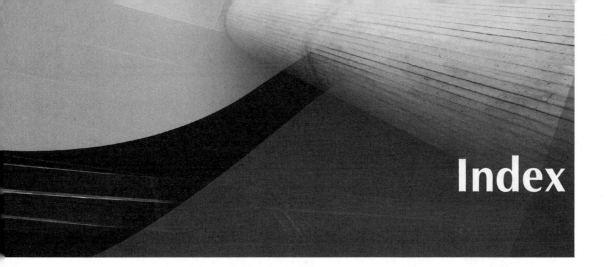

Index

A

abort shutdowns, 85
ACFSUTIL command, ASM, 60
Active Data Guard, 290–291
Active Session History (ASH) view, AWR, 236
active standby databases, 290–291
active/active clustering, SQL Server, 276–277
active/passive clustering, SQL Server, 276
activity monitors, AWR, 224
Address Windowing Extensions (AWE), 19
administrator client, 120
Administrators section, of Enterprise Manager Configuration, 111–112
advanced queues, Oracle Streams, 305
Advanced Replication, 307
ADVISE FAILURE command, data recovery, 147–148
Advised Recovery section, Oracle, 149
AFTER trigger, 248
AL32UTF8 (Unicode character set), international language databases, 91–92
alert log
    avoiding "checkpoint not complete" alert in, 41, 198–199
    cleaning up older, 204
    DBAs monitoring errors in, 9
    directory for, 36
    invalid object alerts in, 187
    listing errors on OEM home page, 8, 204
    maintaining, 203–204
    resizing, 198–199
    in transaction process flow, 41
    using DBCA, 81

aliases
    overview of, 123–124
    using client network utility with, 123–124
ALL_ permission, catalog views, 23
ALTER DATABASE BEGIN BACKUP, hot backup, 130
ALTER DATABASE DATAFILE, resizing datafiles, 200
ALTER DATABASE END BACKUP, troubleshooting backup, 142
ALTER DATABASE OPEN RESETLOGS, point-in-time recovery, 145
alter statements, spfile.ora file, 34
ANALYZE command, consistency checks, 173–174
ANALYZE TABLE table_name VALIDATE STRUCTURE CASCADE command, Oracle
    detecting corruption, 173–174
    evaluating if index should be rebuilt, 182
apply engine, Oracle Streams, 306
archive logs, 41
    directory for, 36
    hot backups and, 130
    log switching through redo logs and, 41
    recovering to specific, 144
    redo logs and, 38–39
    running backups of, 135, 137–138, 152–154
    running out of archive space, 39, 138

ARCHIVELOG mode
    customizing OEM backup jobs, 138–139
    FULL transaction logs similar to, 34–35
    Oracle DBCA backups, 128–129
    point-in-time recoveries, 145
    redo logs and, 38–39
ASH (Active Session History) view, AWR, 236
ASM (Automatic Storage Management)
    background processes, 31
    creating database with DBCA, 81
    overview of, 57–61
    using duplicate database to migrate to, 150–151
ASM (Automatic Storage Management), in RAC
    configuration parameters, 298–302
    as high-availability solution, 275
    managing disk groups, 297
    viewing information, 302–303
ASM Configuration Assistant (ASMCA), 297
ASM_DISKGROUPS parameter, ASM, 298
ASM_DISKSTRING parameter, ASM, 298
ASM_POWER_LIMIT parameter, ASM, 298
ASMCA (ASM Configuration Assistant), 297
ASMCMD command, disk management, 60, 299–300
asmdba (Automatic Storage Management administrator) group, Oracle installation on Linux, 50
ASMLib, ASM configuration, 298
ASMM (Automatic Shared Memory Management), 17–20
ASSM (Automatic Segment Space Management)
    evaluating if index should be rebuilt, 182
    reducing fragmentation of tables, 184
attributes, cursor processing, 255
audit logs
    directory for, 36
    setting up for grants, 189
AUTO_UPDATE_STATISTICS option, 176
autoextend setting, datafiles, 201–202
Automated Maintenance Tasks, Oracle Scheduler, 109
automatic failover, 292–296
Automatic Shared Memory Management. See ASMM (Automatic Shared Memory Management)
Automatic Storage Management. See ASM (Automatic Storage Management)
Automatic Storage Management administrator (asmdba) group, Oracle installation on Linux, 50
Automatic Workload Repository. See AWR (Automatic Workload Repository)
autonomous transactions, PL/SQL, 265
Availability tab, OEM, 106

AWE (Address Windowing Extensions), 19
AWR (Automatic Workload Repository)
    Active Session History view, 236
    activity monitors in, 224
    library cache for SQL statements, 236–238
    overview of, 233
    reports, 233–235

B

background processes
    running in Oracle, 30–32
    setting up when database is created, 82
background_core_dump parameter, directories, 204
background_dump_dest parameter, directories, 36, 204
BACKUP ARCHIVELOGS command, purging obsolete files, 156
backups. See also restore and recovery
    backup and restore commands, 129–131
    backup and restore of objects, 156–161
    configuring with RMAN, 131–135
    DBA responsibility for, 3
    examples of, 137
    in OEM, 106, 137–141
    options, 135–137
    platform differences, 6
    preparedness for multiple platforms and, 311
    SQL Server/Oracle tools for, 104
    storage setup for files, 56
    strategies, 128–129
    testing RAC, 283
backupset type, RMAN, 133
base backups, 134–135
batch files, SQL*Plus in, 113
bcp utility, database migrations, 9
BEFORE trigger, 247–248
BEGIN CATCH block, SQL Server, 264
BEGIN statement, PL/SQL, 251
BEGIN TRAN block, SQL Server, 251
BEGIN TRY block, SQL Server, 264
best practices, and DBAs, 4
BIN$, recycle bin, 162–163
blocks, database
    backup strategy for corrupted, 142
    recovering with RMAN, 146–147
    sizing SGA memory, 22
    validating with consistency checks, 173–174

breakpoints, debugging in PL/SQL with, 263
b-tree indexes, for primary key indexes, 212
BULK COLLECT
    cursor processing, 256
    using PL/SQL FORALL loop, 257
bulk update locks, SQL Server, 220

C

cache
    database using memory for, 16
    defining functions in Oracle to use
        result, 261
    library, for SQL statements, 236–237
case sensitivity, choosing character set, 89
CASE statement, conditions, 250
cat or more command, Linux, 49
catalog owner, RMAN backups, 131–132
catalogs
    containing system-level information, 23
    RMAN configuration for backups,
        131–132
catalog.sql script, data dictionary, 23
catproc.sql script, data dictionary, 23
CBO (cost-based optimizer)
    creating execution plans with gathered
        statistics, 177, 209, 229–230
    improvements to, 229
    statistics for tables/indexes and, 230–231
    useful database parameters, 231–232
cd command, Linux, 49
Cd command, Windows, 49
chained row analysis, Segment Advisor,
    182–183
chains
    creating jobs with DBMS_SCHEDULER,
        195–196
    creating jobs with Oracle Scheduler,
        193–194
character sets
    changing, 93
    choosing, 89
    NLS parameters for, 89–92
    setting environment variable for NLS_
        LANG, 92–93
checklists
    common migration tasks, 12
    database installation, 5–6
    DBA monitoring, 9
    setting up Windows for Oracle
        installation, 48
    troubleshooting multiple platforms, 311

chgrp command, Linux, 49
chmod command, Linux, 49
chown command, Linux, 49
CI value, NLS_SORT parameter, 89
client connections
    configuring, 120–123
    in JDBC, 123
    setting up aliases in tnsnames.ora file,
        123–124
    tools for, 119–120
client failover, Oracle RAC, 283–285
cloning database, 151–152
Cluster Verification Utility. See CVU (Cluster
    Verification Utility)
clustering. See also RAC (Real Application
    Clusters)
    indexes, 182, 211
    naming examples, 76–77
Clusterware (crs) group, Oracle installation
    on Linux, 50
Clusterware software, RAC configuration,
    278–282
coding
    backup strategy for poor, 142
    database practices, 240–243
    DBA responsibility for, 3–4
    Oracle functions, 258–259
cold backups, 130–131, 145
command-line commands
    Automatic Storage Management, 60
    backup and restore, 129–131
    Linux vs. Unix, 48–49
    SQL*Plus, 112–117
commit points
    explicit cursors handling size of, 255
    PL/SQL error handling with, 265
    for PL/SQL transactions, 253–254
COMPATIBLE parameter, 35
components, Oracle
    choosing database, 63–64
    choosing for installation, 66–67
    managing in Database Configuration of
        OEM Server tab, 108
composite indexes, 213
conditions, PL/SQL, 250
Configuration Manager, My Oracle
    Support, 124
CONNECT role, Oracle, 97–98
connections
    client, 119–123
    JDBC, 123
    testing RAC, 282–283
consistency checks, 173–174

constants, declaring in PL/SQL packages, 243
constraints, database migrations and, 10
control files
        backing up in Oracle, 135
        backup strategy for loss of, 142
        created with database, 82
        managing in Storage category of OEM
            Server tab, 108
        not included in full backups, 135–136
        RMAN backups of, 131
        RMAN restore and recovery of, 143
        storage requirements, 56–57, 62–63
CONTROL_FILES parameter, 36
conversions, database migration, 9–10
copy backup type, RMAN, 133
Copy command, Windows, 49
CPU (Critical Patch Update), 70
create operations, 241, 243
CREATE PROCEDURE role, 100
CREATE SESSION permission, CONNECT role,
    97, 98
CREATE TABLE statement, ASM, 300
Critical Patch Update (CPU), 70
cross-checks, archive log backups, 138
crs (Clusterware) group, Oracle installation on
    Linux, 50
csscan utility, changing character set, 93
cumulative database backup option,
    RMAN, 134
CURSOR_SHARING parameter, 36, 237
cursors
        declaring in PL/SQL packages, 243
        in PL/SQL transactions, 254–257
custom shell database template, 80
CVU (Cluster Verification Utility)
        configuring RAC, 278, 280
        testing RAC, 282

D

Data Definition Language. See DDL (Data
    Definition Language)
data dictionary
        capturing object statistics in, 180–181
        capturing system statistics in, 177
        containing system-level information,
            23–26
        views, 26–27, 189
Data Guard. See Oracle Data Guard
Data Guard broker, automatic failover,
    294–295
Data Movement tab, OEM, 106

Data Pump Utility, 157–161
data warehouse template, creating with
    DBCA, 80
database
        defined, 74
        terminology used in this book, 310
database administrator (dba) group, Oracle
    installation on Linux, 50
database administrators
        roles of. See DBAs (database
            administrators), role of
        tools. See DBA (database administrator)
            tools
Database Configuration Assistant. See DBCA
    (Database Configuration Assistant)
Database Configuration category, OEM Server
    tab, 108
database identifier (DBID), 76
database owner, SQL Server, 101–102
Database Upgrade Assistant (DBUA),
    68–69, 79
Database Upgrade Guide, Oracle, 69
Database Vault, Oracle, 96
databases, creating
        choosing character set, 89–93
        creating listener, 85–89
        DBA planning/managing installation
            of, 5
        with DBCA, 79–82
        duplicating with templates and scripts,
            83–85
        instances, 74–75
        name definitions, 76–77, 80
        naming uniquely, 119
        overview of, 74
        parameters, 35
        schema, 74–75
        shutdown options, 85
        SQL Server vs. Oracle setup, 77–78
datafiles
        backing up in Oracle, 135
        backup strategy for loss of, 142
        cold backups and, 131
        consistency checks in, 173–174
        creating database with DBCA, 80
        moving to another location, 149–150
        recovering with RMAN, 146–147
        resizing, 198–201
        RMAN hot backups and, 130
        shrinking and resizing, 198
        storage management with ASM, 57–62
        storage setup for, 56–57
        tablespace monitoring of, 200–202

datatypes, converting during migration, 10–11
dates, validation after database migration, 11
DB_BLOCK_CHECKSUM parameter, 174
DB_BLOCK_SIZE parameter, 35
DB_CACHE_SIZE parameter, 17
DB_FLASHBACK_RETENTION_TARGET
  parameter, 165
DB_NAME parameter, 35
DB_RECOVERY_FILE_DEST_SIZE
  parameter, 165
DB_WRITER_PROCESSES parameter, 37
dba (database administrator) group, Oracle
  installation on Linux, 50
DBA (database administrator) tools
    aliases, 123–124
    client connections, 119–123
    JDBC connections, 123
    My Oracle Support, 124
    OEM. *See* OEM (Oracle Enterprise
      Manager)
    for performing common tasks, 104–105
    SQL Developer, 117–119
    SQL*Plus, 112–117
DBA role, Oracle, 96–98
DBA_ permission, 23
dba_audit_statement view, 189
dba_col_privs view, grants, 189
dba_datapump_jobs view, 157
dba_objects, querying, 24–26
dba_objects table, invalid object alerts,
  187–188
dba_recyclebin view, 162–163
DBA_SCHEDULER _JOBS, 28
dba_scheduler_chain_steps view,
  DBMS_SCHEDULER, 196
dba_tab_privs view, grants, 189
dba_views, data dictionary, 26–27
DBAs (database administrators), role of
    database installation planning, 5
    database migrations, 9–13
    dividing privileges, 101–102
    general skills of, 2–3
    leveraging skills, 5–8
    mental preparedness for multiple
      platforms, 310–314
    monitoring checklist, 9
    overview of, 2
    permissions required, 96
    placement within organization, 4
DBCA (Database Configuration Assistant)
    ASM installation with, 59
    creating different passwords for system
      users, 94

creating Oracle database with, 28
    database creation with, 79–80
    removing databases with, 82
DBCC CHECKALLOC command, SQL
  Server, 174
DBCC CHECKDB command, SQL Server,
  173–174
DBCC CHECKTABLE command, SQL Server,
  173–174
DBCC procedures, SQL Server
    evaluating if index should be
      rebuilt, 182
    performing consistency checks, 173
    recovering tablespace, 146
DBCC SHOWCONTIG command, SQL Server,
  182, 184
dbconsole process, DBCA, 81
DBID (database identifier), name
  definition, 76
DBMS packages, PL/SQL, 270–271
DBMS_AUTO_TASK_ADMIN, 197
DBMS_DDL.ALTER_COMPILE, 188
DBMS_JOB package, 196
DBMS_METADATA package, 270
DBMS_OUTPUT package, 263, 270
DBMS_REDEFINITION package, 186, 270
DBMS_REPCAT package, advanced
  replication, 307
DBMS_SCHEDULER package
    converting jobs created with DBMS_
      JOB to, 196
    overview of, 194–196
    scheduling jobs after database
      migration, 11
    scheduling jobs with, 28, 191–192
DBMS_SQL package, 270
DBMS_STATS package, 176–177, 179–188
DBMS_STREAMS_ADM package, 305
DBMS_STREAMS_AUTH package, 304–305
DBMS_UTILITY package, 188
DBUA (Database Upgrade Assistant),
  68–69, 79
DBVERIFY utility, Oracle, 146–147, 173–174
DDL (Data Definition Language)
    dictionary lock, 221
    setting up Data Pump export
      job, 157
    SQL Server vs. Oracle, 246
deadlocks, 219
debugging, stored procedures in PL/SQL,
  262–264
DECODE function, conditions, 250
Del command, Windows, 49

delete operations
    backup options, 155–156
    databases, 82
    with PL/SQL `FORALL` loop, 257–258
    purging obsolete files, 155–156
    SQL Server vs. Oracle triggers for, 247
    using implicit cursors, 255
design, DBA responsibility for, 4
destination parameters, 36
developers, SQL Developer tool, 117–119
development DBAs, 4
/dev/shm file system, Linux, 18
`dgmgrl` command, automatic failover,
    294–295
DHCP (Dynamic Host Configuration
    Protocol), 47
differential backups, 134–135
`Dir` command, Windows, 49
directories
    duplicating databases with scripts using,
        83–84
    location and destination parameters
        for, 36
    maintaining trace files in, 204
disaster recovery. *See* backups; restore and
    recovery
disk groups
    ASM, managing, 297
    ASM configuration, 298–302
    ASM installation, 59–61
    creating database with DBCA and
        ASM, 81
disks
    clustering with RAC. *See* RAC (Real
        Application Clusters)
    estimating space for Data Pump jobs,
        158–159
    Oracle installation requirements, 45
    setting up storage for, 56–57
`dm_db_index_physical_stats`, SQL
    Server, 182
DML triggers, 246
downstream capture, Oracle Streams, 305
downtime, patching RAC, 286
`DUPLICATE` command, RMAN, 149–151
Dynamic Host Configuration Protocol
    (DHCP), 47

E

echo `$ORACLE_HOME` command, Linux, 48
enterprise architect, DBA as, 3

Enterprise Manager (EMCA)
    configuring in OEM, 111–112
    upgrades with, 79
`env` command, Linux, 49
environment variables, for `NLS_LANG`, 92–93
error handling
    cursor processing and, 255–256
    at package level in PL/SQL, 243–245
    PL/SQL, 264–269
error logs, SQL Server, 203–204
error messages
    alert logs. *See* alert log
    PL/SQL `SQLERRM` function
        returning, 265
    PL/SQL standard, 268–269
/etc/pam.d/login file, 51
/etc/security/limits.conf file, 51
event triggers, 246–247
EXCLUDE parameter, Data Pump jobs,
    157–158
exclusive locks
    Oracle, 221
    overview of, 219
    SQL Server, 220
`EXECUTE IMMEDIATE` statement, 247
`EXP/IMP_FULL_DATABASE` role,
    Oracle, 101
expire backup options, 155–156
explain plans
    tuning using, 228–230
    viewing for queries, 226–228
explicit cursors, Oracle transactions, 254–255
exporting
    with Data Movement tab in OEM, 106
    with Data Pump utility, 157–161

F

failover, Oracle RAC
    configuring automatic failover,
        294–296
    Data Guard standby database
        option, 290
    as high-availability solution, 275–278
    setting up client, 283–284
    testing, 282
failover, SQL Server log shipping, 289
FAN (Fast Application Notification), client
    failover in RAC, 283, 285
Fast Application Notification (FAN), client
    failover in RAC, 283, 285

Fast Connection Failover (FCF), client failover in RAC, 283
Fast-Start Failover, 295
FCF (Fast Connection Failover), client failover in RAC, 283
file maintenance
    datafiles, 199–200
    error logs, alert logs and trace files, 203–204
    logs, 198–199
    shrinking and resizing, 197–198
    tablespace monitoring, 200–203
files
    backup options, 135
    storage requirements, 56, 61–62
    Windows installation setup, 47
flash recovery area, creating database with DBCA, 82
flashback
    configuring recovery area for, 82, 163–166
    of database, 166–168
    as high-availability solution, 275
    of queries in undo area, 39
    restoring tables from recycle bin, 163
flashback command, 164–168
flashback recovery area (FRA)
    configuring, 164–166
    flashing back items, 166–168
    overview of, 82
flashback table command, from recycle bin, 163
flashback_transaction_query view, 168
FOR loops, cursor processing, 256
FORALL loop, PL/SQL transactions, 257–258
format, RMAN configuration for backups, 132–133
forward slash (/), database coding, 242
4GB RAM Tuning, 19
FRA (flashback recovery area)
    configuring, 164–166
    flashing back items, 166–168
    overview of, 82
FULL backups
    SQL Server and Oracle options, 128–129, 136–137
    of SQL Server transaction logs, 34
full or fast scans, tuning indexes, 229
FULL=Y parameter, exporting full database with Data Pump job, 157
function-based indexes, 212–214, 260
functions, PL/SQL, 243–245, 258–261

G

GATHER_STATS_JOB, automatic statistics gathering, 176
general transaction database template, creating with DBCA, 80
global database name, 76
global partitioned indexes, 217
global views, RAC instances, 288
GRANT SELECT ANY CATALOG to USER role, 23
grants, 188–190
grep command, Linux, 49
Grid Control, deploying RAC, 286–287
Grid Infrastructure
    ASM installation, 58, 60
    Oracle installation of components, 278–279
groups
    Automatic Storage Management. See disk groups
    managing redo logs, 108
    for Oracle installation on Linux, 50–52
    shrinking and resizing redo logs, 198–199
gv$ views, RAC, 287–289

H

hardware
    backup strategy for, 141–142
    DBA decisions about, 4
    Oracle installation requirements, 45
health checks
    with Configuration Manager, 124
    database maintenance, 174–175
    platform differences for, 7–8
high-availability architecture
    advanced replication, 307
    ASM in RAC environment, 297–303
    clustering with RAC. See RAC (Real Application Clusters)
    options, 274–275
    overview of, 274
    primary and standby databases, 289–296
    streams, 304–307
history cleanup, in general maintenance, 173

home directory
    ASM installation on, 58
    Oracle installation in Linux on, 51
    Oracle installation in Windows on,
      46–47
    Oracle software installation on, 64
hot backups, 130

I

identity column, SQL Server, 242
immediate shutdowns, 85
implicit cursors, Oracle transactions, 254–255
importing
    with Data Movement tab in OEM, 106
    with Data Pump utility, 157–161
incremental backups, 134–135
Independent Oracle User Group (IOUG), 124
index_stats table, 182
indexed views, 214–215
indexes
    bitmap, 215–216
    detecting corruption between tables and,
      173–174
    enabling monitoring, 210
    function-based, 212–214, 260
    general tasks, 173
    invisible, 218–219
    overview of, 209–210
    partitioned, 217
    primary key, 211–212
    rebuilding, 181–184, 191–192, 218
    reorganizing tables, 184–187
    reverse key, 216–217
    tuning using explain plans, 228–230
    types of, 210–211
    updating statistics for, 178–181, 230–231
    views, 214–215
index-organized table (IOT), creating primary
    key index with, 211–212
Initialization Parameters, OEM Server tab
    Database Configuration, 108
init.ora file, 287–288
insert operations
    with PL/SQL FORALL loop, 257–258
    triggers for, 247
    using implicit cursors, 255
inst_id parameter, RAC, 288
instance, terminology used in this book, 310
Instance Activity, OEM, 224–225
INSTANCE_TYPE parameter, ASM, 298

instant client, 120
integrity, database, 173
intent locks, SQL Server, 220
interface, DBAs responsibility for, 4
internal locks and latches, 221
Internet Directory, Oracle, 121–122
invalid objects, database maintenance,
    187–188
invalid synonyms, database maintenance, 189
invisible indexes, 218–219
I/O events, storage for, 56
IOT (index-organized table), creating primary
    key index with, 211–212
IOUG (Independent Oracle User Group), 124
IP addresses, configuring RAC, 279–280
ipcs-b system command, 19
isolation, SQL Server, 219

J

JAVA_POOL_SIZE parameter, 17
JDBC (Java Database Connectivity)
    client failover in RAC, 284
    connections, 123
    managing SQL Server databases, 10
JOB_QUEUE_PROCESSES parameter,
    scheduling jobs, 37, 82
jobs
    Data Pump, 157–158
    scheduling. See scheduling jobs

K

kernel parameters, Oracle installation on
    Linux, 54–55

L

languages, choosing character sets, 89–91
large pages, and memory, 19
LARGE_POOL_SIZE parameter, 17
LCRs (logical change records), Oracle
    Streams, 306
ldap.ora file, 122
.ldf files, 62
least recently used (LRU) blocks, sizing SGA
    memory, 22
library cache for SQL statements, AWR,
    236–238

Linux, Oracle installation setup
  disk storage, 57
  hardware, 45
  kernel parameters, 54–55
  required packages, 53–54
  software, 64
  useful commands, 48–50
  users and groups, 50–52
LIST command, backup views with, 152–155
LIST FAILURE command, data recovery advisor, 147–148
listeners
  client connection configuration, 85–89, 121
  configuring automatic failover, 294–295
  in service list for Oracle, 29
  setting up RAC, 285
local partitioned indexes, 217
Local Service account, Windows installation, 47
LOCAL_LISTENER parameter, RAC listeners, 285
location
  choosing for database files, 81–82
  database parameters for, 36
  file system in Windows for Oracle installation, 47
locking data, 219–221
log groups, creating with database, 82
LOG_ARCHIVE_DEST parameter, 35–36
logical change records (LCRs), Oracle Streams, 306
logical standby databases, 290–291
logs
  alert. See alert log
  archive. See archive logs
  audit, 36, 189
  overview of, 38
  primary/standby databases and, 290–296
  redo. See redo logs
  resizing, 198–199
  SQL Server and Oracle backup options, 135
  storage requirements for, 56–57, 62
  transaction logs. See transaction logs, SQL Server
  transaction process flow and, 40–42
LRU (least recently used) blocks, sizing SGA memory, 22
ls command, Linux, 49
lsnrctl utility, 87

M

MAA (Maximum Availability Architecture), Oracle, 274, 296
maintenance, database, 171–205
  consistency checks, 173–174
  files. See file maintenance
  grants, 189–190
  health checks, 174–175
  index rebuild, 181–184
  invalid objects, 187–188
  job scheduling. See scheduling jobs
  mental preparedness for multiple platforms, 311
  Oracle/SQL Server backup plans, 128–129
  in SQL Server, 172
  synonyms, 190–191
  table reorganization, 184–187
  tasks, 172–173
  update statistics, 176–181
Maintenance Plan Wizard, SQL Server, 172
maintenance window schedules, system and user job setup, 196–197
man (manual) pages, Linux commands in, 49–50
man command, Linux, 49
Manage Scheduler privilege, 197
master database
  backing up in SQL Server, 135
  not existing in Oracle, 22
  system-level information in Oracle vs., 23–26
materialized views, creating indexes on, 214–215
MAX_JOB_SLAVE_PROCESSES parameter, 37
MAXDATAFILES parameter, 35
Maximum Availability Architecture (MAA), Oracle. See also high-availability architecture, 274, 296
Maximum Availability, Oracle Data Guard, 290
Maximum Performance, Oracle Data Guard, 290
Maximum Protection, Oracle Data Guard, 290
MAXLOGFILES parameter, database creation, 35
.mdf files, 62

memory
    designing storage and, 55
    managing in OEM Server tab, 108
    Oracle installation requirements, 45
    parameters, 17–20
    sizing PGA, 22
    sizing SGA, 20–22
    structures for, 16
Memory Advisors, Database Configuration in
    OEM Server tab, 108
MEMORY_MAX_TARGET parameter, 18
MEMORY_TARGET parameter, 18, 20
MEMORY_TARGET parameter, 36
mental preparedness for multiple platforms,
    310–314
Microsoft Loopback Adapter, Windows for
    Oracle installation, 47
Migration Wizard, database, 10–11
migrations, database
    overview of, 9–11
    tasks for, 12
    validation of data after, 11
mkdir command, Linux, 49
Mkdir command, Windows, 49
MMALCHER, 26
model database, backing up in SQL
    Server, 135
monitoring
    checklist for, 9
    DBA responsibility for, 7–8
    tools for, 104
most recently used (MRU) blocks, sizing SGA
    memory, 22
MOVE command, tables, 186
Move command, Windows, 49
MRU (most recently used) blocks, sizing SGA
    memory, 22
msdb system database, SQL Server
    backing up, 135
    job scheduling in, 191
    not existing in Oracle, 22
multimaster replication, 307
mv command, Linux, 49
My Oracle Support
    managing patches, 70–71
    overview of, 124

N

naming conventions
    Data Pump jobs, 157
    Linux disk storage, 57
    listeners, 85–89
    Oracle database, choosing unique
        name, 80

Oracle database, name definitions,
    76, 119
recycle bin objects, 162
navigation, OEM, 105–107
Net Configuration Assistant (NETCA), creating
    listener, 85–89
NETCA (Net Configuration Assistant), creating
    listener, 85–89
network configuration
    DBAs working with, 4
    Real Application Clusters, 279–280,
        282–283
    Windows for Oracle setup, 47
NLS (National Language Support) parameters
    choosing character set for database,
        89–93
    setting environment variable for
        NLS_LANG, 92–93
NLS_COMP parameter, 89
NLS_LANGUAGE (NLS_LANG)
    parameter, 90
NLS_SORT parameter, 89–90
NO_DATA_FOUND error, SELECT INTO, 255
NOARCHIVELOG mode, Oracle
    customizing backup job in OEM,
        138–139
    Oracle DBCA backup strategy,
        128–129
    point-in-time recovery in, 145
    redo logs and, 39
    transaction logs and, 35
noconfig option, response files, 68
nonclustered indexes, Oracle, 182
normal shutdowns, 85
%NOTFOUND attribute, cursor processing, 255
nowait option, response files, 68
nowelcome option, response files, 68
NTFS file system, installing database software
    on, 47

O

object maintenance
    grants, 189–190
    index rebuild, 181–184
    invalid objects, 187–188
    overview of, 181
    synonyms, 190–191
    table reorganization, 184–187
objects
    backing up and restoring, 156–161
    granting individual permissions
        against, 189
    importing with OEM, 160–161

querying information about database, 24–25
recompiling invalid, 187–188
OCR (Oracle Cluster Registry), configuring RAC, 278, 280
OEM (Oracle Enterprise Manager)
    activity monitors, 224–225
    ASM disk groups and files, 300–301
    AWR reports, 233–235
    backup settings, 133–134
    backups, managing, 154–155
    backups, scheduling jobs, 137–141
    configuring table reorganization, 184–186
    copying database, 151–152
    database configuration, 108
    database creation with DBCA, 81
    Enterprise Manager Configuration area, 111–112
    home page, 8
    importing objects, 160–161
    invalid object alerts, 187–188
    navigation, 105–107
    Oracle Scheduler interface, 28, 109
    overview of, 105
    RAC database management, 282
    RAC deployment, 286–287
    Resource Manager, 109
    restore and recovery, 147–148
    scheduling jobs, 191–193
    scheduling jobs, backups, 137–141
    scheduling jobs, Data Pump, 158–160
    security, 109–110
    setting up Oracle streams, 305
    statistics management, 109
    storage management, 107–108
    tablespace monitoring, 111, 201–203
    viewing background processes, 31
oinstall (Oracle installation) group, on Linux, 50
OPATCH method, Oracle patches, 286
operating systems
    DBAs working with configuration of, 4
    Oracle installation preparation, 44–46
optimizer parameters, 36
Optimizer Statistics Gathering task, 176
OPTIMIZER_INDEX_COST_ADJ database parameter, 232
OPTIMIZER_MODE parameter, 36, 232
options, retrieving values of, 33–34
Options tab, Oracle Scheduler, 193
"ORA-1555: snapshot too old" error, 40

Oracle
    PL/SQL language in. See PL/SQL
    skills needed for managing, 6–7
    SQL Server database migration to, 9–13
    SQL Server vs. See SQL Server vs. Oracle
    storage requirements for files, 61–62
Oracle, internal structures
    data dictionary views, 26–27
    database creation parameters, 35
    jobs and schedules, 28
    location and destination parameters, 36
    master, msdb and tempd not existing in, 22
    memory parameters, 17–20
    memory structures, 16
    optimizer and performance parameters, 36–37
    other parameters, 37–48
    parameters. See parameters
    services and processes, 29–32
    sizing SGA and PGA, 20–22
    some basic parameters, 35–36
    system-level information, 23–26
    templates and temporary tables, 28–29
    transaction log parameters, 34–35
    transaction logs vs. redo logs, 38–39
    transaction process flow, 40–42
    undo area, 39–40
    viewing and setting parameters, 33–34
Oracle Cluster Registry (OCR), configuring RAC, 278, 280
Oracle Configuration Manager, 64, 70–71
Oracle Data Guard
    configuring automatic failover, 294–296
    failover using standby database option, 290
    as high-availability solution, 274–275
    server design, 290–291
Oracle Database Upgrade Guide, 69
Oracle Database Vault, 96
Oracle Enterprise Manager. See OEM (Oracle Enterprise Manager)
Oracle Grid Control, deploying RAC, 286–287
Oracle home directory
    planning location of, 47
    Windows for Oracle installation setup, 46
Oracle Internet Directory, client connections, 121–122

Oracle Scheduler, OEM
creating job in, 191–194
overview of, 191
Server tab, 109
Oracle Server installation
Linux setup, 50–55
Linux/Unix commands, 48–50
operating system preparations, 44–46
Oracle database components, 63–64
overview of, 44
Windows setup, 46–48
Oracle SQL Developer
creating new package framework,
243–245
creating unit test, 263–264
database development with, 117–119
database migrations, 10
debugging procedures, 262–263
developing, unit testing and version
control, 242
managing SQL Server databases, 10
viewing explain plan, 228
Oracle Streams
background processes, 31
defined, 304
as high-availability solution, 275
setting up, 304–305
using, 306–307
Oracle Universal Installer (OUI), 64, 68
oracle user, 51–52, 95–98
ORACLE_BASE directory, DBCA, 81
ORACLE_HOME directory, DBCA, 79–80, 81
ORACLE_HOME environment variable, 46–47
ORACLE_SID, Windows installation setup, 46
OUI (Oracle Universal Installer), 64, 68

P

packages
error handling, 266–268
Oracle installation requirements for
Linux, 53–54
PL/SQL package bodies and, 243–245
using DBMS, 270
PAE (Physical Address Extension), 19
parameters
ASM, 298
backing up, 135
basic, 35–36
database creation, 35
duplicating databases with scripts, 83
function-based index, 213

location and destination of, 36
managing in Database Configuration of
OEM Server tab, 108
materialized views, 215
memory, 17–20
optimizer and performance, 36–37
Oracle Streams, 304
other, 37–38
overview of, 32–33
performance tuning using, 231–233
RAC, 287–289
storage requirements, 62
transaction log, 34–35
viewing and setting, 33–34
partitioned indexes, 217
partitioned tables, 183–184
passwords
securing schema by not giving out, 101
storage requirements, 62
Patch Set Updates (PSU), 70–71
patches
applying, 70–71
applying with Software and Support tab
in OEM, 106
Configuration Manager for assistance
in, 124
for RAC environments, 286
patchsets, 70
peer-to-peer, multimaster replication as, 307
Performance tab, OEM, 106, 224–225
performance tuning
Automatic Workload Repository,
233–238
better-performing systems and,
208–209
with current activity views, 221–226
of indexes. *See* indexes
locking, 219–221
Oracle Data Guard protection mode
for, 290
parameters, 36
SQL plans. *See* SQL plans
troubleshooting multiple platforms, 311
troubleshooting with system
statistics, 177
permissions
catalog view, 23
Data Pump, 157
debugging procedures by
checking, 262
grant, 189–190
Oracle Streams, 304–305
oracle user, 51–52

schema, 98–101
server, 95–98
SQL Server database owners, 99
SQL Server vs. Oracle, 243
viewing session, 51–52
pfile, 34
PGA (Program Global Area) memory, 17–18, 22
PGA_AGGREGATE_TARGET parameter, 22
PGA_AGGREGATE_TARGET parameter, 36
Physical Address Extension (PAE), 19
physical standby databases, 290–291
pipelined table functions, 259–261
platforms, mental preparedness for multiple, 310–314
PL/SQL
    database coding, 240–243
    debugging procedures and unit testing, 262–264
    error handling, 264–269
    functions, 258–261
    overview of, 240
    packages and package bodies, 243–245
    triggers, 246–248
    updates and conditions, 249–250
    using DBMS packages, 270–271
PL/SQL transactions
    beginning, 251–253
    cursor processing, 254–257
    defining commits, 253–254
    overview of, 250–251
    processing with FORALL loop, 257–258
PMON background processes, 30
point-in-time recoveries
    flashing back database to, 166–168
    overview of, 145
    recovering tablespace to, 146
port numbers, listeners, 87
ports, Oracle client connections, 119
prerequisite checks
    Oracle installation requirements, 45
    Windows for Oracle installation, 48
primary databases
    as high-availability solution, 275
    overview of, 289–296
    setting up standby database, 292–296
primary key indexes, 211–212
private IP addresses, RAC, 279–280
privileges
    Oracle streams, 304–305
    PL/SQL debug mode, 262–263
    unlimited tablespace, 111
    user jobs, 197

processes, running in database, 29–32
PROCESSES parameter, 35
processors, Oracle installation requirements, 45
Profiler, SQL Server, 209
Program Global Area (PGA) memory, 17–18, 22
programs, job, 28
protection modes, Oracle Data Guard, 290
ps -ef command, Linux, 49
PSU (Patch Set Updates), 70–71
public IP addresses, RAC, 279–280
purging recycle bin, 163–164
pwd command, Linux, 48

Q

QMN0 process, Oracle Streams, 31
queries
    executing in SQL*Plus, 112–117
    exporting with Data Pump, 157
    flashing back, 167–168
    invisible indexes testing performance of, 218
    reducing time with indexes. See indexes
    tools for, 104
    troubleshooting on RAC database, 289
QUERY_REWRITE_ENABLED parameter, 37
QUERY_REWRITE_ENABLED=TRUE parameter, 213, 215
QUERY_REWRITE_INTEGRITY=TRUSTED parameter, 213, 215
queues, Oracle Streams advanced, 305

R

RAC (Real Application Clusters)
    Automatic Storage Management in, 297–303
    background processes, 31
    configuring, 278–282
    configuring/monitoring instances of, 287–289
    deploying, 286–287
    as high-availability solution, 274–275
    overview of, 276–278
    patching, 286
    setting up client failover, 283–285
    setting up RAC listeners, 285
    testing, 282–283

RAM, Oracle installation requirements, 45
range scans, tuning indexes, 229
RBO (rule-based optimizer), 229
read-only tables, bitmap indexes for, 215
read-write snapshot, converting to, 291
Real Application Testing, Software and Support
    tab, 106
recompiling
    invalid objects, 187–188
    invalid synonyms, 189
`record` parameter, response files, 68
`recover database` command, 143
recovery. *See* backups; restore and recovery
recovery catalog
    purging obsolete files, 155–156
    RMAN restore and recovery options, 143
Recovery Manager. *See* RMAN (Recovery
    Manager)
`RECOVERY WINDOW` parameter, purging
    obsolete files, 155–156
`RECOVERY_CATALOG_OWNER` role, 131
recycle bin, 37, 161–164
`RECYCLEBIN` parameter, 37
redo logs
    created with database, 82
    managing in Storage category of OEM
        Server tab, 108
    planning backup strategy for, 142
    resizing, 198–199
    transaction logs vs., 38–39
    transaction process flow, 40–41
`REDUNDANCY` parameter, purging obsolete
    files, 155–156
`REF CURSOR`, 256–257
`RELIES_ON` clause, Oracle, 261
`REMOTE_LOGIN_PASSWORDFILE`
    parameter, 38
`REPAIR FAILURE` command, data recovery
    advisor, 149
`REPAIR FAILURE PREVIEW` command, data
    recovery advisor, 149
replace operations, 241, 243
replication
    as high-availability solution, 275
    Oracle Advanced Replication, 307
    setting up Oracle Streams, 305
reports
    AWR, 233–235
    backup status, 155–156
resizing. *See* sizing
Resource Governor, SQL Server, 109
Resource Manager category, OEM Server
    tab, 109
`RESOURCE` role, Oracle, 96–97, 100

response files, 67–68
restore and recovery. *See also* backups
    copying database, 149–152
    Data Recovery Advisor, 147–149
    DBA responsibility for, 3
    knowing length of time for, 144
    in OEM, 147–148
    options, 143
    platform differences for, 6
    protecting users with flashback,
        164–168
    protecting users with Recycle Bin,
        161–164
    purging obsolete files, 155–156
    recovering to specific point, 144–145
    SQL Server/Oracle tools for, 104
    tablespaces, datafiles, and blocks,
        146–147
    testing RAC, 283
    using standby database for, 291
    viewing available backups for,
        152–155
    what can go wrong, 141–143
`restore database` command, 143
restore point
    creating in OEM, 139–141
    flashing back database to, 166–168
    recovering to, 145
result cache, 261
retention policies
    OEM configuration for backups,
        133–134
    purging obsolete files, 155–156
    RMAN configuration for backups,
        132–133
    undo, 39–40
reverse key indexes, 216–217
`rm` command, Linux, 48–49
`rm -r` command, Linux, 49
RMAN (Recovery Manager)
    backup and restore commands,
        129–131
    configuration for backups, 131–134
    configuring/scheduling backup jobs in
        OEM, 137–141
    copying database in, 149–152
    flashing back items with, 166–168
    managing backups in, 152–156
    restore and recovery options, 143–147
roles. *See also* DBAs (database
  administrators), role of
    granting user access to catalog
        views, 23
    maintaining grants, 189

rollbacks
    beginning transactions, 251–253
    defining commits in PL/SQL
        transactions, 254
    PL/SQL error handling with, 265
rolling patches, RAC, 286
row exclusive table locks, 221
row locks, 221
row share table locks, 221
row-level triggers, 247–248
rpm -q *package_name* command, 53–54
rule-based optimizer (RBO), 229
runtime client, 120

S

sa account, SQL Server, 98
savepoints
    beginning transactions in Oracle with,
        251–253
    PL/SQL error handling with, 265
scalar-valued functions, Oracle, 258–259
Schedule tab, Oracle Scheduler, 193
scheduling jobs
    for automatic statistics gathering, 176
    after creating database, 82
    after database migration, 11
    defined, 28
    in OEM, for backups, 138–140
    in OEM, for Data Pump, 158–160
    overview of, 191
    for system and user jobs, 196–197
    for table reorganization, 186
    tools for, 104
    using DBMS_SCHEDULER package,
        194–196
    using DBMS_STATS package, 179–180
    using Oracle Scheduler, 109, 191–194
schema locks, SQL Server, 220
schema owner, 75
Schema tab, OEM, 106, 184–186
schemas
    creating backups of, 156–157
    exporting with Data Pump, 157
    implementing Oracle Streams for, 305
    overview of, 74–75
    permissions, 98–101
    recompiling invalid objects at level
        of, 188
    updating statistics for, 178–181
SCN (system change number)
    flashing back database to, 166, 168
    listing details about archive logs,
        153–154

    point-in-time recovery to, 145
    recovering to, 145
scripts
    cold backups and, 131
    creating for other platforms, 8
    duplicating databases with, 83–84
    reviewing RMAN in OEM, 139–140
    using SQL*Plus command-line,
        113, 114–117
Secure Backup, integration with RMAN, 132
security
    considerations, 95
    overview of, 94
    patches, 70–71
    permissions for schemas, 98–101
    permissions for server, 95–98
    privileges for DBA roles/responsibilities,
        101–102
Security category, OEM, 109–110
Segment Advisor
    rebuilding indexes, 182–183
    table reorganization, 184–185
SELECT ANY CATALOG role, system
    DBA, 101
SELECT FOR UPDATE statement, locking
    data manually, 219
SELECT INTO, using implicit cursors, 255
SELECT statement
    cursor processing in PL/SQL,
        255–257
    setting up client failover in RAC,
        283–284
    UPDATE statement in Oracle vs., 249
semicolon (;), database coding, 242, 262
sequences, Oracle, 241–243
server
    defined, 74
    naming, 76–77, 119
    permissions for, 95–98
server log, DBAs monitoring, 9
Server tab, OEM
    Database Configuration category, 108
    defined, 106
    Oracle Scheduler, 109
    Security category, 109–110
    SQL Server Management Studio
        vs., 107
    Statistics Management category, 109
    Storage category, 107–108
services, running in database, 29–32
Session Monitor, SQL Server, 209
SESSION_CACHED_CURSORS parameter, 37
SESSIONS parameter, 35
Set command, Windows, 49
SET commands, SQL*Plus, 113–114

SGA (System Global Area) memory
  defined, 17
  Oracle parameters for, 17–20
  sizing, 20–22
SGA_MAX_SIZE parameter, 17–18
SGA_TARGET parameter, 17–18
SGA_TARGET parameter, 36
share row exclusive table locks, Oracle, 221
share table locks, Oracle, 221
shared locks
  Oracle, 221
  overview of, 219
  SQL Server, 220
SHARED_POOL_SIZE parameter, 17
SHOW RECYCLE BIN, 163
shutdown
  database options, 85
  of listener, 87
  triggers used for, 246
SID (system identifier)
  client connections and, 119
  configuring/monitoring RAC instances,
    287–289
  database name definitions, 76
  disk storage setup in Linux, 57
  ORACLE_SID, 46
  SQL Server vs. Oracle, 76
SIMPLE option, SQL Server
  backup strategy, 128
  point-in-time recovery in, 145
  transaction logs, 34
single-instance database, patching RAC
  like, 286
sizing
  configuring flashback recovery area, 165
  datafiles, 198–201
  files, 197–198
  logs, 198–199
  SGA and PGA memory, 20–22
  tablespaces, 108
SMON background process, 30
snapshot database configuration, 291
software, configuring RAC with
  Clusterware, 278
software, installing Oracle
  overview of, 64–67
  patches, 70–71
  removing software, 68
  upgrading database, 68–70
  using response file, 67–68
Software and Support tab, OEM, 106
sort order, choosing character set, 89
sp_configure, SQL Server parameters, 33

sp_updatestats, update statistics, 176
sp_who command, 113
SPFILE parameter, 37
spfile.ora file
  configuring/monitoring RAC, 287–288
  defined, 34
spool command, SQL*Plus, 113
SQL Developer. See Oracle SQL Developer
SQL plans
  database parameters, 231–233
  overview of, 226
  statistics for tables and indexes,
    230–231
  tuning using explain plans, 228–230
  viewing explain plans, 226–228
SQL Server Agent, scheduling jobs, 191–192
SQL Server Integration Services (SSIS),
  migration, 9
SQL Server Management Studio
  defined, 104
  OEM vs., 105
  Server tab of OEM vs., 107
SQL Server vs. Oracle
  backup and restore, 128–131
  client connection tools, 119–120
  clustering, 276–278
  Data Definition Language, 246
  database coding practices, 240–243
  database creation, 77–78
  database definitions, 74–77
  database migrations, 9–13
  delete and expire backup options, 156
  error functions, 265
  function types, 258–259
  general maintenance tasks, 172–173
  health checks, 175
  high-availability options, 274–275
  index types, 211
  installation checklists, 6
  lock types, 220–221
  locking, 219–221
  memory structures, 16
  mental preparedness for multiple
    platforms, 310–314
  performance tuning, 209
  querying database objects, 24
  scheduling jobs, 192
  server roles, 96–98
  setup, 77–78
  SID (system identifier), 76
  system-level information, 23–26
  tools for database tasks, 104–105
  transaction logs vs. redo logs, 38–39

triggers, 246–247
UPDATE statement, 249–250
update statistics procedure, 178
viewing and setting parameters, 33–34
SQL statements, library cache for, 236–237
SQL*Loader
database migrations using, 9
repairing unusable index caused by, 183–184
SQL*Net message, 225
SQL*Plus
overview of, 112–117
viewing ASM information, 303
viewing explain plan for query, 226–228
SQLCODE error function, PL/SQL, 265
SQLERRM error function, PL/SQL, 265
sqlnet.ora file, 122–123
SSIS (SQL Server Integration Services), migration, 9
staging area, Oracle Streams, 306
standard installation document, 5
standby databases
configuring existing database with, 292–296
as high-availability solution, 275
overview of, 290
using active, 290–291
STAR_TRANSFORMATION_ENABLED database parameter, 232
startup, triggers used for, 246
startup mount command, cold backups, 131
statistics
gathering object, 178–181
gathering system, 177–178
maintenance tasks, 173
overview of, 176–177
performance tuning by viewing, 209
validating for performance, 230–231
Statistics Management category, OEM Server tab, 109
STATISTICS_LEVEL parameter, 37, 176
Storage category, Server tab of OEM, 107–108
storage requirements
disks, 56–57
managing with ASM, 57–61
for Oracle files, 61–62
overview of, 55–56
stored procedures
database migrations and, 10
debugging, 262–264
declaring in PL/SQL packages, 243–245
validation after database migration, 11

streams. See Oracle Streams
synchronous capture, Oracle Streams, 306
synonyms, database maintenance, 190–191
SYS, 24–25
sysadmin role, SQL Server, 97–98
SYSASM role, Oracle, 98
SYSAUX tablespace
creating with database, 82
monitoring, 203
viewing/changing, 107–108
SYSDBA role, Oracle
auditing grants, 189
managing RAC databases with OEM, 282
overview of, 96–98
preferences, 101
SYSMAN, 25
SYSOPER role, Oracle
auditing grants, 189
defined, 98
of system DBA, 101
SYSTEM, 26
system change number (SCN). See SCN (system change number)
system DBAs, 4
System Global Area. See SGA (System Global Area) memory
system identifier. See SID (system identifier)
system maintenance, job setup, 196–197
system monitoring, with SMON background process, 30
system statistics, 176–178
SYSTEM tablespace
creating with database, 81–82
monitoring, 203
viewing/changing, 107–108
SYSTEM user, Oracle, 98
system views. See views, current activity
System V-style shared memory, 19
system-defined errors, PL/SQL, 265
system-defined functions, 259–260

T

tables
backups of, 156–157
creating with flashed back data, 167–168
detecting corruption between indexes and, 173–174
locks, 221
partitioned indexes for, 217

tables *(cont.)*
    primary indexes for constraints in, 211
    recompiling invalid synonyms on,
      189–190
    reorganizing fragmented, 184–187
    restoring from recycle bin, 163
    triggers on, 247–248
    tuning using explain plans, 228–230
    updating statistics, 178–181
    validating performance with statistics,
      230–231
tablespaces
    backup options, 135
    created with database, 81–82
    datafile storage requirements, 62
    exporting with Data Pump, 157
    maintaining, 311
    monitoring, 200–203
    RMAN backup configuration, 131
    RMAN hot backups, 130
    RMAN recovery of, 146–147
    setting quotas, 110–111
    viewing/changing, 107–108
TAF (Transparent Application Failover)
    configuration, RAC, 284–285
target database, RMAN backups, 132
TEMP tablespace
    creating with database, 81–82
    overview of, 29
    viewing/changing, 107–108
tempdb database
    not existing in Oracle, 22
    not included in SQL Server backups, 135
    SQL Server database vs. Oracle, 28–29
tempfiles, 28
templates
    creating databases with DBCA, 80
    duplicating databases with, 83–84
    overview of, 28–29
    SQL Server vs. Oracle, 82
temporary tablespaces
    monitoring, 202
    not included in Oracle backups, 135
    overview of, 28–29
test environment
    avoid mixing production and, 160
    copying database for, 149–150
    importing system statistics into, 177–178
    PL/SQL unit tests, 263–264
    Real Application Clusters, 282–283
thick clients, JDBC, 123
thin clients, JDBC, 123

TIME_WAITED column, AWR Active Session
    History view, 236
times, validating after migration, 11
timestamps, validating after migration, 11
TNS Listener service, 29
tnsnames.ora file
    overview of, 121–123
    possible connection issues, 124
    setting up client failover in RAC, 284
    setting up database alias, 124
    setting up RAC listeners, 285
TO_functions, Oracle, 259–260
TOO_MANY_ROWS error, SELECT INTO, 255
tools, DBA. *See* DBA (database administrator)
    tools
Top Activity, OEM, 224–225
trace files, maintaining, 204
trace sessions, tools for, 104
transaction logs, SQL Server
    hot backups and, 130
    parameters for, 34–35
    redo logs vs., 38–39
    SQL Server and Oracle backup
      options, 135
transactions
    PL/SQL. *See* PL/SQL transactions
    process flow, 40–41
    shutdown of, 85
Transparent Application Failover (TAF)
    configuration, RAC, 284–285
triggers
    disallowing table updates using, 268
    generating IDs for primary keys,
      242–243
    overview of, 246–248
troubleshooting
    copying database for, 149
    DBA responsibility for, 3
    mental preparedness for in multiple
      platforms, 311
    restoration of files vs. full recovery, 142
TRY CATCH block, SQL Server, 264
T-SQL (Transaction SQL), 240–241
Type command, Windows, 49
TYPE setting, TAF configuration, 284–285

U

undo area, 39–40
UNDO tablespace
    creating with database, 81–82
    monitoring, 202

overview of, 39–40
transaction process flow, 41
viewing/changing, 107–108
UNDO_MANAGEMENT parameter, 36
UNDO_RETENTION parameter, 39–40
UNDO_TABLESPACE parameter, 36
Unicode character set (AL32UTF8),
　international language databases, 91–92
unique scans, tuning indexes, 229
unit test, PL/SQL, 263–264
Unix commands, 48–49
UNLIMITED TABLESPACE role, 100
"until time," recovering to, 145
update locks, SQL Server, 220
update operations
　PL/SQL conditions and, 249–250
　with PL/SQL FORALL loop, 257–258
　triggers for, 247
UPDATE statement
　SQL Server vs. Oracle, 249–250
　using implicit cursors, 255
update statistics
　maintenance tasks, 173
　objects, 178–181
　overview of, 176–177
　systems, 177–178
upgrades
　backup strategy for, 142
　creating restore point in OEM for,
　　139–140
　overview of, 68–70
　using Configuration Manager, 124
　using Upgrade Companion, 69–70
user accounts, Windows for Oracle
　installation, 47
User Manager, Linux, 51
USER tablespace, 107–108, 110
USER_ permission, catalog views, 23
user_dump_dest parameter, directories,
　36, 204
user_recyclebin view, 162
user_scheduler_ view, 197
user-defined errors, PL/SQL, 265
user-defined functions, 259–260
users
　creating for ASM installation, 58
　creating for Oracle installation on Linux,
　　50–52
　DBA responsibility for adding, 3
　job setup for, 196–197
　planning backup strategy for errors of,
　　141–142
　protecting with recycle bin, 161–164

Users area, Security category of OEM Server
　tab, 109–110
utlrp.sql script, 188

V

v$ views, ASM information, 302–303
v$database view, 142, 145
v$db_cache view, 21
v$flash_recovery_area_usage view,
　165–166
v$flashback_database_log
　view, 165
v$log_history view, 41, 198–199
v$object_usage table, 210
v$pga_target_advice view, 22
v$pgainfo view, 22
v$process view, 22
v$recovery_file_dest view, 166
v$session view, 222
v$session_wait view, 225, 236
v$sga view, 20
v$sgainfo view, 20
v$sgastat view, 21
v$undostat view, 40
validation of data, in database migration, 11
variables, declaring in PL/SQL packages,
　243–245
version control, SQL Developer tool, 242
View Database Feature Usage, OEM
　Server tab, 108
views
　ASM disk group and file, 300–301
　background process, 31
　backup, 152–155
　catalog, 23
　data dictionary, 26–27
　Data Pump job, 157
　flashback recovery area, 165–166
　indexed, 214–215
　parameter, 33
　RAC instance, 287–288
　recycle bin, 162
　sizing SGA memory, 20–22
　statistics for undo area, 40
views, current activity
　activity monitors, 223–224
　current sessions, 222
　defined, 221
　wait events, 225–226
VIP (virtual IP) addresses, RAC, 279–280
virtual columns on tables, 213–214

VLM, using on Windows, 19
voting disk, RAC, 278, 280

W

wait events
    acquiring locks/performing
      transactions, 219
    AWR Active Session History view, 236
    AWR library cache for SQL statements,
      236–237
    AWR reports in OEM, 234–235
    checking performance issues, 225
WAIT_TIME column, AWR Active Session
  History view, 236

whoami command, Linux, 49
Windows, Oracle installation setup
    checklist for, 48
    command-line commands, 49
    file system, 47
    hardware, 45
    network connectivity, 47
    Oracle home directory, 46
    software, 64
    user account, 47
WITH RECOVERY option, 145
WORKAREA_SIZE_POLICY=AUTO parameter,
  PGA memory, 22
workload repository, managing with
  OEM, 109

Are You Oracle Certified?

Professional development and industry recognition are not the only benefits you gain from Oracle certifications. They also facilitate career growth, improve productivity, and enhance credibility. Hiring managers who want to distinguish among candidates for critical IT positions know that the Oracle Certification Program is one of the most highly valued benchmarks in the marketplace. Hundreds of thousands of Oracle certified technologists testify to the importance of this industry-recognized credential as the best way to get ahead—and stay there.

For details about the Oracle Certification Program, go to oracle.com/education/certification.

Oracle University — Learn technology from the source

ORACLE
UNIVERSITY

Join the World's Largest Oracle Community

With more than 5 million members,
Oracle Technology Network
(otn.oracle.com) is the best place online
for developers, DBAs, and architects to
interact, exchange advice, and get software
downloads, documentation, and
technical tips — all for free!

Registration is easy;
join Oracle Technology
Network today:
otn.oracle.com/join

ORACLE
TECHNOLOGY NETWORK

GET YOUR FREE SUBSCRIPTION TO *ORACLE MAGAZINE*

Oracle Magazine is essential gear for today's information technology professionals. Stay informed and increase your productivity with every issue of *Oracle Magazine*. Inside each free bimonthly issue you'll get:

- Up-to-date information on Oracle Database, Oracle Application Server, Web development, enterprise grid computing, database technology, and business trends

- Third-party news and announcements

- Technical articles on Oracle and partner products, technologies, and operating environments

- Development and administration tips

- Real-world customer stories

If there are other Oracle users at your location who would like to receive their own subscription to *Oracle Magazine*, please photocopy this form and pass it along.

Three easy ways to subscribe:

① Web
Visit our Web site at **oracle.com/oraclemagazine**
You'll find a subscription form there, plus much more

② Fax
Complete the questionnaire on the back of this card
and fax the questionnaire side only to **+1.847.763.9638**

③ Mail
Complete the questionnaire on the back of this card
and mail it to **P.O. Box 1263, Skokie, IL 60076-8263**

ORACLE®

Copyright © 2008, Oracle and/or its affiliates. All rights reserved. Oracle is a registered trademark of Oracle Corporation and/or its affiliates. Other names may be trademarks of their respective owners.

Want your own FREE subscription?

To receive a free subscription to *Oracle Magazine*, you must fill out the entire card, sign it, and date it (incomplete cards cannot be processed or acknowledged). You can also fax your application to **+1.847.763.9638. Or subscribe at our Web site at oracle.com/oraclemagazine**

O **Yes, please send me a FREE subscription *Oracle Magazine*.**   O No.

O From time to time, Oracle Publishing allows our partners exclusive access to our e-mail addresses for special promotions and announcements. To be included in this program, please check this circle. If you do not wish to be included, you will only receive notices about your subscription via e-mail.

O Oracle Publishing allows sharing of our postal mailing list with selected third parties. If you prefer your mailing address not to be included in this program, please check this circle.

If at any time you would like to be removed from either mailing list, please contact Customer Service at +1.847.763.9635 or send an e-mail to oracle@halldata.com. If you opt in to the sharing of information, Oracle may also provide you with e-mail related to Oracle products, services, and events. If you want to completely unsubscribe from any e-mail communication from Oracle, please send an e-mail to: unsubscribe@oracle-mail.com with the following in the subject line: REMOVE [your e-mail address]. For complete information on Oracle Publishing's privacy practices, please visit oracle.com/html/privacy.html

X	
signature (required)	date

name / title

company / e-mail address

street/p.o. box

city/state/zip or postal code / telephone

country / fax

Would you like to receive your free subscription in digital format instead of print if it becomes available? O Yes O No

YOU MUST ANSWER ALL 10 QUESTIONS BELOW.

(1) WHAT IS THE PRIMARY BUSINESS ACTIVITY OF YOUR FIRM AT THIS LOCATION? (check one only)

- □ 01 Aerospace and Defense Manufacturing
- □ 02 Application Service Provider
- □ 03 Automotive Manufacturing
- □ 04 Chemicals
- □ 05 Media and Entertainment
- □ 06 Construction/Engineering
- □ 07 Consumer Sector/Consumer Packaged Goods
- □ 08 Education
- □ 09 Financial Services/Insurance
- □ 10 Health Care
- □ 11 High Technology Manufacturing, OEM
- □ 12 Industrial Manufacturing
- □ 13 Independent Software Vendor
- □ 14 Life Sciences (biotech, pharmaceuticals)
- □ 15 Natural Resources
- □ 16 Oil and Gas
- □ 17 Professional Services
- □ 18 Public Sector (government)
- □ 19 Research
- □ 20 Retail/Wholesale/Distribution
- □ 21 Systems Integrator, VAR/VAD
- □ 22 Telecommunications
- □ 23 Travel and Transportation
- □ 24 Utilities (electric, gas, sanitation, water)
- □ 98 Other Business and Services _____

(2) WHICH OF THE FOLLOWING BEST DESCRIBES YOUR PRIMARY JOB FUNCTION? (check one only)

CORPORATE MANAGEMENT/STAFF
- □ 01 Executive Management (President, Chair, CEO, CFO, Owner, Partner, Principal)
- □ 02 Finance/Administrative Management (VP/Director/Manager/Controller, Purchasing, Administration)
- □ 03 Sales/Marketing Management (VP/Director/Manager)
- □ 04 Computer Systems/Operations Management (CIO/VP/Director/Manager MIS/IS/IT, Ops)

IS/IT STAFF
- □ 05 Application Development/Programming Management
- □ 06 Application Development/Programming Staff
- □ 07 Consulting
- □ 08 DBA/Systems Administrator
- □ 09 Education/Training
- □ 10 Technical Support Director/Manager
- □ 11 Other Technical Management/Staff
- □ 98 Other

(3) WHAT IS YOUR CURRENT PRIMARY OPERATING PLATFORM (check all that apply)

- □ 01 Digital Equipment Corp UNIX/VAX/VMS
- □ 02 HP UNIX
- □ 03 IBM AIX
- □ 04 IBM UNIX
- □ 05 Linux (Red Hat)
- □ 06 Linux (SUSE)
- □ 07 Linux (Oracle Enterprise)
- □ 08 Linux (other)
- □ 09 Macintosh
- □ 10 MVS
- □ 11 Netware
- □ 12 Network Computing
- □ 13 SCO UNIX
- □ 14 Sun Solaris/SunOS
- □ 15 Windows
- □ 16 Other UNIX
- □ 98 Other
- 99 □ None of the Above

(4) DO YOU EVALUATE, SPECIFY, RECOMMEND, OR AUTHORIZE THE PURCHASE OF ANY OF THE FOLLOWING? (check all that apply)

- □ 01 Hardware
- □ 02 Business Applications (ERP, CRM, etc.)
- □ 03 Application Development Tools
- □ 04 Database Products
- □ 05 Internet or Intranet Products
- □ 06 Other Software
- □ 07 Middleware Products
- 99 □ None of the Above

(5) IN YOUR JOB, DO YOU USE OR PLAN TO PURCHASE ANY OF THE FOLLOWING PRODUCTS? (check all that apply)

SOFTWARE
- □ 01 CAD/CAE/CAM
- □ 02 Collaboration Software
- □ 03 Communications
- □ 04 Database Management
- □ 05 File Management
- □ 06 Finance
- □ 07 Java
- □ 08 Multimedia Authoring
- □ 09 Networking
- □ 10 Programming
- □ 11 Project Management
- □ 12 Scientific and Engineering
- □ 13 Systems Management
- □ 14 Workflow

HARDWARE
- □ 15 Macintosh
- □ 16 Mainframe
- □ 17 Massively Parallel Processing
- □ 18 Minicomputer
- □ 19 Intel x86(32)
- □ 20 Intel x86(64)
- □ 21 Network Computer
- □ 22 Symmetric Multiprocessing
- □ 23 Workstation Services

SERVICES
- □ 24 Consulting
- □ 25 Education/Training
- □ 26 Maintenance
- □ 27 Online Database
- □ 28 Support
- □ 29 Technology-Based Training
- □ 30 Other
- 99 □ None of the Above

(6) WHAT IS YOUR COMPANY'S SIZE? (check one only)

- □ 01 More than 25,000 Employees
- □ 02 10,001 to 25,000 Employees
- □ 03 5,001 to 10,000 Employees
- □ 04 1,001 to 5,000 Employees
- □ 05 101 to 1,000 Employees
- □ 06 Fewer than 100 Employees

(7) DURING THE NEXT 12 MONTHS, HOW MUCH DO YOU ANTICIPATE YOUR ORGANIZATION WILL SPEND ON COMPUTER HARDWARE, SOFTWARE, PERIPHERALS, AND SERVICES FOR YOUR LOCATION? (check one only)

- □ 01 Less than $10,000
- □ 02 $10,000 to $49,999
- □ 03 $50,000 to $99,999
- □ 04 $100,000 to $499,999
- □ 05 $500,000 to $999,999
- □ 06 $1,000,000 and Over

(8) WHAT IS YOUR COMPANY'S YEARLY SALES REVENUE? (check one only)

- □ 01 $500, 000, 000 and above
- □ 02 $100, 000, 000 to $500, 000, 000
- □ 03 $50, 000, 000 to $100, 000, 000
- □ 04 $5, 000, 000 to $50, 000, 000
- □ 05 $1, 000, 000 to $5, 000, 000

(9) WHAT LANGUAGES AND FRAMEWORKS DO YOU USE? (check all that apply)

- □ 01 Ajax
- □ 02 C
- □ 03 C++
- □ 04 C#
- □ 05 Hibernate
- □ 06 J++/J#
- □ 07 Java
- □ 08 JSP
- □ 09 .NET
- □ 10 Perl
- □ 11 PHP
- □ 12 PL/SQL
- □ 13 Python
- □ 14 Ruby/Rails
- □ 15 Spring
- □ 16 Struts
- □ 17 SQL
- □ 18 Visual Basic
- □ 98 Other

(10) WHAT ORACLE PRODUCTS ARE IN USE AT YOUR SITE? (check all that apply)

ORACLE DATABASE
- □ 01 Oracle Database 11*g*
- □ 02 Oracle Database 10*g*
- □ 03 Oracle9*i* Database
- □ 04 Oracle Embedded Database (Oracle Lite, Times Ten, Berkeley DB)
- □ 05 Other Oracle Database Release

ORACLE FUSION MIDDLEWARE
- □ 06 Oracle Application Server
- □ 07 Oracle Portal
- □ 08 Oracle Enterprise Manager
- □ 09 Oracle BPEL Process Manager
- □ 10 Oracle Identity Management
- □ 11 Oracle SOA Suite
- □ 12 Oracle Data Hubs

ORACLE DEVELOPMENT TOOLS
- □ 13 Oracle JDeveloper
- □ 14 Oracle Forms
- □ 15 Oracle Reports
- □ 16 Oracle Designer
- □ 17 Oracle Discoverer
- □ 18 Oracle BI Beans
- □ 19 Oracle Warehouse Builder
- □ 20 Oracle WebCenter
- □ 21 Oracle Application Express

ORACLE APPLICATIONS
- □ 22 Oracle E-Business Suite
- □ 23 PeopleSoft Enterprise
- □ 24 JD Edwards EnterpriseOne
- □ 25 JD Edwards World
- □ 26 Oracle Fusion
- □ 27 Hyperion
- □ 28 Siebel CRM

ORACLE SERVICES
- □ 28 Oracle E-Business Suite On Demand
- □ 29 Oracle Technology On Demand
- □ 30 Siebel CRM On Demand
- □ 31 Oracle Consulting
- □ 32 Oracle Education
- □ 33 Oracle Support
- □ 98 Other
- 99 □ None of the Above